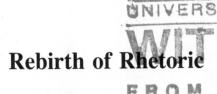

Rebirth of Rhetoric

Rebirth of Rhetoric brings together contributions from several fields to provide a forum in which a unifying theory for language and literature studies can be debated.

The book does not aim to resurrect classical or Renaissance rhetoric, but to remake rhetoric within a contemporary context. The context of texts (both spoken and written) is one of the main emphases of this collection, whether it is the ideology informing the text, or the way in which a text is transformed by its audience. The book also presents a range of practical approaches to the study of texts of all kinds (literary, televisual, film and photographic).

The book argues a case for development in the Arts and Humanities which will bring together people working in Education, Linguistics, Composition, Literature and Cultural Studies.

Richard Andrews is senior lecturer in the School of Education and Director of the Centre for Studies in Rhetoric at the University of Hull, England.

Rebirth of Rhetoric

Essays in language, culture and
education

Edited by
Richard Andrews

London and New York

First published in 1992 by
Routledge
11 New Fetter Lane, London EC4P 4EE

Simultaneously published in the USA and Canada
by Routledge
a division of Routledge, Chapman and Hall, Inc.
29 West 35th Street, New York, NY 10001

Phototypeset in 10/12pt Times by Intype, London
Printed in Great Britain by T.J. Press (Padstow) Ltd, Padstow, Cornwall.

British Library Cataloguing in Publication Data
Rebirth of Rhetoric: Essays in language, culture and education
I.   Andrews, Richard
808

Library of Congress Cataloging in Publication Data
Rebirth of Rhetoric: essays in language, culture and education /
edited by Richard Andrews.
        p.   cm.
Includes bibliographical references and index.
1.   English language – Rhetoric – Study and teaching.
2.   English philology – Study and teaching.   I.   Andrews,
Richard
PE1404.R377   1992   91–47147
808′.042 – dc20

ISBN 0 415 06261 6
        0 415 06262 4 paperback

Contents

List of contributors		vii
Acknowledgements		xi
1	**Introduction** *Richard Andrews*	1
2	**Aristotle's *Poetics* and *Rhetoric*: narrative as rhetoric's fourth mode** *Douglas D. Hesse*	19
3	**Persuasive forces: language, ideology and education** *Ian Frowe*	39
4	**Rhetoric in the university** *Evelyne d'Auzac*	59
5	**Voice/text/pedagogy: re-reading the writing classroom** *Pam Gilbert*	67
6	**Issues of audience: egocentrism revisited** *Deborah P. Berrill*	81
7	**On teaching non-fiction** *Carla Asher*	102
8	**Narrative, argument and rhetoric** *Richard Andrews*	116
9	**Intertext or inner text? How children learn to read and talk together** *James McGonigal*	129
10	**A rhetoric of reading** *James E. Seitz*	141

11 **Shakespeare's rhetoric in action**　　　　　　156
Rex Gibson

12 **Reading across media: the case of *Wuthering Heights***　172
Patsy Stoneman

13 **Weathertexts on Spanish, French and English language**　197
television
Jerry Booth

14 **The power of a dress: the rhetoric of a moment in fashion**　212
Prudence Black and Stephen Muecke

Bibliography　　　　　　　　　　　　　　　228
Index　　　　　　　　　　　　　　　　238

Contributors

Richard Andrews is Senior Lecturer in English Education and Director of the Centre for Studies in Rhetoric at the University of Hull, England. His recent publications include *The Problem with Poetry* and *Narrative and Argument* and, with Angela Fisher, *Narratives*.

Carla Asher is Director of School Programs at the Institute for Literacy Studies at Lehman College, City University of New York, where she also directs the New York City Writing Project. Her articles have appeared in *English Education* and the *Quarterly* of the Center for the Study of Writing.

Evelyne d'Auzac is currently Professor of English Social History at the University of Jean Moulin – Lyon III (France). After her Agrégation she wrote her doctoral dissertation on P.G. Wodehouse. She taught at Paris III, then at the City University of New York. She is also interested in short-story narratology.

Deborah P. Berrill teaches at the Faculty of Education, Queen's University, Canada, and is interested in both spoken and written argument. She co-authored *Spoken English Illuminated* with Andrew Wilkinson and is presently editing a new book, *Perspectives on Written Argument*. In addition, she has published and presented papers in England, Canada and the United States.

Prudence Black is a textual historian working in Sydney in the field of Australian fashion.

Jerry Booth is the author of *The Invisible Medium* (with Peter Lewis) and *Books and Publishers* (with M. Lane). He has combined his interests as film-maker, educationalist and committed European in a European Audiovisual Production programme with partners in three countries. He is also a Principal Lecturer and European Coordinator in the School of Art, Architecture and Design at the University of Humberside.

Ian Frowe read philosophy at the Universities of Wales, Exeter and Liverpool. After several years' teaching in primary and middle schools he is now Lecturer in Education at Homerton College, Cambridge.

Rex Gibson is Director of the Shakespeare and Schools Project and a Tutor at Cambridge Institute of Education. He is Series Editor of *Cambridge School Shakespeare*. His books include *Structuralism and Education* and *Critical Theory and Education*.

Pam Gilbert is a Senior Lecturer in Education at James Cook University of North Queensland, Townsville, Australia. Her interests are in language education, in critical discourse analysis, in gender and literacy, and in the application of contemporary theories of textuality and subjectivity to the language classroom. She has published widely in these fields (*Writing, Schooling and Deconstruction*; *Gender, Literacy and the Classroom*; *Fashioning the Feminine: Girls, Popular Culture and Schooling*).

Douglas D. Hesse is Director of Writing Programs and Associate Professor of English at Illinois State University. Among his publications are chapters on rhetorical and narrative theory in *Essays on the Essay*, *Narrative and Argument*, *Literary Nonfiction* and *Writing Theory and Critical Theory* and articles in *English Journal*, *College Composition and Communication* and *Journal of Advanced Composition*.

James McGonigal is Head of English at Jordanhill College of Education, Glasgow. His interests include modernist poetics, special needs in the National Curriculum, co-operative teaching and learning, and Scottish religious verse. He is currently editing *Sons of Ezra: British Poets and Pound* and *Hard Words and Fancy Words: English Teaching in Residential and Secure Units*.

Stephen Muecke is Associate Professor in the School of Humanities, University of Technology, Sydney, where he teaches Writing and Textual Studies. He is the co-author of *Reading the Country: Introduction to Nomadology* and the co-editor of *Paperback: An Anthology of Black Australian Writings*.

James E. Seitz serves as Director of Writing and teaches writing and literature at Long Island University in Brooklyn, New York. His forthcoming book, *Metaphor, Reading, and Composition: Toward a Rhetoric of Suggestion*, concerns the role of metaphor in the rhetoric of literary and composition studies.

Patsy Stoneman is Senior Lecturer in English at Hull University. She has written a book on Elizabeth Gaskell and articles on the Brontës, George Eliot and teaching postgraduate women. She is Reviews Editor of the *Journal of Gender Studies*.

Acknowledgements

I am grateful to several colleagues and friends for conversations which have helped to inform my thinking about rhetoric and the shape of this book: to Professor Brian Vickers of ETH, Zurich, for his generosity in correspondence and in sending materials to Hull; to Professor Francis Cairns and Malcolm Heath of the Department of Classics and to Lynette Hunter of the Department of English at the University of Leeds for their interest and encouragement; to colleagues in the English and Education departments at the University of Hull, particularly Professor Alan McClelland and Robert Protherough for their unstinting support; to Angela Fisher and David Strickland, Linda Combi, Jerry Booth, Stephen Clarke, Peter Medway and other friends for conversations and collaborations; to the contributors for their enthusiasm and efficiency in the undertaking of the project; to Professor Gordon Pradl for reading the manuscript with such a clear critical eye and for suggesting several improvements which I have tried my best to incorporate; to Anita Roy, Claire L'Enfant and Louise Snell at Routledge for their editorial vision and guidance in the preparation of the book; and finally, to Dodi Beardshaw, David and Zoë for giving me space and atmosphere in which to work on it. Any shortcomings in the book must, of course, remain my own.

1 Introduction

Richard Andrews

I first became aware of rhetoric and its history in the mid-1980s, as head of an English faculty in an international school. In conversations with history and maths teachers on a small research project, I realized that we had more in common in the ways our different subjects were framed than I had assumed. The historian spoke at length about narrative; the mathematician about syntax. On an earlier occasion, another maths teacher had commented on the mathematical structure of a story I had told in an assembly.

These connections seemed more profound than those I had associated with 'language across the curriculum' which always appeared to want to apply a notion of language skills to other subjects in the curriculum, rather than to look at the identity of each subject in terms of its discourses.

The more I reflected on the nature of discourse in different subject areas, the more it struck me that, since undergraduate days (and perhaps before), my interest in 'English' had been not so much one in pure literature, but one which could embrace both literary productions and those outside literature. I was passionate about poems, but also about what made a poem different from other kinds of written or spoken discourse.

This does not mean to say that my embryonic model of English language study was a very rich one. Indeed, *language* then (in the 1960s and 1970s) as a subject had an impoverished feel about it simply because it did not include the fictional or the rhythmic. The chasm between 'lang.' and 'lit.' seemed too wide and somehow unbridgeable at the time, partly because it was reinforced by groupings in school, college and university which privileged literature over language study.

On my undergraduate course in 'English Language and Literature', however, I was lucky enough to be 'farmed out' – the metaphor is telling – to spend a year with a tutor whose interest was linguistics. I can now see that my 'discovery' of rhetoric fifteen years later owed a great deal to the sessions spent exploring language at its several levels. Rhetoric embodied what I had been interested in all along: the way discourses are framed at the 'text' level, the way they are shaped by their context and the differences between them. When I realized that this was also a concern in history, mathematics – and for that matter in music, architecture and other disciplines – it seemed worth exploring further.

'Rhetoric' is not a term to embrace lightly; it is too pockmarked by a century in which it has been deemed to be associated merely with sophistication (in the less positive sense of *that* word), cant and emptiness. It has seemed to suggest a state in which language floats free of its context and thus becomes deracinated, superfluous – perhaps inflated – and ultimately meaningless. This palsied view of rhetoric is not new, however. The earliest recorded pejorative reference to rhetoric in English, according to the *OED*, dates from the mid-sixteenth century. Plato was fiercely critical of it.[1] It seems that the epithetic phrase 'sweet rhetoric' has been particularly far from people's mouths in the last hundred years or so.

It is not the intention of this book to argue the case at the level of style. Indeed, it seems to me wholly justified to criticize and ostracize speakers and writers for uses of language which seem divorced from context and meaning – except in play. If the term 'rhetoric' has been narrowed to refer simply to this level of language use, it is inevitable that such a pejorative feel should have been acquired.

The contributors to this book and I see more than the surface of rhetoric. Underneath the pockmarked skin, as it were, we see a frame that is alive and strong. The cardinal points of the frame are the speaker(s) or writer(s) or maker(s) (e.g. film-makers, fashion designers); the audience (a term that describes theatre-goers, television-watchers and so on, but whose etymology is aural) or reader; and the subject-matter, the 'world' that is to be communicated, however 'real' or fictional or selective that 'world' is. Mediated by these three agencies and central to the whole business is the 'text', however tightly or loosely that is defined. This is no more than a classic communication triangle of the kind posited by Charles Morris. But it is essentially the same triangle that has informed thinking in classical rhetoric and in modern linguistics.

It is illuminating and indeed energizing to conceive of rhetoric in this way because not only does such a conception – taking in as it does a great deal more than 'style' – link itself in an unbroken tradition running back to Isocrates and beyond (and no doubt to other theoreticians and practitioners of the art in other cultures), but it also enables us to conduct a kind of archaeological dig to unearth the way in which any communicative act is shaped in the present. At any moment the way in which a situation is framed in terms of language (in the broad sense) can be explored. Take the following situations: a class in a school in New South Wales is being read to by a teacher. The 'text' comes in a book, encased in a cloth binding. There are only so many words on each page. The text is, say, *Poona Country* by Farrukh Dhondy.

Already there are various rhetorical questions (in the fullest sense of those terms) that can be asked: some of these are extratextual and some are intratextual; some may even be intertextual. For example, who has chosen this text? Is the reading the only way the students will experience the text? Will they take the book home to continue by themselves or will the reading always be controlled by the teacher? Dhondy is an Indian by birth and lives in England: what significance has that for students reading him in Australia? Is the book being read for pleasure? Does the way a book encases a text have any bearing on the way the text is structured (e.g. into 'chapters' or 'sections') and read? Could we conceive the same text in a completely different embodiment? Would it still be the 'same' text? How does this text compare to others by Dhondy? to others by Indian writers? to others in the same genre? to the lives of its 'readers'? All these questions result from a consideration of the text within a communication triangle. Consequently, all these questions are rhetorical and invite a response (unlike the so-called 'rhetorical question').

If rhetoric takes in context as well as text, then the educational contexts in which language operates and in which literature is read will be a natural part of the network to be studied. Education in institutions appears to be very text-oriented, in the narrower sense of the term 'text'. Not all the contributions to this book are explicitly educational in focus, but all of them can be applied to educational contexts. It is partly because this book as a whole is most likely to be read in educational contexts that such an assumption can be made, and why the word education appears in the subtitle. Such a situation is itself rhetorical; James Seitz argues in this volume that reading is as much constructed rhetorically as writing or any other 'productive' linguistic art.

There is a danger in this enterprise that 'rhetoric' could be taken to mean anything to do with communication; that is not how it is seen in the present collection.

Nor is this a book in which readers will find a resuscitation of classical or Renaissance or even nineteenth-century Scottish rhetoric. Each of these traditions has contributed to the present state of the art, but no single one of them can claim to provide a model suited to the present context. Rather, the essays collected here suggest a remaking – or, to choose a more organic, more dramatic metaphor – a rebirth of rhetoric at the end of the twentieth century. Rebirth has been chosen above the more mechanical metaphor to avoid the suggestion that the book will contain taxonomies of devices with which to analyse or compose.

For Aristotle, rhetoric was the possible means of persuasion on any subject in a given situation. The emphasis is clearly on the suasive, on bringing about the desired outcome or effect. Its domain was largely political, and certainly public. Winterowd, on the other hand, suggests that rather than being confined to the persuasive, rhetoric is 'a meta-subject that can serve to unify the diverse aspects of the study of discourse of all kinds' (Winterowd 1968: vii). He then goes on to argue that all communication is persuasive, and therefore that all communication is rhetorical.

Here, at once, we have the difference between the historians of rhetoric and the proponents and students of classical rhetoric on the one hand, and those who would link rhetoric to discourse production and analysis on the other.

Let us examine how Winterowd argues the case for the persuasiveness of language. Having accepted that not all language is an appeal to do something or accept some idea, he establishes that some communication fulfils the role of courtship: the overcoming of social estrangement. This very purpose is seen to be rhetorical. Even dictionary definitions or minimal instructions are seen to be persuasive if one reads or attends to them in a communicative context. Rhetoric is a term used by Winterowd to mean virtually 'the use of language', 'communicative acts in language'. He also imbues language with a moral dimension: language is not only a suasive act but a moral one too.

Winterowd has been cited here for at least three reasons. First, to suggest that the present claims for rhetoric are not new. Second, to forge the link between the use of language and the art of rhetoric. Third – and most importantly – to act as a basis from which we can build a stronger and more specific case for rhetoric.

Nash is worth quoting at length at this point, because he gives rhetoric an equally wide brief but somewhat different emphasis:

> Since 'rhetoric' has for some time been a suspect (not to say pejorative) term, let us be quite clear what we mean by it. . . . We do not mean empty verbal gesture – mere grandiloquence – and we do not use the term in restricted reference to the figures and tropes of poetic language. The word is used here [in his book] in an old-fashioned and honourable sense, as a general designation for the techniques of composition.
>
> (Nash 1980: 8–9)

Let us take this a stage further. The aspect of composition is certainly an important element of rhetoric, and the present book includes much on composition, but a rhetorical perspective must also give due weight to the audience in the communicative act. Neither is it enough to equate rhetoric with the use of language or with 'language acts'. Linguistics is better placed to fulfil that function now that it embraces not only the phonemic, morphological, lexical and syntactic levels, but also language at the level of the 'text' – or discourse analysis. The major difference between rhetoric and linguistics is that rhetoric is concerned with *the arts of discourse* and with context. If there is to be a working definition for the purposes of this book, then this one serves best, incorporating as it does those definitions already cited. Strictly speaking, 'discourse' can include the visual and aural as well as the linguistic: from Hockney (an inveterate explorer of the rhetoric of art) to Madonna, from Wordsworth to weather forecasts.

Perhaps one of the strongest statements in support of rhetoric in recent years has been that of Eagleton (1982). Having argued that 'English' as a subject is more or less bankrupt, he suggests that its unity is to be found in its political ends, in its intentional practices. This political literary criticism – but one that includes 'non-literary' texts – is rhetoric. As well as 'providing a whole course in the humanities, incorporating the art of speaking and writing well in any discourse whatsoever' (Eagleton 1982: 52), it developed into an approach to reading texts (criticism) until 'Textual analysis is seen as preparatory to textual composition: the point of studying literary felicities and stylistic devices is to train oneself to use them effectively in one's own ideological practice' (52). From this point of view, rhetoric is seen both as a theory of effective discourse and the practice of it and is defined as 'the study of the ways in which any discourse whatsoever produces its effects' (53). According to Eagleton, 'our present aim should be to abolish "literary criticism" and revive rhetoric in its place' (53).

Is rhetoric, then, primarily about the *production* of 'texts' (by which I mean to include spoken utterances)? Hernadi thinks so: 'I find it tempting to say that rhetoric concerns the active beginning of communication and interpretation concerns its productive end' (Hernadi 1990: xiii). Hernadi's reflexive title (*The Interpretation of Rhetoric and the Rhetoric of Interpretation*), however, suggests otherwise. Indeed, a rhetorical perspective allows us to see that writing has a similar reciprocity with reading as speaking does with listening. Not the same kind of reciprocity, because speech and writing are different (another aspect of rhetoric) as is listening from reading. The reciprocity is simply there, as has been suggested by Barthes and more recently and fully for an educational context by Jones (1991).

This move to see writing and reading in terms of speech has many implications and multiple contributing influences, and is partly responsible for the revival of interest in rhetoric. One aspect of this move is the emergent understanding of the social context and determination of writing and reading, which is less obvious in these modes than in speech and listening. Bakhtin offers a dangerously neat, almost syllogistic argument here for justifying a rhetorical stance in relation to texts. Opening proposition: stylistics, as a branch of literary studies, has cornered itself into a study of, in Bakhtin's phrase, 'private craftsmanship' (Bakhtin 1981: 226). This over-specialized field is thus cut off from a sociological approach to its problems and has 'become bogged down in stylistic trivia', ignoring the wider discourses that take place in 'the open spaces of public squares, streets, cities and villages' (Bakhtin 1981: 226). Following proposition: discourse is fundamentally social in nature. Stylistics is but one level of linguistic (discursive) analysis and diminishes itself if it does not link itself to generic, modal, functional and other 'higher' levels of such analysis, which in turn have historical and political significance. Conclusion: literary study needs to take on a rhetorical dimension so that the political and aesthetic context of the text can be explored. The delicious irony of this approach is that far from diminishing the role of literature in society, it enhances it.

What Bakhtin perceived was that rhetoric had been reduced to stylistics, and consequently that, post-Ramus, it was seen to operate only at lexical and syntactic levels and via metaphor and metonymy. A good example of this reductionism is the search-and-destroy technique of targeting metaphors and similes in poems. Of the five elements of classical rhetoric, only diction remained as the area of practice. *Inventio* or invention, and *dispositio* or arrangement (macro-structure) at the productive end of the spectrum, and memory and delivery at the performative end seemed to have been forgotten. In fact, in recent years, some of these various elements of rhetoric have been afforded more attention. The 'process' movement in the teaching of writing, represented for example in the work of Graves (1982) and Calkins (1986), has shed more light on the beginnings and early stages of composition, particularly on the processes of drafting and revising; 'ideas' for composition have been generated by the writers themselves rather than being 'given' (as in the *Progymnasmata*, a rhetorical textbook for apprentice writers which is discussed below, and in typical practice of the 1940s, 1950s and early 1960s in Britain). Arrangement has received less attention. Pringle and Freedman (1985) noted in their report on research into two modes of writing at grades 5, 8 and 12 that very little revision was taking place above the level of the sentence in schools in Ontario. This aspect of rhetoric, though it might have been given renewed momentum by structuralism, and operates at the meeting point of intention, function and form, has been largely neglected. Memory has probably received even less attention and delivery has been limited largely to finishing schools and to coaching in verse-reading and public speaking.

At least the first three of these elements – *inventio*, *dispositio* and *elocutio* – are worth bringing together again under the umbrella of rhetoric. Such reunion suggests that one of the advantages of reconsidering writing practices in a rhetorical light is not so much that there will be manuals for the guidance of apprentice writers, but that the very bringing together of these disparate traditions and practices at a theoretical level will inform and enliven the teaching and learning of composition and reading, and provide an overarching dialogic theory to frame knowledge *about* language and language use.

How are the notions of dialogue and context different from those which examine the 'historical background' to a text? They are

different in that rather than look at a text as totally or partially
(according to your political perspective) informed by its historical/
social/political context, they see the text as *acting within society*, as
part of a dialogue with other voices and texts.

[margin note: *Like Discourse Analysis*]

This brings us on to Bakhtin's second major contribution to the
reconsideration of rhetoric. Rhetorical discourse, in 'all its living
diversity . . . cannot fail to have a deeply revolutionizing influence
on linguistics and on the philosophy of language' (Bakhtin 1981:
269) because of the 'internally dialogic quality of discourse'. This
dialogic quality renders less than useful the primarily monologic
models of communication that inform educational institutions like
schools and programmes like English in the National Curriculum
in England and Wales. This point is made by Maybin, for example,
in her discussion of children's talk in schools. She suggests that:

> we need a model of language which acknowledges the collabor-
> ative production of dialogue, and the centrality of context to its
> meaning. The model of language which is currently influential in
> educational policy and practice is strongly focused on ideas about
> individual speakers and their purposes and capabilities. It is this
> model which has propagated the idea of certain children being
> 'impoverished' in their use of language. I would suggest however
> that it is the model itself which is impoverished.
>
> (Maybin 1991: 48)

One implication of this is that the language that goes on in schools
and colleges must be examined, not only within the classroom or
lecture room in the tradition of Barnes *et al.* (1969), but of these
rooms within the institution as a whole. How is the language of
the playground different from or similar to the language of learning?
In which areas of the school does language have perlocutionary
effect? Sheeran and Barnes (1991) explore this question in *School
Writing*; Maybin's article is one of a number that are beginning to
re-explore the nature of school *talk* (e.g. Summers 1991; Stratta
and Dixon 1992).

A consequence of the interest in speech and dialogism is the
renewed attention paid to argument and argumentation, and to
non-fictional forms of argument like the essay. After a period in
which the individual voice has been celebrated and privileged (see
Pam Gilbert's chapter for a critique of this position) and which has
therefore put narrative centre-stage, it is now the turn of argument
to receive fuller critical attention in an attempt to open it up to
students of all ages. There is a direct link with classical rhetoric

here in that Aristotle's *Rhetoric*, Cicero's *De Oratore*, the *Rhetorica ad Herennium* and other texts deal with various types of argumentation. The social and political context for these types of argument has changed, as have the functions of argument. We argue not only to persuade, but to clarify, to discover real issues under ostensible reasons for arguments, to prove, to win and to resolve, and we use a wide range of spoken and written means for achieving these ends. One advantage of reconsidering rhetorical categories and their interrelationships is that we can reinterpret classical rhetoric, as does Douglas Hesse in his chapter on the *Rhetoric* and the *Poetics*.

Another point made by Bakhtin – with specific regard to the novel but applicable to all genres – is the very eclectic nature of genres. The novel, with its borrowings from 'extra-literary genres' like letters, journals and manifestos, is symptomatic of all genres in that although it has certain basic characteristics, it is able to embrace other forms within it, to adapt itself to different forms and contexts. A rhetorical view of genre would accept this flexibility rather than wanting to categorize distinct and rigid forms. In teaching terms, it would encourage students of all ages to find an appropriate form of expression for the task in hand but also to invent, to experiment, to use inappropriate forms and genres at times in order to subvert convention and throw new light on a communicative act.

An attempt to view texts, utterances and so on in a rhetorical light is simply an attempt to return to a moment of excitement in the history of the teaching of language, namely the emergence of literary studies in the second half of the nineteenth century and the establishment of 'English (Literature)' as the central pillar of the humanities from about 1920 (marked, for example, by the publication of Sampson's *English for the English* in 1921). As Eagleton (1991) suggests, this is the very nature of the subject 'English' and of the humanities in general: they and 'crisis' are almost synonymous because they provide a critique of existing assumptions about the relationship between society and its language products. And as Dixon makes clear in the first part of *A Schooling in 'English'* (1991), this 'moment of excitement' took place in the university extension programmes in response to grassroots public demand rather than being the brainchild of the university departments themselves.

To maintain the view, however, that 'literature' should be at the heart of the educational enterprise in schools or that it should form the major part of university undergraduate courses is holding on to the right principle for the wrong reasons.[2] Just as 'Eng. Lit.' struggled to establish itself against philology and diachronic language study in the late nineteenth century (forming the divide between 'Literature' and 'Language' disciplines of the twentieth century), so too a broader discipline is now trying to establish itself with reference to the existing orthodoxies. 'English', in schools in England and Wales at least, is at the same time dividing into (again) 'English' (embracing media studies, information technology and literature as well as documentary types of spoken and written language) and 'English Literature'. The latter has been marginalized by making it optional; we seem to be returning to a situation in which only the 'more able' will have access to the novels of Austen, the autobiographies of Gorky or the poetry of Derek Walcott. 'Literature' (it can hardly be called '*English* Literature') will be the preserve of an elite.

Similarly 'English' seems a misnomer for what is going on, even now, in schools, colleges and universities. The terms themselves carry a moral and pedagogical legacy which is hard not to include, even though practice in composing a letter, writing minutes for a meeting or interviewing someone might be forms common to many languages. The connection with a *national* curriculum makes it clear why 'English' as such has been retained. Readers in other countries might reflect on the politics of 'English' in their own contexts. What values accrue to the subject? What is its role in the curriculum as a whole? How is literature seen in relation to the English language and to the subject 'English'?

What else can rhetoric offer what we might loosely term 'English studies'? Perhaps the most important element is unity. 'English' is now – in schools at least – a term which embraces language work, literature, media studies, information technology, drama, communications and the modus operandi of other disciplines. It is a huge field, but one which needs to argue its corner in whichever institution it operates. There have been various movements or attempts to unite the school subject over the last twenty-five years. One is the 'skills' or 'Lego' approach which builds 'from the bottom upwards'; that is to say, you cannot write a sentence until you have mastered the dictionary, and you cannot write a whole piece until you have mastered every possible permutation of a sentence. Then there is the 'cultural heritage' approach, the one in which you can only study the works of English writers, born in England, writing in 'standard' English and covering themes like tea on the lawn, croquet and being a butler. Perhaps the dominant approach over the last generation has been that of 'personal growth', though the closest to a rhetorical perspective is that of English as 'cultural studies'.

If we array these various approaches we can see them as complementary rather than oppositional. Not only that; they each inhabit a distinct area of the rhetorical field. The 'personal growth' tradition is closely tied to the self, to the expressive, to the writer or speaker. The 'skills' approach is the narrowest of the four, focusing on the 'product' (language and language competence) and how to acquire it. 'Cultural studies' and the 'heritage' approach share common ground in that they are concerned also with products; one delimits itself to the products of a particular literary culture, whereas the other takes all products from all cultures as its field. We only need to cite other areas of interest to English, like reader-response, dialogism and what happens to language when it is deployed in the real world, to realize that these are partial accounts of the subject. Each of these approaches can be embodied within a rhetorical model which not only gives the subject a unity and therefore the ability to defend itself, but also the possibility for commerce between the various subjects. Such is the reflexive nature of the subject that simply being aware of the relationships between these various and seemingly diverse aspects can be part of the pleasure of rhetoric itself.

How does the 'lang./lit. split' look from a rhetorical point of view? In rhetoric, the distinction between 'language' and 'literature' is an interesting one, but not one which need split the subject in two, nor give rise to formulae like 'we teach language through literature'. Literature – in its full range – is one form of expression in language. A rhetorician would ask: why does fiction nearly always take narrative form? What is a poem? What is the difference between recorded speech and speech as represented in script? What is the social context of poetry? One important area that rhetoric would want to explore further has already been charted by Pavel (1986). In *Fictional Worlds*, he discusses the landscape and constitution of these worlds in terms of their 'distance', 'borders' and conventions. From a philosophical perspective, fictions have been taking on increasing significance:

> philosophers of logic and language [have] started to question the soundness of limiting the inquiry to plain referential discourse. The reorientation brought about by research in modal logic and possible-world semantics has drawn the attention of logicians towards the close kinship between possibility and fiction; formerly underrated, fiction begins to serve as a means of checking the explanatory power of logical hypotheses and models . . . a severe testing ground for formal semantics.
>
> (Pavel 1986: 2–3)

While it is not acceptable to say simply that fictions are possible real worlds, it is interesting to speculate as to the exact relationships between fictional worlds and 'real' ones. These are examples of theoretical questions which, because they are generated from day-to-day issues confronted by teachers in classrooms, can be translated into pedagogical approaches.

Pedagogically, rhetoric has much to offer. However, it is important to make clear that teaching methods are not fossilized and that there is no intention to return to the grammar school approach of the 1580s or the 1950s. The approach of the rhetoric manual is no longer appropriate for at least three reasons. First, the cataloguing of which rhetoric manuals are very fond seems to belie the fact that when we write or speak, we are pressed by function and *inventio*: the context from without and the urge to communicate something from within. Second, many of the forms described in rhetoric manuals have outlived their usefulness. They no longer apply within the present social context. This is a larger question than might at first appear, particularly if we consider which forms and genres are made accessible to students in schools and colleges, and what legacy these forms bring with them. Third, the modelling technique used, for example, in the *Progymnasmata*,[3] is too cumbersome. The basic technique is definition, division into the variations of the genre or form, a few words of advice about its structure or deployment and then an exemplary text. Modelling of this kind is useful and sometimes necessary, but it almost always cramps expression initially and must be seen as just one of the approaches in the pedagogical repertoire.

What rhetoric offers is an overview of the relationship between speaker/writer and audience, subject-matter and text or utterance. This theoretical perspective, like all good theory, suggests practical possibilities and alternatives. Given a particular situation, it can array the possible routes a speaker/writer can take to achieve his or her end. It can service propriety, but also generate humour through impropriety. It can also provide a perspective on the internal structure of texts: the whole area of *dispositio* was devoted to questions of arrangement, and we are now in a position to play much more inventively with arrangement than the classical treatises suggest.[4]

In exploring the possibilities offered by a rhetorical perspective, *Rebirth of Rhetoric* moves from a consideration of the relationship between Aristotle's *Rhetoric* and *Poetics* to an analysis of the effect of Jean Shrimpton's arrival in Melbourne in 1965, the 'rhetoric of a moment in fashion'. Each of the contributors takes a different angle on the question of the relevance of rhetoric to contemporary situations, ranging from the teaching and learning of argument, the nature of the essay, the teaching of non-fiction, and how children learn to read and talk together to a consideration of Shakespeare's rhetoric in action, the nature of weather forecasts in Europe, versions of *Wuthering Heights* and the power of a dress.

Douglas Hesse's chapter, 'Aristotle's *Poetics* and *Rhetoric*: narrative as rhetoric's fourth mode', charts the late nineteenth-century demise of rhetoric in the light of the ascendancy of literary studies, challenges Knoblauch and Brannon's (1984) position on the relationship between poetics and rhetoric, and argues for a fresh look at the *Poetics* as a branch of rhetoric. One of the key perceptions this realignment allows is the viewing of poetic mimesis as 'a productive mode of composition able to change the world, one whose success depends not on an objective reality but on the reader's perceptions of the mode itself'. The breaching of the wall between rhetoric (the common language of the world used to 'get things done', the language of persuasion) and poetics (aesthetic, contemplative, self-referring language) enables us to see the aesthetic dimension of everyday language and the persuasive, enactive dimension of artworks. Hesse not only breaches the wall, but steps through to suggest that the poetic, represented by narrative, informs the rhetorical or 'argumentative' as well as being a form of argument in itself. At a more fundamental level still, 'both . . . the poetic and rhetorical exist within their readers' narratives, mediating past and future'.

The social context of language is part of the subject of Ian

Frowe's chapter on language, ideology and education, the first part of which examines the relationship between language and social reality. The ideological nature of dictions used in intelligence testing and in the language of management in schools is examined. That the adoption of such 'languages' is necessary to advancement in this latter field is indicated by the suggestion that 'those who refuse to adopt the "official language" of managerialism, who constitute a challenge to its dominance, represent an objection' and may be 'punished' by denial of advancement. Thus the chapter serves as a reminder that 'rhetorics' can be constructed, and that their embodiment of particular ideologies must be looked at critically.

After these two general essays, the next section of the book examines more closely questions of rhetoric in educational contexts. In 'Rhetoric in the university', Evelyne d'Auzac traces the link between the notion of rhetoric and the history of education in France, and then considers the contemporary situation for students in higher education. Via an exploration of the significance of digital coding and a discussion of Derrida's notions of the instability of discourse, she argues that students would have a greater appetite for culture if they were more aware of the ways in which messages were constructed and relayed; in other words, if the rhetorical underpinning of acts of communication were made more explicit. The chapter ends by looking at the mismatch between students' and teachers' perceptions of the rhetorical field.

Pam Gilbert's chapter critiques the notion of 'voice' in writing, a notion that might be seen as a late Romantic construct. It seems to me that Gilbert is right in putting this self-oriented theory of writing into perspective. It is not so much the element of 'voice' that is at issue here – indeed, there are fascinating and important connections between speech and written composition – but its over-emphasis in the writing process or act, and the notion that in some way one's voice determines the nature of one's writing. Gilbert sees the privileging of 'voice' as part of a simplistic binarism (like man/woman) which gives it the advantage over the second part of the pair, writing. This essay identifies the effect such an approach has on the writing classroom, and argues for the framing of practices of this kind through discourse theory: 'texts that are produced within the classroom site need to be read from within the discursive network that such a site represents'.

Such a shift away from the self to a more social theory of writing and reading practice – and thus to a more rhetorical position – is reflected in Deborah Berrill's essay, 'Issues of audience: egocentrism revisited'. This chapter examines the differences in final-year undergraduates' ability to construct theses and acknowledge alternative points of view, and draws on two traditions: that of classical rhetoric, with its focus on the persuasion of an audience, and theories of cognitive development (principally the notion of decentring). Comparison is then made with the kind of egocentrism exhibited in the writing of 11-year-olds, as revealed in an earlier study. This comparison leads to a refining of what is meant by egocentricity, a consideration of the work of Piaget and Vygotsky and a conclusion that is illuminating in its suggestion that, far from being merely an audience-oriented mode, argument can help young adults gain a clearer sense of their own identities.

By this point in the book, we have moved well away from the orthodox position of those defending a subject ('English') predicated upon literature and 'personal response'. Carla Asher's account of her work on the evaluation of a language arts programme of a school district north of New York City, and of a course taught with Gail Kleiner on non-fiction, describes successful attempts to infuse exposition with the liveliness usually found in good literary or autobiographical work. Three questions were raised that the course tried to answer: what is the range of non-fiction and what do we enjoy about it? What are the processes of *writing* non-fiction? And how might collaboration play a part in the composition of non-fictional texts? Further light is shed on the question of 'personal voice' in this chapter, and though in some ways this piece seems to disagree with Pam Gilbert's, we have to remember that it is returning to the liveliness afforded by the inclusion of 'voice' from a school writing tradition that has almost eliminated the personal imprint: that of the exposition or 'essay'. Thus a rhetorical perspective has helped to restore balance and energy to a rapidly enervating form.

My own chapter reports recently completed research on the writing of 12/13-year-olds in a small town in north-east England. It tries to suggest that writing in two broad modes – narrative and argumentative – need not be a constraint upon young writers, particularly if they are encouraged to play and experiment with the arrangement of their work.

James McGonigal's chapter, 'Intertext or inner text?', explores what happens to young children's minds as they read. It draws on the work of Gordon Wells and Margaret Meek, setting their findings in a postmodernist context and thereby revealing an increased intertextuality between books, billboards and everyday imagining and speech. The development of an 'inner dialogue' with language is an important step in becoming a reader, and McGonigal charts the development of such a dialogue through a survey of children's books, each of which displays rhetorical patterns. This exposure to and enjoyment of rhetorical patterning can help to widen the repertoire available to children as they *write*: not slavishly following models but drawing on a fund of possibilities and making connections between words and sounds; creating a rich texture of language awareness.

The question of a rhetoric of reading is further explored in James Seitz's chapter. Acknowledging that the rhetoricity of writing has been the primary advance in contemporary theories of language and education (supported, but not fully theorized, by advances in the understanding of speech and listening), he turns his attention to the rhetorical stances afforded to, or developed by, readers. Here, rhetoric is defined as 'the relationship one assumes between oneself and the addressed' as mediated through language of whichever kind, and thus the claims of the reader are met. The relationship is clearly reciprocal, and again this is how rhetoric can provide a balance between the claims of reader-oriented theories of communication (e.g. 'reader-response') and writer- or speaker-oriented theories (e.g. 'process' writing). As Jones (1991) suggests, models of reading which operate separately from those of writing, and vice versa, are impoverished. What Seitz is offering here is an insight into processes of reading that include an understanding of attitudinal 'stance' and therefore of a reader's ethos: 'Reading, like writing, is an invigorating, dialogic, imaginative act of composition.'

The last section of the book looks specifically at four clusters of texts from a rhetorical perspective: plays by Shakespeare, particularly *Macbeth*; *Wuthering Heights* and versions of it in different media; television weather forecasts in three European countries; and newspaper stories and photographs of Jean Shrimpton's arrival in Melbourne in 1965. The range is deliberately eclectic – rhetoric can embrace this range – and the individual contributions playful, scholarly and incisive at the same time.

Rex Gibson's chapter on the persuasive use of language in Shakespeare derives from unparalleled experience in bringing Shakespeare off the page for countless schoolchildren and teachers. It is this embedding in *action* that makes the essay so telling. From the start, Gibson is at pains to point out that the rhetoric with which he is concerned is not so much that of the classification of linguistic devices, however interesting that is, but the enactment of possibility in the language that Shakespeare provides. Furthermore, he indicates that Shakespeare, though schooled in textbook rhetoric, 'broke the rules cheerfully'. What emerge from applying a rhetorical perspective to Shakespeare are three questions: how does Shakespeare persuade his audience? How do characters persuade others? And how do characters persuade themselves? Answering these questions leads Gibson to the conclusion that rhetoric, tentatively redefined as 'all the ways in which speakers or writers seek to persuade a listener or reader, by appealing to their reason, their emotions, their imagination and their confidence in the speaker or writer', sends us back to Shakespeare with new eyes.

In 'Reading across media: the case of *Wuthering Heights*', Patsy Stoneman examines how Emily Brontë's novel has been mythologized, 'transformed by the real history' which it has also helped to construct. She focuses on representations of Catherine and Heathcliff out of doors, to which there are only two references in the original novel. These representations include the Monty Python semaphore version, William Wyler's Hollywood film version of 1939, Clare Leighton's 1931 woodcut illustration and critical accounts by David Cecil and others. In her analysis of these various texts, Stoneman reveals the ideologies that inform them and, as a result, sheds more light on *Wuthering Heights* itself. The chapter ends with an account and analysis of a recent novel, Jane Urquhart's *Changing Heaven* (1990), which transforms the themes of Emily Brontë's novel and thus 'accepts that novel's challenge to evade closure'.

In a very different but not unrelated look at weather – a topic which might be said to link these last four chapters, if we include the symbolic dimension of weather in *Macbeth* and the antipodal significance of Australian seasons from an English point of view – Jerry Booth looks at weather forecasts on British, French and Spanish television. Here we have a fairly containable popular genre that is relatively 'pure'; that is to say, there is less scope for transformation or distortion between the source of the information and its delivery on the television screen. This genre is examined in detail and similarities and differences between the various presentations noted. What emerges is an analysis of the way verbal and visual languages combine in this genre, and how – for example – the camera is used to convey a feeling that this is a serious 'factual' programme we are watching. As with all rhetorical studies, we are made aware in Booth's essay of the possibilities in weather forecasts that are *not* taken up; and so get a clearer sense of the forms as they stand at the moment.

The volume closes with an analysis of 'a moment in fashion'. In this chapter, Prudence Black and Stephen Muecke explore the text and context of a photograph of Jean Shrimpton wearing a mini-skirt in Melbourne in 1965; a moment and a photograph which evidently sent shock-waves through Australian society. Apart from the analysis of the moment itself, the authors suggest that rather than set up a general model of rhetoric for language and communication purposes, each text 'needs to be taken in its own historical and social context'.

This comment helps to clarify the direction that this book as a whole is attempting to map: that rhetoric, while on the one hand providing a meta-disciplinary unity for the arts of discourse and indeed a necessary unity at a time when the arts and humanities are from time to time having to defend their patch, at the same time is a pragmatic, modest art concerned with both the production of appropriately framed, clearly expressed messages and the reception of such messages. According to Lloyd Bitzer, writing in the journal *Philosophy and Rhetoric*, rhetoric's pragmatism means that 'it comes into existence for the sake of something beyond itself; it functions ultimately to produce action or change in the world'. It is able to decode more powerfully than conventional criticism, looking beyond the concrete evidence of the text to the ideologies that inform the making of that text. It is also able to suggest possibility, and in that respect goes beyond the oiling of the conventional. It links the receptive to the productive, opening the door between criticism and composition. What heartens me most, I think, is the humour, insight and imagination that it affords in places that other approaches have not reached.

In the spirit of rhetoric (and of criticism) the title of the book should have been *Rebirth of Rhetoric?* It is hoped that the essays included here will generate in you, the reader, your own questions and responses.

NOTES

1 For a defence of rhetoric against the criticisms of Plato and a recent account of the history of rhetoric, see Vickers (1988).
2 For a defence of the study of literature in the academy, see Bergonzi (1990).
3 The *Progymnasmata* of Aphthonius has been translated by Nadeau (1952) and more recently in an unpublished version by Malcolm Heath.
4 See, for example, Andrews (1991b).

2 Aristotle's *Poetics* and *Rhetoric*: narrative as rhetoric's fourth mode

Douglas D. Hesse

To hear rhetoric and composition scholars tell it, for the past century poetics has wantonly displaced rhetoric in the English departments of American universities. However, there are signs of rhetoric's new respectability. Literary theorists critical of an 'apolitical' view of literature have joined the compositionist tale, with scholars like Stanley Fish and Terry Eagleton calling for rhetorical criticism at an historical moment when Great Culture aestheticism no longer suffices.[1] And yet, the movement is not only from poetics to rhetoric, for even as literature has noticed rhetoric, composition has courted aesthetic texts. In particular 'literary non-fiction' has emerged as a focus of interest within the Conference on College Composition and Communication.[2] Changed teaching and critical practices have been accompanied by deconstructions of the rhetoric/poetic dichotomy, to the extent that several models of English studies being proposed for American colleges and universities invoke a perspective of these two theoretical traditions as complementary.[3]

Such a perspective is latent in Aristotle's *Rhetoric* and *Poetics*. To say so is not to call wistfully for the wisdom of noble ancients ignored and corrupted by post-Renaissance scholarship. Rather I observe that the valorization of poetic and trivialization of rhetoric cannot be grounded as classical and fundamental. Sharing a similar status as *techne* or productive arts and a similar ontology in which language truths are measured by consensus of the 'probable' rather than verification of the 'real', the *Rhetoric* and *Poetics* resist clean separation from one another. This chapter will explore one particularly important way in which these texts interweave, arguing that the *Poetics* offers a fourth mode of persuasion – the mimetic or narrative – that complements and completes the logical, ethical and pathetic forwarded in the *Rhetoric*, sharing affinities with but ultimately differing from them.

A BROAD-STROKE BACKGROUND

Two familiar versions of the changing fortunes of rhetoric and poetics – and the reasons therefore – are Berlin's (1987) *Rhetoric and Reality* and Eagleton's (1983) *Literary Theory*. Using the case of Harvard University in the late nineteenth century, Berlin links the demise of writing instruction to the ascendancy of 'literature' as a field of study. Literature climbed a complexly braided rope. The hero strand begins with Harvard's hiring of Francis James Childs as Boylston Professor of Rhetoric and Oratory. An editor of Spenser and of English and Scottish popular ballads, Childs took the Harvard position with the stipulation that he need not teach freshman composition. At the same time, English departments were seeking a disciplinary identity in the new university, an identity, moreover, grounded in practices less labour-intensive than the teaching of writing. A third strand was Harvard's institution of an entrance exam in writing, which promoted expectations that the ability to write was 'prior to' the experience of higher education and therefore beneath the purview of college professors. The combined result was the devaluing of writing instruction, and as Harvard went so went American education. And as went writing instruction, so went rhetoric (Berlin 1987: 21–4).

At least two other factors influenced the relative positions of rhetoric and poetic. The first, growing out of Romanticism, privileged originality and 'personal' vision in the creation of works. Classical rhetoric, its taxonomies and methods available for public use, seemed rather base and common against the measure of genius. With the rhetor cast as a manipulating 'automaton', rhetoric was transformed from an art to a science, and a limited science at that. Even such a celebrated text as Blair's *Lectures on Rhetoric and Belles Lettres* asserted that nothing could be said regarding invention, thus effectively dismissing one-third of Aristotle's *Rhetoric*. A second factor was the high moral and cultural function attributed to literary texts. Terry Eagleton uses Matthew Arnold as touchstone for a view of the literature professor as priest. English departments could justify emphasizing poetic over rhetoric (and poetic regarded narrowly as reading, reception and interpretation, rather than as a productive art) because the former held a crucial position as an acculturating moral force. That poetic-as-literature also satisfied personal, political and disciplinary desires did not, of course, hurt its rise. Berlin argues that for literature fully to occupy a position of prestige in the academy, there needed to exist inferior oppositional texts as foil. There can be no master without slaves, no high art without low. One subtle and 'politically unconscious' effect (to echo Fredric Jameson) of literature's rise and poetic's translation into interpretation was the depriviliging of rhetoric and the 'common texts' assumed to be its domain.

These factors converge only in retrospect (and only in ways interested observers would have them). However, by the mid-twentieth century, there seem to exist several broad, if unexamined, understandings about the provinces and qualities of rhetoric and poetics. Poetic is aesthetic, transcendent of politics, and as a result, pure and disinterested. Rhetoric is pragmatic, political and, as a result, susceptible to bias and manipulative. Poetic texts exist to 'be', rhetorical to 'do'; the latter are 'transactional' in Britton's terms (Britton *et al.* 1975), the former, well, 'poetic'. Poetic is concerned with interpreting works already established as poetic, rhetoric with producing new texts; given the differing status of texts, interpreting is valued over producing (see Lloyd-Jones and Lunsford 1989: 26). Producing poetic texts is an act of genius, organic, an art; producing rhetorical texts an act of following a method, mechanical, a science. The end of poetic is contemplation; of rhetoric, action. Poetical works are imaginative and unbound except by the author's inspiration; rhetorical works are rational and fettered by reality.

These dichotomies have been challenged for both ideological and epistemological reasons. Eagleton (1983) summarizes arguments that aestheticized views of literature are no less political than others; the aesthetic stance, furthermore, tends to be conservative in the broadest sense, perpetuating the cultural status quo under the ideological cloak of texts 'apart' from the material world. Rhetoric, on the other hand, has traditionally been connected to 'the real world' but regarded as suspiciously manipulative of it, with the only recourse, ironically, being an appeal to the reality rhetoric is said to manipulate. The presumption that discourse can be measured against an external stable reality has been thoroughly challenged by epistemic and transactional rhetorics, which draw a double-pointing arrow between language and world, whereby truth is established by agreement, not by direct appeal to 'pure' facts (see the discussion of epistemic rhetorics in Bineham 1990). The normal and natural and realistic and reasonable are historically determined, not absolutely. This epistemological challenge offers a crucial point of contact between Aristotle's *Rhetoric* and the *Poetics*. Both have been glibly dismissed as presuming a direct correspondence between language and reality. But in fact Aristotle deftly avoids this reduction, and a close reading pushes rhetoric and poetic more closely together than many would prefer.

READING ARISTOTLE

Probably the most controversial attack on Aristotle's *Rhetoric* (and classical rhetoric in general) is Knoblauch and Brannon's (1984) *Rhetorical Traditions and the Teaching of Writing*, whose anticipated impact can be seen in its triggering not one but three critical reviews in *College Composition and Communication*. Knoblauch and Brannon observe that:

> Zeus and Jove have been demoted to mythological figures. Almost no one assumes that the earth is the center of the universe, or that animal entrails can be read to foretell the future, or that electricity can cure warts. People have given up, reluctantly, on centaurs and dragons, on the Great Chain of Being, on alchemy, on phlogiston and the 'ether', on witches (for the most part) and on the punitive value of drawing-and-quartering. Of all the intellectual systems that once animated the classical world, only the concepts of ancient rhetoric . . . seem to have survived so vigorously the ravages of time and the usually inexorable processes of evolution.
>
> (Knoblauch and Brannon 1984: 22)

The shortcomings of classical rhetoric, according to Knoblauch and Brannon, derive from its origin in an age when 'human knowledge . . . was regarded as essentially complete and stable, a mirror of the way things "really are" ', an age confident in the stable relationship between language and world (in which the latter precedes and 'judges' the former) and an unproblematic set of shared values among individuals in society (Knoblauch and Brannon 1984: 23). The simplemindedness of classical rhetoric is revealed in aspirations to construct exhaustive taxonomies, representing arguments about the world as products of a finite and codifiable number of operations.

While I agree that such assertions as 'Men's actions are nobler than women's because a man is "a naturally finer being" ' thankfully belong to another age (Aristotle 1924: 1,367a), Knoblauch and

Brannon's characterization of Aristotle's language view conflicts with the *Rhetoric* itself. One rebuttal is definitional or tautological. The province of rhetoric is probabilistic reasoning. If all could be demonstrated by fitting the right words to an objective reality, rhetoric need not exist at all. To put it another way, rhetoric exists – and exists as distinct from logic or science – precisely because matters *do* escape universal agreement or direct demonstration. That the sun rises in the east or that water extinguishes fire are not propositions of rhetoric.

The second challenge to Knoblauch and Brannon's complaint concerns Aristotle's understanding of the enthymeme, which Grimaldi regards as 'the master structural idea' of the *Rhetoric* (Grimaldi 1972: 136). Recall that the *Rhetoric* describes two main forms of logical argument, by example and by enthymeme or 'rhetorical syllogism'. Enthymemes depend on listeners supplying premises, drawing on their established sense of what is the case (Aristotle 1924: 1,356b–1,357a). Consider, for example, the assertion that: the United States justly attacked Iraq because Saddam Hussein had invaded Kuwait. This enthymeme is compelling only insofar as a reader accepts its many unstated premises, for example, that: Military action against a country that has invaded a third is justifiable. Now, it may well be that most readers will 'supply' – and accept – this premise. But many will not, something that Aristotle anticipated: 'There are few facts of the "necessary" type that can form the basis of rhetorical syllogisms. Most of the things about which we make decisions, and into which therefore we inquire, present us with alternative possibilities' (Aristotle 1924: 1,357a).

Argument by enthymeme, then, is not a means of discovering objective general truth but of selecting arguments that listeners/readers will accept as true. The 'available means of persuasion' in Aristotle's famous definition of rhetoric has less to do with finding arguments that exist than finding those that work. There is considerable profundity in Aristotle's simple observation that a statement 'is persuasive because there is somebody whom it persuades' (Aristotle 1924: 1,356b). Knoblauch and Brannon overstate Aristotle's belief in the universal validity of enthymemes when they contend such reasoning was preferred 'because of ancient confidence in the stability of general truths' (Knoblauch and Brannon 1984: 38). Perhaps these truths were general in the sense of being widely accepted, but little in Aristotle's discussion of the enthymeme suggests he regarded them as inherently true by nature. If so, to return to the point above, they would exist beyond the bounds of rhetoric.

I have dwelt on *Rhetorical Traditions and the Teaching of Writing*, which has among several fine qualities an incisive critique of writing pedagogy, because it represents a view of classical rhetoric that has contributed to the separation of rhetoric and poetic. In *The Contemporary Reception of Classical Rhetoric: Appropriations of Ancient Discourse*, Welch (1990) labels this view 'the Heritage School'. Among its several characteristics are a positivistic belief that classical rhetoric is stable and changeless, aloof from modern re-readings (Welch 1990: 9); a dependence on the use of formulas, usually numbered taxonomies, for presenting classical rhetoric (10), one effect of which is to render it simple, stilted and naive (23); the dichotomizing of thought and discourse and the reduction of intertwining ideas and categories to simple and separate ideas (26); and the conflation of 700 years of rhetorical theory into a single idea, as if all classical rhetoricians and texts spoke with a single voice (28). In contrast, Welch champions the Dialectical School, which resists these tendencies, drawing on various theoretical perspectives to engage classical rhetoric as continually created in each new context in which it is read (29). In my own depiction of rhetoric and poetic at this chapter's outset – in my grand historical narrative synthesis – I confess to having spoken with a Heritage School voice. Ironically, so does Welch herself in setting up the heritage/dialectical dichotomy.

My point in all of this is a simple one. What Aristotle's *Rhetoric* means should not be fixed in ways that truncate readings of the work in a modern context. It is quite in the spirit of the work, for example, to read in Aristotle's discussion of the enthymeme a very postmodern view of 'proof' as socially constituted, not externally and objectively located. Approaching the *Rhetoric* as a still-living text enables closer connections between rhetoric and poetics. After all, the *Poetics*, too, can be read through both Heritage and Dialectical School gazes.

At the Heritage School level of reading the *Poetics* is an historical document valuable only for what it reveals about the way things were 'back then', describing literary works of a type either no longer written or so transformed that Aristotle's dicta offer no reasonable criteria for their production or judging. How strange, for example, to discuss a Samuel Beckett play in terms of its unity of plot, having a whole with a beginning that 'is not itself necessarily after anything else', a middle, and an end (Aristotle 1924: 1,450b). Its very title misleads a modern audience, for 'poetics' promises them at least a discussion of the lyric. But 'poem' in the *Poetics* refers almost exclusively to tragedy and epic poetry (comedy being reserved for a separate, lost, volume), compositions that have a plot. Rhythm and 'poetic language' are discussed, but these are secondary aspects of the topic. Centrally, poetics is the imitation of action. A more accurate modern title might be 'Narrative'. However, to continue the Heritage School reading, the whole business of plot-making and mimesis in the *Poetics* is by now outmoded and naive. The poet appeared as scribe of nature, and as in the *Rhetoric*, the accuracy of his or her transcription was determined by holding the text against the natural world. A unified widespread cultural consensus about the natural made such determinations unproblematic. We lack such a cultural consensus today (indeed, much to the dismay of cultural literacy advocates like E.D. Hirsch or William Bennett who might long for the apparent stability of the world of the Heritage School *Poetics*).[4]

If the *Poetics* is to be recovered for a postmodern context (and I hope to justify such a recovery for reasons beyond theoretical gymnastics), Aristotle's concept of mimesis must support a more sophisticated representation than 'copying the world'. There exists a tradition for doing so. Adams notes that Aristotle contested Plato's criticism of the poet as 'mere imitator of appearances'. For Aristotle

> change is a fundamental process of nature, which he regards as a creative force with a direction. . . . The poet's imitation is an analogue of this process; he takes a form from nature and re-shapes it in a different matter or medium. This medium, which the form does not inhabit in nature, is the source of each work's inward principle of order and consequently of its independence from slavish copying. . . . It is through his peculiar sort of imitation that the poet discovers the ultimate form of actions.
>
> (Adams 1971: 47)

Although Adams highlights Aristotle's poet as creator, the phrase 'taking a form from nature' preserves nature as prior to and controlling the work in a fashion not far removed from the Heritage School complaint. Breaking this circle requires pushing harder the concepts of imitation and nature. Ricoeur's (1984) *Time and Narrative* furnishes the appropriate lever.

Ricoeur begins his discussion of the *Poetics* by noting Aristotle's oblique definition of mimesis or imitation as the 'representation of action' which he replaces quickly with 'the organization of events', or emplotment (Ricoeur 1984: 34). By emphasizing emplotment

(Aristotle's *muthos*), Ricoeur signals the crucial status of mimesis as the dynamic activity of composing, not an artifact or result. The difference between imitation as a process versus as the creation of an imitative artifact is a subtle one. Consider the difference between the 'imitation of action' versus the 'imitation of actions'. The former has the sense of enacting a process, the latter of working from a completed entity to recreate it. Aristotle's definition of tragedy preserves this sense:

> Tragedy is essentially an imitation not of persons but of action and life, of happiness and misery. All human happiness or misery takes the form of action; the end for which we live is a certain kind of activity, not a quality. . . . We maintain that Tragedy is primarily an imitation of action, and that it is mainly for the sake of the action that it imitates the personal agents.
>
> (Aristotle 1924: 1,450a-b)

'Imitation of action' approaches the status of what in the *Rhetoric* Aristotle calls the regular or general 'lines of argument', the *topoi* (Aristotle 1924: 1,358a). Its fundamental nature is manifested in its resistance to elaboration or articulation, for example in discussion of the form of a plot. At first glance, this discussion appears so obvious and vague as to be silly:

> Now, a whole is that which has beginning, middle, and end. A beginning is that which is not itself necessarily after anything else, and which has naturally something else after it; an end is that which is naturally after something itself, either as its necessary or usual consequent, and with nothing else after it; and a middle, that which is by nature after one thing and has also another after it. A well-constructed Plot, therefore, cannot either begin or end at any point one likes; beginning and end in it must be of the forms just described.
>
> (Aristotle 1924: 1,450b)

The profound thing about this definition is its self-referential nature. Ricoeur notes that 'it is only in virtue of poetic composition that something counts as a beginning, middle, or end. . . . [T]he ideas of beginning, middle, and end are not taken from experience. They are not features of some real action but the effects of the ordering of the poem' (Ricoeur 1984: 38–9). Plots are not found in or measured against reality but are rather constructed and measured against existing strategies for constructing. Each plot, then, argues for a possible causal configuration of its constituent events.

If plots argue for possible states of affairs, what gives them form and on what basis are they evaluated? One ultra-New-Critical, ultra-hermeneutical response might answer these questions with 'the work itself', as its parts are read against the unique whole. This effectively solves the 'mimetic of reality' problem but suffers the philosophical shortcoming of ignoring the work's necessary position within a network of language. Ricoeur proposes to solve the evaluative/interpretive problem by characterizing mimesis as a threefold entity. Mimesis (1) is the cultural tradition of storymaking against which one reads and writes, mimesis (2) is the work itself, and mimesis (3) is the intersection of the world of the text and the world of the hearer or reader (Ricoeur 1984: 71).

This answers, in most ways, the charge that Aristotelian imitation is servile and naive, for it characterizes plots as produced and judged against other plots and against the art of emplotment. And yet this does not sever connections between 'reality' and poetry. Ricoeur argues that literary works bring experience to language (and readers and writers experience to literary works), current arguments against the possibility of extralinguistic reference notwithstanding (Ricoeur 1984: 79). Narrative resignifies the world by mediating mimesis (1) and mimesis (3) through mimesis (2), and to deny the impact of this resignification on reality would be to embrace a purely aesthetic view of poetic (Ricoeur 1984: 81). Mimesis (1) changes, and with it reality. Rather than a closed circle, imitation is an 'endless spiral' (Ricoeur 1984: 72). Although Ricoeur's image carries the troubling sense of inherently positive growth, it casts poetic mimesis as a productive mode of composition able to change the world, one whose success depends not on objective reality but on the reader's perceptions of the mode itself.[5]

At this point I return to the nature of language in the *Rhetoric* and *Poetics* which I suspended earlier for this excursion into the nature of mimesis. Both works define successful discourse as the production of the 'acceptable', not that which is 'true to nature' but, rather, 'true to belief'. In the *Poetics* Aristotle observes that 'a likely impossibility is always preferable to an unconvincing possibility' (Aristotle 1924: 1,460a) and defends descriptions that are 'neither true nor of the thing as it ought to be' but 'in accordance with opinion' (Aristotle 1924: 1,460b). In the *Poetics* and the *Rhetoric*, the 'persuasive' is closely linked to the probable, and the probable is a common product of the work and the public (Ricoeur 1984: 50). Plot and enthymeme depend on the author's tapping the readers' sense of what is, a sense that always has the inertia of 'mimesis (1)', in Ricoeur's terms.

Having said this, I would hardly presume to erase objective nature from Aristotle's work. His doctrine of infallible signs and belief that 'those things happen by nature which have a fixed and internal cause' (Aristotle 1924: 1,369a) cannot easily be swept under truth as socially constructed. But even as he preserves objective nature, Aristotle blurs its boundaries. Consider the following discussion:

> We may lay it down that Pleasure is a movement, a movement by which the soul as a whole is consciously brought into its normal state of being; and that Pain is the opposite. . . . It must therefore be pleasant as a rule to move towards a natural state of being, particularly when a natural process has achieved the complete recovery of that natural state. Habits also are pleasant; for as soon as a thing has become habitual, it is virtually natural; habit is a thing not unlike nature; what happens often is akin to what happens always, natural events happening always, habitual events often.
>
> (1,370a)

Aristotle does not replace nature with habit, an equation that remains for modern theories of ideology to make. But as 'virtually natural', habit may have the persuasive force of the natural. Crucially, habit possesses the capacity for change that nature does not. The implications of Aristotle's drawing an indeterminate line between habit and nature are enormous. Consider the depiction of tragedy as having finally attained 'its natural form' (Aristotle 1924: 1,449a). Far different to arrive in some final accord with a stable reality, like a telescope image at last coming into focus, than merely to fit an audience's habituated sense of what is natural.[6]

More significant to rhetoric/poetic interrelations than the status of the natural is Aristotle's invocation of movement in this passage. Persuasion, after all, occurs in time, as the audience is displaced from one position to another and most powerfully when the 'new position' appears to be natural, as in the outcome of enthymemic reasoning. Reading the *Poetics* through the lens of the *Rhetoric* (and vice versa) highlights the temporal dimension of persuasion, the rhetor moving readers through propositions. The rest of this chapter elaborates this point.

POETIC IN/AS RHETORIC

Aristotle lists three divisions of rhetoric: political, which is concerned with decisions about future events; forensic, concerned with legal decisions about past events and the determination of guilt or fault; and ceremonial, which praises or censures somebody. In the former two, the hearer is cast as judge, making a decision about events, in the last as observer, making a decision about the quality of the oratory and skill of the orator (Aristotle 1924: 1,358b). Ceremonial rhetoric clearly overlaps with drama and the epic, whose audiences similarly judge the skill of the author and the production. Obviously, the audience of a ceremonial speech is invited to judge the subject – to whom the discourse 'points' – and so something more than the quality of the artifice holds their attention. Dramatic characters undergo a similar gaze. Further, ceremonial discourse and poetry share an experiential dimension that foregrounds the development of discourse. How can be seen in the way Aristotle ascribes a 'different kind of time' to each of his three main divisions of rhetoric (Aristotle 1924: 1,358a). Political rhetoric focuses on the future, persuasion towards the best course of action. Forensic focuses on the past, the judgement of events already completed. Ceremonial rhetoric is the rhetoric of the present. Now, the past – even the past of the present circumstances which necessitate decision – intrudes in 'future-oriented' political rhetoric. And obviously past events are always judged through their future in the present. So, the distinctness of these 'different times' is suspect from the outset. But consider, at least, the implications of ceremonial rhetoric as inhabiting the present. This may imply that arguments of ceremonial discourse are merely transitory, located in a present with no implications beyond the reading or listening occasion. More powerfully, however, the central aim of ceremonial discourse inheres in the experience of the discourse itself unfolding in 'performance'. W. Rhys Roberts suggests as much in his gloss of Aristotle's word that he translates as *observer*: 'a mere onlooker, present at a show, where he decides no grave political or legal issue . . . and plays no higher role than that of speech taster or oratorical connoisseur' (note to Aristotle 1924: 1,358b). This analysis seduces us, perhaps, to slip poetics under rhetoric as a subcategory of ceremonial discourse. But the interesting consequence is less the imperialistic expansion of rhetoric's territory than the recognition of a means of persuasion largely shadowed in the *Rhetoric*.

Persuasion as experience places us at the crucial juncture of aesthetics and pragmatics. One might well take the position that poetic creates experience important for what it is, not what it leads to, while rhetoric uses experiences for ends beyond the words that carry it. After all, Aristotle counts action or plot as the chief purpose of tragedy and argument the end of rhetoric (Aristotle 1924: 1,450a). Such a definitional solution settles the issue from without and facilitates taxonomizing but shuns the rich complications of individual works.

Consider, for example, the consequence of Burke's formulation of this issue. In defining poetics as 'symbolic action in and for itself' and rhetoric as 'symbolic action in persuasion and identification', Burke may imagine, for the sake of definitional clarity, impossibly 'pure' texts: poetic works that have no persuasive force, rhetorical works devoid of any aesthetic dimension (Burke 1978: 16). Yet more is lost than gained by treating Burke's definition as anything more than a starting point for discussion. Even Aristotle asserts that the value of the poetic object transcends the object itself. Poetry, after all, is 'something more philosophic and of graver import than history, since its statements are of the nature rather of universals, whereas those of history are singulars' (Aristotle 1924: 1,451b). Plays, then, present a case for the way things are in the world, an end beyond 'symbolic action in and for itself'. Drama, too, has specific aims of persuasion and identification, specifically the arousal of pity and fear (Aristotle 1924: 1,452a), its 'tragic pleasure' (Aristotle 1924: 1,453b), while 'affective' aims have been deemed the province of poetic. And yet, pathos is one of the *Rhetoric*'s three primary modes of persuasion. While Aristotle regards it as inferior to logic, he devotes a third of Book II to the emotions, including fear (Aristotle 1924: 1,381b–1,383b) and pity ('a feeling of pain caused by the sight of some evil . . . which befalls one who does not deserve it' (1,385b)). He does not repeat this discussion in the *Poetics* because his analysis in the *Rhetoric* can stand for both, and the two works continually cross-reference one another on this topic, as well as others.

Aristotle's discussions of character and thought more directly complicate Burke's 'action for itself/action for persuasion and identification' division.[7] In both oratory and drama, character is a means to an end, in the former that of persuasion through ethos, in the latter that of action through agency; actors 'do not act in order to portray the Characters; they include the Characters for the sake of the action' (Aristotle 1924: 1,450a). I recognize the slippage between 'character' (the ethos of the rhetor or poet ostensibly 'outside' the text though always present as its creator) and 'characters' (people figured in the text). But both terms, character and characters, locate action or argument as events or thoughts occurring to someone.

The centrality of 'thought' to both rhetoric and poetics is even more obvious. 'Thought' has the sense of propositional content; in the drama it 'is shown in all [characters] say when proving or disproving some particular point, or enunciating some universal proposition' (Aristotle 1924: 1,450b). Aristotle defers to the *Rhetoric* for the discussion of 'thought', noting that 'we may assume what is said of it in our Art of Rhetoric, as it belongs more properly to that department of inquiry', and strategies to 'prove or disprove, to arouse emotion . . . or to maximize or minimize things' are no different in poetry than in oratory (Aristotle 1924: 1,456a). 'Thought' may seem to play a different role in rhetoric and poetics. With the end of rhetorical discourse being the arrival at a judgement, such discourse culminates in one final proposition to which examples and enthymemes, ethical and pathetic appeals have 'converged'. However, 'it is the action in it, i.e. its Fable or Plot, that is the end and purpose of the tragedy' (Aristotle 1924: 1,450a). Epics and tragedies consist, therefore, of a succession of thoughts, propositions whose truth and appropriateness may be judged but whose main function is to steer the course of action, resulting in a changed state of affairs. Propositions in drama, then, are 'dispersed in time', as it were, encountered in the plot's unfolding, caused and causing.

Rhetoric and poetic only *appear* to differ in terms of the status of 'thought'. Actually, rhetorical propositions share poetic's temporality in ways elided by traditionally reductive equations of rhetoric to what Welch calls hierarchical familiar logic (Welch 1990: 37). In his 1926 commentary, Baldwin perceived a shared concept of movement in time:

> To put the contrast with broad simplicity, a speech moves by paragraphs; a play moves by scenes. A paragraph is a logical stage in a progress of ideas; a scene is an emotional stage in a progress controlled by imagination. Both rhetoric and poetic inculcate the art of progress; but the progress of poetic is distinct in kind. Its larger shaping is not controlled by considerations of inventio and dispositio, nor its detail by the cadences of the period. In great part, though not altogether, it has its own technic.
>
> (Baldwin 1989: 135)

Baldwin overstates the role that emotion and imagination are said to play in dramatic progression. Aristotle rather emphasizes reason, naturalness, consistency and causal logic, decreeing, for example, that changes in the hero's fortune most 'arise out of the structure of the Plot itself, so as to be the consequence, necessary or probable, of the antecedents' (Aristotle 1924: 1,452a). And Baldwin misses a similar complexity with his injunction that 'we are to think of poetic composition not as structure, but as movement' (Baldwin 1989: 144). Considerations of structure clearly pervade Aristotle's several discussions of plot unity cast in the formal terms of beginning, middle and end. In defence of Baldwin, his concern for movement over structure is recuperated if 'poetic composition' means the 'act of composing' rather than the result of that act. In these terms, the poet faces the task of moving something (the events? the readers? the characters?) from one point (in time? in space? in attitude?) to another, thereby evoking an emotional response.

NARRATIVE AS RHETORIC'S FOURTH MODE

'Moving the audience' is precisely the task the rhetor faces, in forensic and political discourse as well as ceremonial. The audience begins in one position *vis-à-vis* the 'facts' of some matter (meant in the broadest term) – perhaps one of ignorance, perhaps one informed and of a certain opinion – and is moved, if the rhetor is successful, to another – one of 'informed judgement'. In constructing the discourse, the rhetor must emplot this movement, for conviction is hardly the product of single arguments isolated in time.

Imagine, for example, that persuasion happened in the following manner. At one instant the reader holds a certain position on the issue, say, of whether the United States should bomb Baghdad. This position may be that of 'yes, it should', 'no, it shouldn't', 'maybe under these circumstances', 'I'm not certain', or any similar permutation. Then, at another instant, after some 'encounter with' persuasion, the reader holds a different position. It makes little sense to conceive of persuasion as happening with this kind of gestalt-shift abruptness, but I am posing the most temporally extreme case of now this position, then that. The important thing is that even in this extreme 'succession of instant change' there is a temporal direction, a before and after. One might try to account for change purely in logical terms; at the moment of the shift, the weight of evidence acquired critical mass or a particularly brilliant argument became complete, causing the audience to change its mind. But, to use still-helpful language from structuralist theory, evidence or argument do not exist in a purely 'vertical' or hierarchical dimension. They necessarily unfold, as all language must, in time.

This imagined version of persuasion bears little resemblance to persuasion as it happens, rarely a neat and tidy shift located in a single moment, rarely, in fact, a shift of opinion at all, as illustrated by the intractability of the American public on matters of political debate. Aristotle's *Rhetoric* does not address the question: at what moment does persuasion occur? which seems, after all, an odd thing to ask. Like ethos, it suffuses the discourse, as the whole succession of examples and enthymemes organized in some effective relationship to one another. That the audience has been persuaded or not can be determined only by the outcome of the discourse, the action taken at the end – the jury's decision, the senator's vote, the order to launch cruise missiles.

Does this open a distinction between rhetorical texts and poetic? The answer may hinge on the relationship between the question I posed above: at what moment does persuasion occur? and the question one might ask of narrative: at what moment does catharsis occur? which may seem a less odd thing to ask. However, one cannot equate 'moment of catharsis' with the moment of change or reversal in an Aristotelian plot, for the turning point in a narrative, the instant when Oedipus knows the whole truth about his past, for example, is not necessarily the audience's cathartic moment. 'To follow a story', Ricoeur notes, 'is to move forward in the midst of contingencies and peripeteia under the guidance of an expectation that finds its fulfillment in the "conclusion" of the story' (Ricoeur 1984: 66). But this fulfilment, like persuasion, develops throughout the work, and it is never reducible to a single moment. 'Plot may be translated into one "thought", which is nothing other than its "point" or "theme". However we would be completely mistaken if we took such a point as atemporal' (Ricoeur 1984: 67).

So, persuasive discourses and poems work identically by nature of their shared narrative dimension? No. Poetic figures mimesis directly in the work through characters. As events 'happen to' characters in a narrative, events 'happen to' its audience or readers. Poetic represents temporal causation directly and visibly through characters. Rhetoric does so more covertly, its only 'characters' – the subjects of events recounted in the text – having a role 'prior to' the discourse. Aristotle locates narrative in specific places in oratory, usually in the introduction, and suggests that rhetoric 'comes after' narrative, working on it. He explains that, 'A speech is a composition containing two parts. One of these is not provided by the orator's art, namely the actions themselves, of which the orator is in no sense author. The other is provided by his art, namely, the proof (where proof is needed) that the actions were done, the description of their quality or of their extent or even all three of these together' (Aristotle 1924: 1,416b). Whereas the poet 'creates' the action, the rhetor merely transcribes it; the poet's end is the rhetor's beginning. What Aristotle calls 'narrative' in this section of the rhetoric is very like plot in the *Poetics*, enacted through characters. But there are subtle complications here. If everything were so simple as mere transcription, the rhetor would have no need to prove that the actions were done; but the narrative depends on the 'rest' of the oratory for verification. Furthermore, while the 'events' of rhetoric precede the text in one sense, in another they are given presence in the discourse, experienced in the same time as the arguments that 'accompany' them. In Book II, chapter 16, Aristotle describes how the narrative may be dispersed throughout ceremonial discourse, especially, for effect. While it may seem, then, that poetry is narrative, with 'thought' sprinkled through, like raisins in a cake, and oratory is of a different flour, flavoured with chunks of narrative, I propose a more radical view. Namely, a narrative dimension underlies the entire text, even the structure at the very heart of Aristotle's rhetoric, the enthymeme.

Enthymeme shares the same epistemological ground as plot, both depending on the configuration of wholes from parts through causal connection in time. The 'unstated premises' of enthymemes, the socially constituted beliefs so widely held as to appear natural or fundamental and therefore assumed in the argument, serve as a 'first event'. As Gates puts it, these premises cause 'the method and selection of facts which together explain (that is, they "cause") the conclusion' (Gates 1988: 139). Or, at least they *appear* to cause, for the enthymeme is, after all a rhetorical syllogism, arguing probability and leading to conclusions of a status different from those of logic. Just as 'plot mediates between individual events and a story taken as a whole', configuring heterogenous factors through a chronological dimension (Ricoeur 1984: 65–6), the enthymeme connects present facts to a prior theoretical ground, enabling a conclusion. Enthymemes are not static, hierarchical structures, as one might be inclined to say of the syllogism (although, obviously, its propositions, too, progress in time), because their claims are of probability. In forwarding his case for the interdependence of poetic and argument, Kauffman reaches a conclusion similar to mine, namely, that 'poetic is enthymematic' (Kauffman 1981: 407), depending on the 'willing participation of the audience' (415). However, Kauffman endows enthymemic premises with a nearly absolutist quality that wilts in the light of recent critical theory. He contends that 'if poetic-rhetorical discourse approaches the universal, it does so because all, or nearly all, human beings share in the experiences from which the premises of the poet's enthymemes are drawn' (Kauffman 1981: 414). As any number of theorists have demonstrated, the canon's 'universality' is itself a rhetorical construct. In contrast, Ricoeur's threefold mimesis explains the universal as always an historical formation judged not against reality but the tradition of textuality against which it is read. The challenge is to enact that tradition without transparently reproducing it. Like the poet, the rhetor must transcend the obvious. In the *Rhetoric* Aristotle observes that 'of all syllogisms . . . those are most applauded of which we foresee the conclusions from the beginning, so long as they are not obvious at first sight' (Aristotle 1924: 1,400b).

Narrative elements in argument, including its enthymemes, support a 'larger' narrative level. From the reader's viewpoint, each element in a text has the status of event towards the text's conclusion. The 'pure' rhetorical discourse of logical appeals might be considered a sort of 'meta-enthymeme', the rhetor not explicitly calling attention to the way she moves readers through success propositions in time. It is dangerously abstract to press further, but Aristotle's *Rhetoric* may be read as a meta-meta-enthymeme, letting pass virtually unaddressed (Book III's discussion of the arrangement of parts notwithstanding) the very possibility of persuasion through emplotment, of propositions 'causing' other propositions in the discourse.

CONCLUSION

As the source of logical and emotional effects, emplotment functions in the *Poetics* as a persuasive mode. This mode, more familiarly called the narrative, complements the three modes of persuasion discussed in the *Rhetoric*. It underlies pathos and ethos as a means of achieving those effects, and it shares with logical argument the combination through succession of disparate ideas and events. But narrative does more than 'serve' the 'fundamental' means of persuasion; rather, it is a form of argument, presenting textual elements as purposefully organized by time, both the time of the text (in the before and after of sequence) and the time of the reader (as those elements and the very mode of their presentation are read against the reader's past).

In 1968, when I was twelve years old, I wrote a spirited essay in my English class in which I argued that college students protesting against the Vietnam War should be summarily expelled and either sent to jail or to the front lines. My reasoning at the time probably had something to do with what they owed society as a result of the opportunity for higher education, though I don't recall the piece in any great detail. What I do recall is rediscovering this piece in the mid-1970s when, as an undergraduate, I sifted through old papers. I could scarcely remember the self who wrote the piece and was appalled that I had ever been him. And yet I realized then – and this is my point now – that the views we hold are the views of a time and context. Our ideas and beliefs exist temporally, in a then-and-now relationship, as well as cumulatively, and sometimes we are persuaded (the hazy passive construction is quite intentional here) despite the vast inertia of experience to modify an old or take a new position. The narrative dimension of a text, in which enthymemes and examples build on one another to cause a particular position, is mimetic of life itself, for through it ideas exist in temporal relation to one another. But it is mimetic in the most complex fashion, since the arrow of representation goes both ways. Our ideas and beliefs exist in time, caused by the experiences, ideas and beliefs that preceded them. Yet the very possibility of causation is learned, not 'natural', and one of its teachers is our experience with texts.

Linking rhetoric to poetics foregrounds the way that all discourse, even the aesthetic, argues for a version of things – at the very least its own legitimacy – using strategies not of its own or its author's making. And linking poetics to rhetoric foregrounds the way that all discourse, even the transactional or overtly persuasive, has an experiential dimension, by which means authors disrupt their readers' time, interposing a new sequence of events or ideas that modify, however incrementally, time after the text. Some discourse wears time on its sleeve, figured through characters who do things or have things done to them *in* the text, and we traditionally label such works narrative. Other discourse presents itself as timeless, as logical construct delivered sequentially only because of the constraints of language. Yet succession is more than an inconvenience, for it carries the force of extension through time, one example or argument succeeding (as if entailed by) and leading to (as if entailing) another. At a more pervasive level, both discourses, the apparently timeful and timeless, the poetic and rhetorical, exist within their readers' narratives, mediating past and future. These narratives are socially and historically constituted, not natural and given. Exploring their production is jointly the work of rhetoric and poetic.

NOTES

1 Slevin (1988) has argued, however, that rhetoric and composition should warily view Eagleton's embrace of rhetoric, since Eagleton downplays, in Slevin's eyes, the student production of writing in favour of the rhetorical interpretations of texts.

2 For a discussion of causes for and consequences of interest in literary non-fiction, see my article 'The recent rise of "literary nonfiction"' (Hesse forthcoming).

3 Berlin has explored the rhetoric/poetic dichotomy most prominently of late, in two articles, 'Rhetoric and poetics in the English department' (Berlin 1985) and 'Rhetoric, poetic, and culture' (Berlin 1991), as well as in *Rhetoric and Reality* (Berlin 1987), which I discuss in this chapter. Kinneavy cautions against overly conflating rhetoric, contending that 'there is . . . something to be said for modern movements which militate against a rigid compartmentalization of the arts, but there is also something to be said for a respect of the different terrains of the arts. Science and literature and rhetoric overlap. . . . [But] overlaps do not constitute equalities' (Kinneavy 1985: 77). Perhaps the most ambitious recent attempt to rethink the English curriculum took place in a meeting of English associations in Maryland in 1987. The recommendations of that conference are reported in Lloyd-Jones and Lunsford (1989).

4 Two compelling explanations and critiques of this cultural nostalgia can be found in the introductory chapters of Aronowitz and Giroux's (1991) *Postmodern Education* and Brantlinger's (1990) *Crusoe's Footprints*.

5 Consigny characterizes rhetoric's transformative dynamic in language that echoes Ricoeur's spiral imagery: 'For reality in the rhetorical domain is a product of a cultural framework and its discourse; and this framework is always open to change. The rhetor, through a shared inquiry with his audience, may actively transform and recreate that framework, and hence their perception of reality. Every rhetorical inquiry is fundamentally a new inquiry, in a new place and time. The rhetor's discernment of commonplaces, development of enthymemes and examples, and articulation of new metaphors, may potentially alter the ways in which his audience perceives of and lives in the world' (Consigny 1989: 286).

6 Narrative theory has similarly wrestled with 'realism' as a set of conventions versus as a mode somehow more faithful to the world than others (see W. Martin 1986: chapter 3).

7 Character and thought are the second and third most important elements of poetry, the complete list, in descending order of importance, consisting

of plot, character, thought, diction, melody and spectacle (Aristotle 1924: 1,450a–b).

3 Persuasive forces: language, ideology and education

Ian Frowe

> Think of the tools in a tool box: there is a hammer, pliers, a saw, a screw-driver, a rule, a glue pot, glue, nails and screws. – The functions of words are as diverse as the functions of these objects. (And in both cases there are similarities.)
>
> (Wittgenstein 1958: section 11)

> Our language can be seen as an ancient city: a maze of little streets and squares, of old and new houses, and of houses with additions from various periods; and this surrounded by a multitude of new boroughs with straight regular streets and uniform houses.
>
> (Wittgenstein 1958: section 18)

The tool-box analogy is useful. Just as tools perform diverse operations, so words can be employed to fulfil a variety of tasks. The same tools in different hands can fashion objects and modify materials with varying degrees of skill and craftsmanship; from chipboard to Chippendale. Tools can also be misused, either intentionally or through sheer ignorance, and the effects of such misuse may be trivial or of some moment. Those whose errors are the result of ignorance attract no opprobrium but require experience and instruction; those whose deviations are consciously engineered may require different treatment. Our 'ancient city' – the product of the use of tools – is forever a battlefield between the developers and the conservationists, each with rival suggestions as to the content and interpretation of planning regulations. Some structures sit on firm foundations and are of sound build, others are not but may still attract a stream of willing buyers won over by the developers' assurances and guarantee certificate. The jerry-builder often incorporates aspects of the well-built property into his own construction, but these may be inappropriate or of a degenerate, superficial kind.

This essay is an attempt to investigate certain issues relating to the use of language for ideological purposes – a sort of linguistic structural survey of certain properties.

LANGUAGE AND PRACTICE

The uses of language are myriad. I can describe, explain, command, praise, question, threaten, console, exhort, joke, etc., through different modes. Language also enables me to conceal, distort, convince, mystify, control, impress, deceive, intimidate, etc. Despite the best efforts of various groups and individuals who perceive almost any change in the stock and use of linguistic artifacts as an aberration to be strenuously resisted, the vocabulary and idioms available are subject to continual revision and change. The linguistic cross-fertilization that occurs through cultural mixing following wars, migration and exploration are obvious examples of this process. The growth and development of academic disciplines, artistic movements, popular culture all contribute to the linguistic battery. Sometimes new words are coined or ones that have fallen into disuse revived. In many cases existing terms are imbued with a new meaning or their meaning retained whilst their reference is extended. Often these changes are short-lived, trivial and of little consequence. However, in other instances alterations in linguistic behaviour need to be viewed more carefully, for the ramifications of such modifications may be highly significant.

The relationship between language and social change is examined in some detail by Skinner (1980). Skinner is critical of what he takes to be the view of Raymond Williams as outlined in Williams's (1976) book *Keywords*. Skinner attributes to Williams a rather crude, mechanistic perspective on the relationship between the social world and the language by which we delineate and characterize that world. In certain instances Williams does speak as if he sees language as the outcome or result of certain social practices. For example, in his discussion of capitalism Williams notes how this gave rise to 'interesting consequent uses of language' (Williams 1976: 43), thus implying that the relation between the two is contingent and that social events took priority. If we denote a social practice as P (in this case capitalism) and the attendant language as L, then the situation could be represented as

$$P \rightarrow L \tag{i}$$

It could be objected that to attribute such a simplistic model of the

relationship between language and practice to Williams is to ignore
the far more sophisticated ideas to be found in his work. Even if
schema (i) is unrepresentative of Williams's position it may seem a
reasonable assumption to make; social changes produce linguistic
ones. But is this all there is to be said? Skinner argues that such
a model is misleading because it assigns far too passive a role to
language. 'It is true that our social practices help to bestow meaning
on our social vocabulary. But it is equally true that our social
vocabulary helps to constitute the character of those practices'
(Skinner 1980: 576).

In other words, rather than simply seeing language as the product
of certain practices, as a mirror of social reality reflecting the processes of change, language actually affects and shapes the character
of those practices. Thus schema (i) is incomplete and needs to be
expanded.

$$P_1 \rightarrow L_1 \rightarrow P_2 \qquad\qquad (ii)$$

where P_1 and P_2 will be different due to the influence of L. Skinner
illustrates his point by reference to the case of Elizabethan merchants who employed the term 'religious' as a way of 'commending
punctual, strict and conscientious forms of behaviour' (Skinner
1980: 570). The practices of sixteenth-century commerce were being
described in a way that attempted to increase their acceptability in
the public gaze by trading on the reverence and praiseworthiness
attaching to the term 'religious'. For this project to be successful it
is not sufficient simply to adopt the vocabulary of devotion and
keep the practices the same. The merchant cannot hope to describe
just any action he performs as being 'religious' and therefore by
adopting this terminology he effectively restricts the range of
behaviour open to him. If he wishes to reap the benefits of com-
mendatory language then his actions must have some connection,
however tenuous, with the normal criteria governing the employment of such terms. (As Skinner points out, this particular enterprise was a failure because the public were unconvinced that the
practices of commerce met these criteria. The result was a new
meaning of the term 'religious'.) We can see how this case fits
schema (ii). The practice P_1 (commerce) adopted a vocabulary or
language, L (religious) which then influenced subsequent practices,
P_2. However, this schema may still be incomplete, for the process
of influence may continue, thus requiring the inclusion of more
terms in the series. It also assumes that the practice is the initial
term when, in fact, this may not be easy to determine. Skinner

claims that 'our social vocabulary and our social practice mutually prop each other up' (Skinner 1980: 576), so that perhaps the term 'language-practice' best describes the situation:

$$L_1/P_1 \rightarrow L_2/P_2 \rightarrow L_3/P_3 \tag{iii}$$

The central point raised by Skinner is that far from being a passive, enervated consequence of practices, language plays a vital role in shaping and characterizing these practices. Therefore, how we choose to conceptualize our activities, the language and vocabulary we employ, will be of paramount importance and deserving of close scrutiny. The failure of the Elizabethan merchants' project to increase the status of their activities by adopting a specific vocabulary can be seen as resulting from a poor 'fit' or 'match' between the practices and the language. People were not persuaded that this linguistic framework could be appropriately applied to such enterprises. The merchants' motivation was clearly one of increased legitimation, i.e. to make their actions more acceptable and respected by portraying them as rightly understood in terms of piety. Had they been merchants in our own age they would no doubt have turned their attention away from religion to science and technology for inspiration.

Of course there is nothing to stop people describing their activities in any way they please, as Stoppard (1975) shows in *Travesties*. In the play Carr employs the word 'flying' to describe a set of actions that are precisely those that do not involve flying in any accepted sense. We are all 'free' to use words in such a way but at the expense of intelligibility. If we can see no connection between the language and the practice we will be unconvinced that this is an appropriate way to characterize such behaviour. In the case of Carr the language and the practice are diametrically opposed, but between this 'total mismatch' and 'perfect fit' (should such a state exist) there are those examples where the degree of match is the crucial question; how appropriate is it to use *this* language when discussing *these* practices? A further complication arises due to the existence of sub-practices within practices. For example, if we take the practice 'financial transactions' and consider the high street banks on the one hand and the black market on the other, then conventional banking and the black market constitute two sub-practices, each with its characteristic language and behaviour. The bank manager who conducted his business using the language of the spiv would produce an incongruity between language and practice that would rightly be condemned. However, the spiv who talks and acts as a black-marketeer cannot be accused of operating with any language-practice mismatch; his practices are precisely those appropriate to his vocabulary. The criticism of the spiv must be that his language-practice as a whole is an inappropriate way of conducting financial transactions, not that he is guilty of some rhetoric-practice gap, i.e. of *not* practising what he preaches. In practices with many sub-practices, such as politics, religion, education, although we may accuse practitioners of hypocrisy in some instances, in others our complaint may be that consistency is no guarantee of validity. That is, the sub-language-practice as a whole is an inappropriate framework for characterizing the activity in question. Why people should adhere to such inappropriate frameworks will now be examined.

IDEOLOGY

'Ideology', as Hall once remarked, 'is a term which does not trip lightly off the English tongue. It has stubbornly refused to be naturalised' (Hall 1977: 9). More recently Simon has described it as a term in 'semantic disarray' (Simon 1984: 382). Both these observations contain a good deal of truth. Part of the discussion surrounding 'ideology' is one of definition. In this respect, however, it is no different from 'justice', 'democracy', 'equality' or 'education'. The purely descriptive or neutral sense of the term, where it simply refers to a set of beliefs such that all beliefs are, *ipso facto*, ideological, renders it otiose. Similarly restricting it to describe only political positions, perhaps its most widespread use, ignores other areas and can lead to a somewhat misconceived characterization of its pejorative connotations as nothing more than knee-jerk reactions. I have beliefs; my opponents, ideologies. The notion of ideology as something to be exposed and removed, as an impediment to critical inquiry and understanding, is one that I feel needs to be retained, so, whilst acknowledging the position of writers who see ideology as an ineliminable level of social formations, such as Althusser, I do not intend to adopt such a view myself.

To describe something as 'ideological' entails the conclusion that it is unsatisfactory in some way; that it provides an incomplete or deficient understanding of the situation. 'Incomplete' and 'deficient' are important, for to gain any purchase in the minds of its adherents an ideology must provide *some* kind of understanding of the situation. Just as the plausible liar does not lie all the time but trades a manufactured bank of trust and integrity, so the plausible ideologist must enable some fit between his account and reality to be perceived. This point is illustrated by Bambrough:

> No account of anything that is large and complex, however much error and falsehood it may contain, can be 'completely false', since in order to be seen as representing or misrepresenting its object it must be seen as referring to that object, and it could not be seen to refer to an object concerning which it contained no truth at all. . . . If my map of Treasure Island is literally *all* wrong it is not a map of Treasure Island.
>
> (Bambrough 1975: 199)

This idea of 'plausibility' is important, for unless enough people think that 'there could be something in this' the project is doomed to failure; an ideology cannot be 'completely false'. Plausibility can be achieved in many ways but central to ideology is the use of language. Thompson proposes that 'to study ideology is to study the ways in which meaning (signification) serves to sustain relations of domination' (Thompson 1984: 130–1). He quotes Bourdieu's observation that 'Language is not only an instrument of communication or even knowledge but also an instrument of power. One seeks not only to be understood but also to be believed, obeyed, respected, distinguished' (Bourdieu, quoted by Thompson 1984: 131).

The ability of language to exercise control and domination provides the link to ideology. It is through language that 'meanings get mobilized', for language is not a fixed, immutable entity but an 'essentially shifting, open, indeterminate phenomenon' (Thompson 1984: 132). Our ancient city is forever subject to change and development.

The notion of 'domination' requires some attention. At first glance it could appear that the strong connotations of overt suppression and force render this concept too blunt an instrument. If the model of military, physical or economic domination is taken then this would certainly be so, for these expressions of power are transparent in their exercise. Obviously a more sophisticated version is needed if the idea of domination through language is to be sustained. Domination can take different forms. I may submit to domination by passive acceptance of the greater power of another whilst still resenting that constraint. Or I may actively subscribe to the values and practices of the dominant group and freely submit. Alternatively, the domination may be of a more subtle, implicit and imperceptible sort where, over a period of time, I come to accept another perspective as being superior to my own. This domination is what Bourdieu terms 'symbolic domination':

> Symbolic domination really begins when the misrecognition (méconnaissance), implied by recognition (reconnaissance), leads those who are dominated to apply the dominant criteria of evaluation to their own practices.
>
> (Bourdieu and Boltanski, quoted in Thompson 1984: 46)

In certain cases it may be that my original criteria for understanding and evaluating my practices were inadequate and in need of revision or replacement. If the new framework does enhance my comprehension of the situation then its adoption would be the rational step to take. Symbolic domination would seem to apply to those instances where the adoption of a new framework is based not on the results of disinterested inquiry but the effects of other 'persuasive forces'. It is not inconceivable that I should be persuaded to adopt a framework that actually does increase my understanding, although my reasons for so doing are not based on disinterested inquiry. However, it may be that I am persuaded to adopt a new framework under the *mistaken* belief that it increases my understanding. I may be attracted to the new framework because it appears to provide solutions to existing problems, or it is fashionable or it will further my career prospects. Because I see it as fulfilling these functions I may be prepared to ignore its limitations and delude myself as to its adequacy. In this sense I connive in my own domination; I am a victim of a 'self-imposed coercion' (Geuss 1982: 60) through the 'free' adoption of certain categories of belief and action, which, under 'ideal circumstances', I would reject.

These 'persuasive forces' may be discursive or non-discursive. I may be overly impressed by the status of the speaker. We might term this the 'prestige index'; the higher the prestige index the more authority and respect that attaches to an utterance simply by virtue of its emergence from a particular set of lips: the party leader, the monarch, the archbishop. The source is, to a greater or lesser degree, self-certificating. The prestige of the speaker may derive from 'expert knowledge', impressive qualifications, wealth, genealogy, power, etc. These non-discursive factors are certainly important, but symbolic domination cannot be explained simply by reference to them alone and it is a justifiable criticism of Bourdieu's position to object that he leans too heavily on the notion that dominating power is a direct function of speaker status. Language spoken, or written, by those of no special status, 'unauthorized' by any institution, can equally engender relations of domination.

As I remarked above, to describe something as ideological implies that it is in some respect unsatisfactory. Exactly what these short-comings consist of is open to debate, but several writers have catalogued key criteria of identification. Concepts such as 'eternaliz-ation' – the conventional portrayed as natural; 'reification' – the reduction of the individual to an object of some kind having certain fixed properties; 'isolationism' – failure to situate events in a wider context; 'dissimulation' – masking relationships of power, etc. (see Miller 1972; Naish *et al.* 1976; Geuss 1982; Thompson 1984). What these indices suggest is that ideologies are, in one way or another, conceptually inadequate; that the 'understanding' claimed is essen-tially partial and incomplete. Edel notes how ideologies traffic in the 'oversimplification of issues and formulations' (Edel 1967: 577). If all ideologies are conceptually inadequate it does not necessarily follow that all conceptually inadequate schemes are ideological. In the case of ideologies the conceptual inadequacy is unacknowledged or ignored by the adherents; its limitations are either not recognized or not able to be recognized. In its ability to inform practice the ideology is perceived as fully prescribing and justifying. For certain, many of our actions are based on partial understanding and imper-fect knowledge of the situation and it is hard to see how this could be otherwise, for the suspension of action pending the fulfilment of these conditions would result in immobility. However, our own cognizance of these problems, of the patchiness of our comprehen-sion, combined with public recognition of these defects, to a large degree removes our conceptual frameworks from the sphere of the ideological.

The oversimplifications mentioned by Edel may be reflected linguistically by the extensive use of slogans or dictums; pat formu-lations and crisp one-liners providing 'solutions' to complex prob-lems. Alexander criticizes the language of child-centred education for its 'addiction to aphorisms and maxims' which involve the 'delib-erate use of fallacy, false dichotomy, category mixing and other devices for creating the illusion in an uncritical audience of a secure argument' (Alexander 1984: 16). The maxims Alexander examines, 'Child, not curriculum', 'Experience, not curriculum', 'We teach children not subjects', are concerned less with imparting under-standing than with a 'direct appeal to anti-intellectualism and "gut" reactions' (Alexander 1984: 17). His conclusion is that such lan-guage no longer constitutes a suitable vehicle for any serious discussion about primary education (Alexander 1984: 20). The appeal of such language is emotional not intellectual. The reasons for the widespread adoption of this language and its attendant practices are no doubt many, but one, and a crucial one for our present inquiry, is that the ideology of Plowden 'seemed to promise solutions to problems that were otherwise intractable' (Scruton 1987: 39). Only 'simple explanations and simple remedies could promise any relief' (Scruton 1987: 40). Simple explanations and simple remedies require a language devoid of a critical edge, hence a vocabulary which 'lulls and cradles, suggesting a romantic conception of the natural order . . . a pot-pourri of firelight and warmth against the cold night' (Alexander 1984: 18).

If one is persuaded to conceive of one's role as a teacher in terms of such language then the freedom of practice resulting is necessarily limited. The maxims are prescriptive; they exhort, suggest, hint that educational activities should proceed only along certain paths and proscribe as anti-educational a range of practices that may have been characteristic of education in the past. For example, P.S. Wilson's comment that 'unless actual situations can become child-centered they cannot become educational' (Wilson 1969: 120) and 'traditional practices are not educational at all, to the extent that they are not child-centered' (Wilson 1969: 124).

The employment of a particular language can be seen as providing the user with a ticket sanctioning entry into a select club. The legitimacy of such language as a framework for understanding is increased as more and more people adopt the terminology. In this way the symbolic domination extends not over individuals or small groups but can determine the terms of discourse for the activity in general, so that all aspects of the enterprise come to be viewed through one perspective. (This intention is clearly seen in Wilson's remarks.) The adoption of a specific vocabulary serves to mask the conceptual shortcomings inherent with the framework, for all ideologies require strategies to protect themselves from critical demolition work. Objections can be dealt with in various ways.

First, issues and problems unable to be dealt with within the framework can be ignored or marginalized; confined, exiled to the periphery of debate. Those wishing to raise such problems may find themselves 'without a voice' or 'dispossessed of the official language' (Thompson 1984: 46) and thus, powerless. Presumably traditionalists' concerns would, in Wilson's eyes, be no longer constitutive of educational issues and therefore capable of summary dismissal; their 'language' merely a repository of archive material meriting nothing more than historical curiosity.

A second ploy is to incorporate the issues into the framework but in a degenerate or contorted form: a procrustean exercise of some sort. In this case the character of the issues may be altered to such an extent that although they are now able to be 'dealt' with, they bear little resemblance to the original article. This process is illustrated by the discussion of intelligence testing below.

Third, it may be the case that the objection is just not perceived as such; the symbolic domination so effective that the problem raised elicits nothing more than blank incomprehension. Kolakowski cites the example of the Soviet catechism, 'a Soviet man does not steal' (Kolakowski 1980: 128), as being prescriptive and descriptive, that is, not simply recommending honesty but a description of reality: Soviet people do not *actually* steal. The objection that theft was rife in downtown Minsk was therefore not seen as any *objection* at all. The appeal of dictums and maxims is their simplicity, so that when faced with unwieldy problems we can rest assured that structure and order are close at hand condensed into a few comforting words. However, these are not the only examples of linguistic persuasive forces, as the discussion of intelligence testing and managerialism will show.

AN HISTORICAL EXAMPLE: INTELLIGENCE TESTING

The debate surrounding intelligence testing and psychometry in general is long-standing and continuing. The language used by certain writers in this field to convince their audience that what was on offer constituted top-quality goods drew heavily on the high esteem pertaining to scientific disciplines.

In his introduction to the 1937 edition of Terman and Merrill's *Measuring Intelligence*, E.P. Cubberly quotes approvingly and at length from the introduction to Terman's 1916 work, *The Measurement of Intelligence*. Cubberly's opinion is that the later work is merely a fine-tuning of the original which 'sets forth scientific facts of far reaching importance, facts which it had cost him, his students, and many other scientific workers years of patient labour to accumulate' (Terman and Merrill 1937: v).

He continues,

> The educational significance of the results to be obtained from careful measurement of the intelligence of children can hardly

be overstated. Questions relating to choice of study, vocational guidance, school room procedure, the grading of pupils, promotional schemes, the study of retardation of children in the schools, juvenile delinquency, the proper handling of sub normals on the one hand and gifted children on the other – all acquire new meaning and significance when viewed in the light of the measurement of intelligence as outlined in this volume . . . such tests give the necessary information from which a pupil's possibility of future mental growth can be foretold . . . the perfection of another important yardstick for evaluating educational practices . . . confident prediction of many students of the subject that, before long, intelligence tests will become as much a matter of necessary routine in school room procedure as a blood count now is in physical diagnosis . . . that all classes of children, but especially the gifted and the slow, will profit from such intellectual diagnosis, there can be but little question.

(Terman and Merrill 1937: v–vi)

The language used in these extracts conveys the impression of a rigorous, well-grounded scientific enterprise – 'measurement', 'necessary information', 'perfection', 'yardstick', 'confident prediction', 'scientific workers', 'intellectual diagnosis', 'facts'. The problems that can now be tackled, delinquency, gifted and slow children, schoolroom practices, vocational guidance, promotional schemes, etc., point to the dramatic effects that will be forthcoming as teachers and educationalists become familiar with the techniques of intelligence quantification. The comparison of intelligence with blood count is the *coup de grâce*, for here intelligence is being portrayed as an identifiable physical property of individuals, as real and quantifiable as anything doctors can measure. A natural feature of the physical world is the object of study. Indeed, so confident were Terman and Merrill as to the ontological status of this property that their tables begin at a 'mental age' of twenty-four months.

The social and political motives behind IQ testing are well documented but concisely summarized by Squibb: 'When the rich man was in his castle and the poor man at his gate there was no need to prove the latter's cognitive inferiority' (Squibb 1977: 80). The epistemological questions regarding the nature and measurement of intelligence are consequently ignored and the conceptual adequacy of the framework assumed. It would be wrong to accuse Terman and Merrill of misology but perfectly justifiable to observe that the intellectual basis for their judgements and actions was open to serious objections. When one considers that children's life prospects were being decided on the results of such tests the charge is not simply sloppy thinking but dangerously sloppy thinking.

The persuasiveness of these extracts comes from their anchoring in 'scientific' language and the almost universal insight into all aspects of educational practice that is promised: 'confident prediction of many students', 'there can be little question', etc. For those dealing with the host of seemingly intractable problems faced by teachers and others, the willingness to be seduced by such a holy grail is not difficult to imagine.

The technical language employed by intelligence testing also serves another important function, that of mystification. The paraphernalia associated with the tests – formulae, tables, graphs, equations – along with 'intelligence quotient', 'mental age', 'standard deviations', 'normal distribution', etc., all helped to create the aura of a highly disciplined technical process that no lay person could hope to understand. The language therefore provides protection from outside scrutiny and also enables the practitioners to acquire some of that all-important commodity, 'expertise'. 'Expertise' or 'technical sophistication' is desirable, for it not only raises professional status in the eyes of the public but proffers the existence of solutions to problems. The procrustean nature of this enterprise is fairly clear. Intelligence is a complex entity whose structure is not easily discerned. If, however, we produce a degenerate notion of intelligence that we can measure, and parade this quantity as the original, it is possible to provide answers to questions. The only drawback is that the 'answer' forthcoming is not related to the original question.

The influence on practice of the scientific/technical language adopted is evident in their instruction for the testing of young children.

> In general it will be found desirable to exclude observers, particularly parents, teachers or brothers and sisters. With a very young child . . . it may be desirable to have one parent present, but never both, and never another child. In such cases parents should be instructed to keep in the background, allowing the examiner to manage the situation and child in his own way. The parent must be warned never to reword a question or to say anything that would suggest an answer.
>
> (Terman and Merrill 1937: 69)

The authority of the examiner, the 'preciseness' and 'sophistication' of the methods, are reinforced by the need to exclude as far as possible untrained, unscientific, members of the public (including teachers). Those who are 'allowed' to be present need to be 'instructed' and 'warned' as to their behaviour; you can observe the operation but your lack of knowledge and subordinate role is quickly established. (The strongly 'medical' nature of this makes one wonder whether the examiners actually wore white coats.)

The widespread acceptance and use of intelligence tests in schools during the decades that followed was in no small way assisted by the language chosen to characterize the activity. The 'guarantee certificates' were sufficiently persuasive to encourage the institutionalization of practices whilst ignoring the serious epistemological defects upon which they were founded. A contemporary example: managerialism.

> Management indeed turns out to mean persuading others to agree with more or less good grace on ends which are systematic and unavailable to question. Technique and skills are the keywords in these trainings, never judgement or reason, nor admiration nor disgust.
>
> (Inglis 1985: 101)

The rise of educational management over the last decade has indeed been meteoric, bringing with it a whole new vocabulary to aid our understanding and guide our practice. Its success as a magnet for finance has been influenced by the way in which its aphorisms, maxims, dictums and metaphors have infiltrated the educational debate, even determined and dominated that debate. A stock reaction to critics of this process is that by attacking management they are arguing for poor or bad management. This is not so and constitutes the rebuttal of a point that has not been raised; sloppy administration serves no one's interests. What can be objected to, however, is the belief that some architectonic notion of 'effective management' should cast its shadow, or 'illuminate', the forum of educational debate; that we must view education more and more through the framework provided by managerialism.

As Inglis points out, ends are assumed and 'technique' and 'skills' posited as the keywords. The value-laden nature of many educational issues renders them unsuited to such mechanisms. As far back as *The Republic* Plato had effectively demolished any notion that morality was a 'skill'. Questions about ends are therefore subsumed in the efficient pursuit of effective means. Apple points out how 'lack of quality' in education is viewed as a 'lack of technical sophistication' (Apple 1979: 112). Human problems may be seen as a 'lack of communication' that can be solved by 'improved communication'; the solution to your problems is more and better management.

Bottery, in an ethical critique of educational management, observes that it is sometimes difficult to pin down 'the insidious and pervasive use of language which creates a prescriptive ethos of hierarchy and manipulation' (Bottery 1988: 342). He then proceeds to give a 'Devil's Dictionary' of management terms with his own interpretation. (I list only a selection.)

effective management	– the head getting his own way in the quickest and most convenient manner
good practice	– what the head/DES/LEA wants
inputs/outputs	– pupils, children
living resources	– teachers
management style	– changing behaviour to get what you want
motivation	– manipulation
pedagogic material	– pupils, children
school management	– the head getting his way
teaching units	– teachers
team work	– getting together a staff who will work towards what the head/DES/LEA wants
resource power	– the bribes available to the head to get the staff to do what he wants them to do.

(Bottery 1988: 343)

The reduction of children and teachers to 'inputs', 'outputs', 'living resources', 'units' and 'pedagogic material' conveys the impression of some manufacturing enterprise at work. This 'depersonalization' is important for 'efficient and effective' decision making and is frustrated by any empathy or sympathy with the particular circumstances of any one individual. As with intelligence testing the social and political background to use of such language is relevant. Once the problems of industry had been firmly placed at the door of ineffective, amateurish management the remedy was effective, professional management. Similarly in education, the problems of truancy, low standards, discipline, low morale could all be solved by better management. Little Puddington Primary School's shortcomings will be best addressed by viewing it as a subsidiary of General Motors and the head as a 'line-manager'. Hence the establishment of 'senior management teams', 'area managers', 'chains of command', 'chief-executives', etc. (the irony of having a 'senior management team' in a small primary school such that its members comprise half the staff seems to have eluded some practitioners). The use of such terms creates the atmosphere of hierarchy and manipulation; of a pressing need to 'get things done', 'meet the objectives', 'deliver the goods'. Martin pinpoints the desire for change as stemming partly from the ambiguous status of the teaching profession. She writes that teachers,

> over invest in the idea of change to prove that like any other profession it has techniques and a body of knowledge which is always being refined and improved. . . . The last thing that the specialist in Education can afford is to be caught purveying the older received wisdom. He must be constantly discovering new truths which through nothing more cogent than the mere passage of time must automatically become invalid. Thus syllabuses, teaching methods, methods of assessment must constantly produce novelty and above all impact.
>
> (B. Martin 1971: 315)

In the light of this it is interesting to note Popper's remarks regarding piece-meal and utopian change. Popper's criticism of radical change was that the number of variables involved rendered effective monitoring of feedback virtually impossible. Wholesale change precludes the possibility of correctly identifying causes and effects and thus increasing understanding. Small-scale modifications with a limited number of variables are more successful in producing refined approaches to complex situations. In this way the pressure for large, dramatic upheavals – novelty and impact – has attractions for the ideologist as the apportioning of responsibility becomes more difficult. Given a framework in which 'accountability' is a key concept the eager pursuit of large-scale change seems somewhat misguided.

This need for change, novelty and impact can be seen as high motivation for the importation of management techniques into education. The idea that change is self-justifying, that the greater the degree of change the more praiseworthy the agent, the pressure to 'make one's mark', 'stamp one's personality on the institution', all these desires can be met through management. However, the changes made need to be portrayed as being based on well-grounded principles in order to gain credibility; the language has to be the sort that will instil confidence in the prospective buyer. The packaging of the 'product' has to be carefully designed. The following extract is from a course entitled 'The effective middle manager' provided by a group of educational management consultants. On the 'configuration of the school' we are told:

> The picture that is suggested is that of the amoeba, that single cell organism with a capacity to change shape in response to external stimuli, or as a consequence of chemical change.
>
> (North West Educational Management Centre 1990)

We are straightaway into a scientific vocabulary: 'amoeba', 'cell', 'organism', 'stimuli', 'chemical change'. Participants are then asked to draw a model of their own school within certain parameters (keywords). These parameters include 'stretch factor', 'mass distribution', 'lines of pace', 'inertia lines' and 'lines of Regression and Progression'. We have now moved from biology to physics.

The need to be able to solve problems is central to ideologies, and, when faced with a situation in which 'people's attitudes and reactions are important', the technique suggested is that of 'Force Field Analysis', which

> uses the concept of apparent immobility in a given situation representing a state of dynamic tension between the needs, drives, aspiration, fears and other feelings of people involved and between technological and environmental forces.
>
> (North West Educational Management Centre 1990)

We are further informed that:

> It is important in the theory that underlies this model that movement in the desired direction can most readily be achieved by reducing or removing restraining forces. Intensifying driving forces before reducing restraining forces often increases the restraining forces in reaction.
>
> (North West Educational Management Centre 1990)

This last sentence has the distinct character of a law of nature, perhaps formulated by the management equivalent of Newton. Notice also how we are informed of a 'theory' underlying the model although this 'theory' is never made explicit. The extensive use of 'forces' as an explanatory model for 'understanding' and 'solving' what are human problems seems highly dubious. Again, to provide solutions the problem has to be suitably transformed into a form that fits the model; a technical solution to what are essentially value-laden issues.

The use of scientific language as a tool of legitimation is not a new phenomenon. Hartnett and Naish (1977) draw interesting parallels between the practices of eighteenth-century physicians and modern-day educationalists. Faced with a medical knowledge that was unable to cope with the maladies of the time, enterprising doctors adopted the terminology of the much respected Newtonian physics to justify their remedies. This improved, 'up-to-date' vocabulary traded on the success of the new physics and presented the physicians' old formulations as based on vigorous, scientific principles:

> just as much 18th century medical theory became displaced in that it took on a social function which in reality bore little relationship to the alleviation of suffering and the cure of disease, so, too, some educational theory may be similarly displaced, and serve for example, as a way of relieving student's stress, or of maintaining professional status, and bear very little on the educational problems towards which it is ostensibly directed.
>
> (Hartnett and Naish 1977: 69)

The language employed by management in the extracts above is one that has 'effected the precipitation of morality' (Inglis 1985: 104) from an area which is bound up in questions of morality. The old Kantian notion of treating people as ends, never as means, has been completely reversed so that people are viewed almost wholly as means; as 'resources' to be used. The teacher is an effective agent required to 'deliver' the curriculum rather as the postman delivers packages the content of which are not his concern. Pattison remarks how business methods carry implicit messages regarding what it is to be human. These messages are 'trivialising and unrealistic about the nature and pluriformity of human beings and human endeavour as well as about the chaotic nature of the world in which we live' (Pattison 1991: 27). From such springs their essential inadequacy when applied wholesale to an activity which concerns itself intimately with the 'nature and pluriformity of human beings'.

This is, of course, denied by various writers who believe that many of the critics of management techniques are mistaken about the true nature of their quarry. Riches and Morgan (1989), in their book *Human Resource Management in Education*, point out that they have dropped the terms 'personnel' or 'staff management' because they have 'restrictive connotations' (Riches and Morgan 1989: 2). Their preferred term is 'Human Resource Management

(HRM)', which takes 'a broader and more integrated view' and 'starts from a consideration of what the strategies of an organization might be then asks how human resources can help formulate and accomplish these strategies, and what human development and motivation is required to meet these ends' (Riches and Morgan 1989: 2–3). The idea that 'Human Resource Management' is to be preferred to 'staff management' is not obvious; teachers may feel less enthusiastic about being a 'human resource' than part of a staff. There also seems to be some confusion regarding 'strategies' and 'ends', for in the above extract the 'strategies' seem to *be* the 'ends'. However, we are assured that the purpose of 'Human Resource Management' 'is not to dehumanize educational processes and products but to ensure that what is most desired is delivered to the recipients of education' (Riches and Morgan 1989: 2). The use of the term 'products' could be seen as precisely achieving what the authors claim to be avoiding; that is, the dehumanizing of education. 'What is most desired' raises questions regarding the nature of democratic participation and an examination of fundamental values, which seems somewhat at odds with systematic management. Indeed, in the same volume of essays Gareth Morgan highlights an important distinction between 'openness' and 'democracy' where 'democracy' is identified with 'nose counting' but 'openness' is the 'vigorous examination of [an] idea that will produce a clear vision – the right answer. That's not democracy . . . [it] is [more] analytical' (Morgan 1989: 73). How the 'right answer' is recognized is not explained. To identify 'democracy' with 'nose counting' seems to be working with a somewhat degenerate conception of what democracy entails. Notice also how Riches and Morgan still choose the word 'deliver' to describe the activity of teaching.

The need to portray such skills and techniques with a human face is motivated merely by the desire for more effective control and manipulation. Inglis remarks how 'the new developments of bureaucratic systems in the forces of managerialism and counselling . . . have to present themselves as warmly and sympathetically concerned with individuals in order to achieve people's compliance' (Inglis 1985: 136). The language of reification which depersonalizes, which models problem solving on a parallelogram or triangle of forces, sees individuals as 'material', 'units' or 'resources', and talks of 'products' and 'outputs' may be attractive to those of a certain frame of mind. The persuasive force of such language may meet a need already held such that the audience is ready, primed, to adopt this framework for understanding and action. When the ladder upwards can only be climbed by adopting 'the official language' the required rationalization of decision is all the more easy to enact. The retreat from considering the fundamental issues in education, which are value issues, indeed the belief that such issues stand outside the scope of rational inquiry conceived on a technical or instrumental basis, signals a desire to luxuriate in the 'comfortable darkness of unreason' (Bambrough 1974: 18), and 'the repression of 'ethics' as a category of life' (Habermas 1971: 112).

Those who refuse to adopt the 'official language' of managerialism, who constitute a challenge to its dominance, represent an objection which may be handled in various ways. At a time when management training is essential for those seeking promotion with educational institutions the 'punishment' for dissent may be simply in terms of lack of advancement. As Ball comments, oppositional activity by individuals is viewed as a 'problem' not of the system but the individual (Ball 1990: 158). 'Collective opposition is systematically misrecognized. . . . The resister is cast as social deviant, and is normalized through coercive or therapeutic procedures' (Ball 1990: 158). Critical argumentation is replaced by psychological analysis; within the artificial neutrality and rationality of the framework the integrity of the opposition is deflected by a feigned concern from those continuing to adhere to the outmoded and outdated; 'flat-earthers' in the modern age.

Although the language of educational management is drawn largely from the scientific and business worlds it is comforting to note that the Elizabethan merchants' bid for spiritual respectability has not been entirely abandoned. Morgan, whose paper is entitled 'Sharing the vision', describes how a group of Canadian managers in an uncertain world felt the need for a 'coherent point of reference' and used expressions such as 'a vision', 'a mission', 'a symbolizing presence' to 'simultaneously energize and focus the efforts of a wide range of actors typically found in modern organizations' (Morgan 1989: 69). Portraying one's activities as a 'mission' or motivated by a 'vision' replaces the need for critical scrutiny with an appeal to faith and trust. Missionaries and visionaries are not renowned for any large degree of self-doubt or scepticism regarding the grounding or purpose of their behaviour. The 'mission statement' has already appeared in education emanating from the Polytechnics and Colleges Funding Committee a few years ago. Colleges were asked to produce a 'strategic plan' outlining their 'mission', presumably in the expectation that a series of banal statements would 'energize and focus the efforts of a wide range of actors'.

CONCLUSION

In an era when 'negative patient care outcome', 'collateral damage' and 'adverse life experience' are the choice of some to signify death, the role of a junk-food vocabulary as social analgesic is a trend to be resisted; the use of tools in the construction of studio sets parading themselves as desirable residences of solid build. Wittgenstein's straight, regular streets and uniform houses suggest an order and propriety that homogeneity alone cannot guarantee. There are always those whose interests lie in the fabrication of the intellectual shanty-town. The purpose of this essay has been to examine some functions of language as the hand-maiden to ideology. The epistemic issues that underpin the critique of ideology have been hinted at although not developed in any structured fashion. Skinner's paper shows how language cannot be viewed as a neutral, passive reflection of practices but actively engages with, informs and fashions those practices. Consequently, the discourse we employ to interpret, describe, understand, explain, analyse and evaluate our actions is significant. Bourdieu's notion of 'symbolic domination' when combined with an examination of the persuasive power of language illustrates how 'inappropriate' frameworks may be adopted when they are seen as counters to pressure and doubt.

As with any treatment of ideology objections can be made in regard to our own ideological blind spots. The claims made within disciplines must always be open to critical examination as to their adequacy and suitability for action. Even if we agree that 'truth' is always provisional, raising questions is essential lest the debate be taken over by those whose first allegiance is not disinterested inquiry but the establishment of a monolithic orthodoxy. A close examination of language is central to any such project.

4 Rhetoric in the university

Evelyne d'Auzac

The word 'rhetoric' is defined in the *OED* as: 'The art of using language so as to persuade or influence others', the next substantive to be used to circumscribe the role of rhetoric being 'eloquence'. The evolution of rhetoric to its present state is described in Douglas Hesse's chapter on narrative as rhetoric's fourth mode.

The question I want to ask here is: what use is made of rhetoric in our universities? Do students reject rhetoric? The answer will vary according to the subject taught and learned. For instance, to the question: is the art of rhetoric useful in the last decade of the twentieth century? the publicist answers affirmatively, since he must convince at all costs, even though it might mean lying in the face of the consumer. Students of advertising, therefore, will learn formulas which are not called rhetorical but which actually are such.

In any country the defender of an accused person will try to persuade the jury and the judge that his/her client is innocent. So the question becomes not so much: is there a rebirth of rhetoric? as: what survives of rhetoric?

In France the notion of rhetoric is linked to the history of education. Rhetoric was indeed taught in secondary schools to pupils of about 16. Indeed, as well as being called, for example, 'the first form' the class in which the teaching of rhetoric was begun was called 'Classe de Rhétorique', while in Belgium this form was called 'Poésie'). The scholastic year which follows 'Classe de Rhétorique' was called 'Classe de Philosophie'. Before reaching the 'Classe de Rhétorique', pupils received a course of teaching that started with textual analysis, in which they were supposed to dissect the elements of a text and show how an author achieved his aim (whether to frighten the reader, to impress with a sense of beauty, to convince of the urgency of a cause, and so on). The last stage of evolution in the teaching of literature was the 'dissertation', in which the pupil had to write an argument that demonstrated his feeling about a 'literary work of art'. The *dispositio* was essential in this exercise, together with thesis, antithesis, synthesis.

This sort of teaching gradually came under a shower of criticism; the argument went that pupils no longer learned how to think by themselves, but were taught merely how to formalize their ideas or a set of ideas supposedly expected by the teacher. As Emile Faguet put it:

> Nous enseignons à écrire et tout style qui n'est pas original n'est pas un style; nous enseignons à penser et toute pensée que nous tenons d'un autre n'est pas une pensée, c'est une formule; et toute méthode pour penser que nous tenons d'un autre n'est pas une méthode; c'est un mécanisme. Nous enseignons à sentir, et tout sentiment d'emprunt est une affectation, une hypocrisie, une déclamation.

The paragon of the system was represented by and embodied in the famous viva voce entrance examination to the Ecole Nationale d'Administration. Students were given exactly two minutes to prepare a question such as: 'How influential was the theatre in the Europe of the fourteenth century?' or 'How important were elephants in the Egyptian thirteenth dynasty?' Needless to say, all the flowers of rhetoric are required to give the illusion of clarity and elegance in such a case, when knowledge is scanty. These examples are extreme ones, but they could be quoted by the adversaries of the teaching of rhetoric as authentic; furthermore, they invited critics of the pedagogical system to demonstrate that rhetoric helps not only those who have something to say but also those who have nothing to say. Rhetoric was thus supposed to put people off the track of 'truth'. So a sort of reverse swing of the pendulum was initiated to solicit more spontaneous reactions to texts and topics. 'Creative writing' was started, sensitivity encouraged, primary reactions celebrated. With the acceleration of cultural events, a typical aspect of our societies, 'creative writing' went along with a new reflection on aesthetics, and, inevitably, a reaction against skin-deep, superficial judgements swept away the critics' sensitivity and what we can call 'postmodernism' took over. Neo-baroque forms in art were the result, such as the creations of Borek Cipek for objects of everyday consumption, true *objets d'art*. In his attempt to escape from the elementary, the artist recreates a world, complete with cross-references and metalanguage, the very image of rhetoric.

But let us go back to the average student at university. Is there anything new in his universe that really differs from the theoretical evolution in the thoughts of his teachers? The answer is most certainly 'yes'. Our industrialized societies register a radical change, that of computer logic. Today, figures, letters, sounds, images, any type of signal may be conveyed through sequences of numbers composed of 0 and 1. This universal language is the crux of our contemporary cross-culture: the digital code reigns supreme and unchallenged.

This new coding of information may be seen to represent the acme of Cartesian logic: 'Diviser une difficulté en autant de parties qu'il sera nécessaire pour la mieux résoudre.' Of course, this new way of coding becomes most gratifying intellectually, because creation is made possible apparently through pure mechanization. Before the era of the computer, information could certainly be transmitted into totally different languages; for instance, the notes on the music sheet could be played on an instrument (or on several instruments), the sound of the music could be captured and pressed into the grooves of a wax disc, which, in turn, set the air vibrating, and the resulting sound waves could be heard by human ears. All these physical phenomena could be transmitted on paper by physicists through the 'classical' medium of handwriting. Now, everything (and music in particular) can be expressed through the all-pervading digital code. The Marquess of Condorcet had intimations of such a universal language when he wrote:

> Peut-être serait-il utile aujourd'hui distiller une langue écrite qui, reservée uniquement pour les sciences, n'exprimant que ces combinaisons d'idées simples qui se retrouvent exactement les mêmes dans tous les esprits, n'étant employée que pour des raisonnements d'une rigueur logique, pour des opérations de l'entendement précises et calculées, fût entendue par les hommes de tous les pays, et se traduisit dans tous leurs idiomes, sans pouvoir s'altérer comme eux en passant dans l'usage commun.
> (Marquess of Condorcet, *Esquisse d'un Tableau Historique des Progrès de l'Esprit Humain* 1793)

The interesting point in our research is that young people in the late 1990s will have been born into the world of the digital code and of a written language 'understood by men from all countries and translated into all their idioms without suffering from the alterations that result from a transfer into their vernacular'.

In other words, our students, even if they are technically unaware of this change in the 'Gutenberg Galaxy', have the impression that they have been nurtured on the digital code. This state of affairs leads them to believe that since there is a universal language there is a universal truth easily detectable through a simplified code: the combination of 0 and 1. This impression is confirmed by their reading of the Ancient Greek philosophers who advocated the immanence of truth. And because the combination of 0 and 1 seems simple and certainly purely mathematical, they infer that the need to be persuasive is of no use; to our students, the external as well as the inner worlds are governed by facts, which can be expressed in exactly verifiable formulae, and to them that is all there is to it. Of course this contradicts the theory of relativity on which they have also been brought up. And things grow even more complicated when they tackle the worlds of literature and language, because linguistics and semiotics do not shun the issue of rhetoric. And since it seems natural to our youngsters to translate 'truth' into easily recognizable signs (0 and 1), they are drawn towards the analyses of the signified behind the signifier in literature and in social sciences.

Jacques Derrida, coming after Genette's remarkable series on *Figures* (translated as 'narrative figures'), went back to the Saussurean principle of the sign in language to open up what he saw as a closed-in system. Saussure considered that signs in language are arbitrary and differential; the sign was formerly considered as a substitute for something, and any metaphor plays this role; the sign carries the signified *and* the signifier, and Saussure insisted on the fact that the signified and the signifier are as inseparable as the two sides of a single sheet of paper. Derrida wanted to go further and show that a signified might have existed prior to its signifier. So, keeping the couple signified/signifier, he created a term that indicates a relation between the two elements; the relation is non-hierarchical, non-substantive, and he invented the word 'differance', from *différer*, which, in French, means 'to defer, postpone, delay' and also 'to be different from, to differ'. In other words, Derrida offers an open concept: according to the structuralist view, a narrative discourse is self-contained, its system is closed and arranged around a centre which plays the role of an organizing agent (in *expositio* any part withdrawn from the whole of the *demonstratio* ruins the general effect). This view may entail an emphasis on *form*: all the elements of the discourse are supposed to explain the meaning of the discourse, but if form is treated as an entity, the analysis suppresses differential values. On the contrary, to Derrida, the elements should be seen as part of a chain of relations, never having the status of an object. If these elements have multiple (or open) meanings, then the text (narrative discourse) is bound to have a different significance from what the author thinks he wants to say. Derrida gives an example and shows how Jean-Jacques Rousseau contradicts himself when trying to explain the difference between 'harmony' and 'melody' as components of music: Rousseau wants to say that melody is authentic because it springs from passion, but to define melody, Rousseau uses the notions of 'articulation' and 'differentiation' which are supposed to be 'corrupt like harmony'. Such is the deconstructive reading of texts. But what else is literary criticism if not a discourse on the 'meaning' of a text; that is to say, a refusal to take a text at its face value?

Derrida goes even further when he not only shows polysemic meaning in narrative discourse, which can be easily accepted by one and all, but also in scientific discourse. According to general belief, the discourses of science and philosophy are *apparently* directed entirely towards some external referent; the significance of these discourses *apparently* depends on their transparency. In fact, according to Derrida, any supposedly scientific discourse wrongly assumes that it is transparent and that its object is a stable entity; indeed neither language nor literature of any kind is a stable object, and the language of the discourse in which any topic is discussed is not exempt from 'differance'.

Derrida's reasoning might be applied to the two visions of scientific discourse that our students have. The first vision is of scientific discourse as consisting merely of facts, as was mentioned earlier; they do not realize that 'facts' must be intelligibly translated and that this may be done in a biased way (for instance, the transmission of 'facts' concerning nuclear energy, the disposal of nuclear waste or the greenhouse effect). The second vision is that of scientific discourse translated into computer language. The latter language seems to offer all guarantees of truth, while it entirely depends on the accuracy of the scientists who created the programme and fed it into the machine. So eventually, readers, either of the programme or of the text, are sent back to square one; they depend on the scientist's ability to reason and on his power of conviction; in other words, on rhetoric. If students were more aware of these phenomena, their appetite for culture would be whetted.

In a chapter concerning 'Literary theory in the graduate programme', Culler analysed the fact that traditional methods of teaching literature no longer attract students and that, in addition, 'If one asks what sort of faculty the departments who hire recent PhDs are likely to need, the most common answer will doubtless be that they need people *who can teach reading and writing* and who can get undergraduates interested in reading and writing' (Culler 1983: 212). Culler also points to the fact that 'students do not take for granted that literature is something they ought to study' (213) and invites teachers to show students that literature relates to other fields, 'such as philosophy, psychology, sociology, anthropology, and history', so that literature can be seen as an 'alternative account of human experience'. And Culler concludes: 'In other words, literary works will appear not as monuments of a specialized high culture but as powerful, elegant, self-conscious or perhaps self-indulgent manifestations of common patterns of sense-making' (217). One can discuss the propriety of the word 'common' since the very fact of being 'common' leads to clichés, and thus to the destruction of literary works as 'monuments'; maybe the adjective 'recognizable' would fit better.

Nevertheless, Culler takes a great step here towards showing the importance of literature and thus, in reference to other subjects taught, the importance of the laws of literature, otherwise called 'rhetoric'. And in some ways we are led back to Derrida's question: is scientific discourse transparent as to its object? The answer is unmistakably 'no' since the digital code depends so much on various factors, including the programmer's ability and liability.

By comparing literary discourse and scientific discourse, a student will realize that scientific discourse is a demonstration and, as such, one that tries to convince, exactly like philosophical discourse; gradually the student will follow Culler when he says: 'Reading a philosophical text as rhetoric is *the authentic* [Culler's emphasis] philosophical move: to read a philosophical text as rhetoric is to put in question its concepts, to treat them as textual strategies or tropes' (Culler 1983: 222). The best examples of scientific textual strategy can be found in the vocabulary of astronomers when they use analogies such as 'black holes' to try to explain verifiable phenomena. Hundreds of such examples could be quoted.

So to the question: what use is made of rhetoric in our universities? one can already answer that rhetoric is indeed used in our universities, irrespective of the subject taught, but that our students are not necessarily conscious of the fact. Their understanding of the different disciplines would nevertheless be enlarged if they were made more aware of it.

The second question, what survives of rhetoric?, draws in

elements that show a discrepancy between the university teachers' culture and that of their students.

First, the means of expressing oneself through the computer has had a heavy impact on the *rapport de force* between teachers and students. Traditionally, an individual who could control language was superior to other people, possessing a power that put him or her in the position of being able to manipulate them. With the advent of the computer, children and, later, adolescents, can hold the reins of a power that was formerly in the hands of their elders, be they parents or teachers. Furthermore, older people sometimes turn out to be less skilful, or slower, than the youngsters in their use of the new techniques. Practically all arts students are now able to handle word-processors, and most science students are trained to write a program. As computerization rapidly evolves, teachers as well as students run after the latest techniques. Neither group wishes to be outwitted or outdistanced in that race in which, more than anywhere else, knowledge is power.

Second, and even more striking, the difference between the cultures of teacher and student lies in the use of tropes. Twenty-five years ago, it was easy for a university teacher to establish interconnections between what was considered to be 'elitist' culture and 'popular' or 'youth' culture. 'Pop music' could be deciphered (or debunked, according to the speaker) using 'classical' music terms, for instance. In the 1990s, the connections still exist, but the words 'decoding' and 'interface' are used, thus revealing the role of the new techniques. Translation from one form of culture to another is still possible, but visual and auditory languages entail many differences in perception. Students, as a result of television, a staple element in their culture and appreciation of the world at large, are nurtured on video-clips and publicity. In what proportion do they discern the logocentric quality of these modes of expression?

To a certain degree they recognize the gimmicks of publicity, but are they in a position to be aware of the fact that of two pieces of information, that which will be best understood is the redundant one? Advertisements, video-clips with endless repetition (as in contemporary popular songs, excepting perhaps some of the 'rap' songs) give rise to a new language, a lingo which, like slang expressions, changes very quickly and can be grasped only by those who are 'in the know'.

As an example, one can quote the American expression 'a send-up', which has come to mean 'a parody', a phrase that a professor of literature can no longer acknowledge as part of his own battery of vocabulary in literary criticism. Like Derrida, the professor may claim that the student is expressing something different from what is really meant. But the student could argue that the professor is wrong, as the expression is a direct inheritance of the television culture. Another remarkable evolution of the language among the students' generation is Shakespeare's line: 'What a piece of work is man'; what was an exclamation of admiration has now turned into an expression of spite: 'What a piece of work she/he is' nowadays means 'What an awful person she/he is'.

The philologist will explain away such an evolution, but the fact remains: in each generation, speakers as well as writers get caught up with fashions and fads, and use contemporary figures of speech. The students might sometimes be like M. Jourdain in *Le Bourgeois Gentilhomme* in that they use rhetoric unawares. In many ways, they do so more than ever; surrounded by a sea of information, speakers will grow more and more choosy about which wave to ride – hence the huge numbers of new expressions.

So again to the second question: what survives of rhetoric in our universities? The answer is that it is linked to what survives of our contemporary culture. Students only partially know the new codification of knowledge: they more and more opt out of the written language and choose forms of expressions linked with comic strips, cartoons, the video-clips, ascribing to them the values of feelings and ideas. University teachers then assume the role of witness and are morally bound to connect the two types of culture. The influence of moving pictures on literature can be seen in, for example, Dos Passos's *Manhattan Transfer*. Thus teachers should be able to open their students' eyes to the devices of their own civilization in their translation of reality: students should be encouraged to remain alert, for fear of being indoctrinated in spite of themselves.

As a conclusion, let us say that what started as a question about the very future of rhetoric in our universities ends with a conviction that rhetoric is alive and widely used by our students. Showing students how to detect rhetoric and its power in the new media is a moral duty and part of any teaching that aspires to objectivity and open-mindedness.

5 Voice/text/pedagogy: re-reading the writing classroom

Pam Gilbert

One of the metaphoric devices that predominates in current discourses on the teaching of writing – particularly the prescriptive discourses advising on acceptable ways to learn to write – is the metaphor that links 'writing' with 'voice'. So apparently natural is the use of this metaphor that, like many other such discursive devices, it has now become one of the dominant ways in which conceptual understanding of the nature of school writing is framed. Both in textbooks written for students, and in coursebooks written for teachers, the metaphor, and the concepts that support it, have become ways of 'knowing' about classroom writing practices. Elbow, for instance, in his guide called *Writing Without Teachers*, advises students that:

> In your natural way of producing words there is a sound, a texture, a rhythm – *a voice* – which is the main source of power in your writing. I don't know how it works, but this voice is the force that will make a reader listen to you, the energy that drives the meaning through his [*sic*] thick skull.
>
> (Elbow 1973: 6; emphasis added)

In similar vein, Graves argues that 'readers can't read voiceless writing when no one is there any more than they can have dialogue with a mannequin' (Graves 1983: 228). He suggests that voice is the 'driving force' of the writing process: 'the imprint of ourselves on our writing'; 'the person in the piece'.

> Voice . . . is that part of the self that pushes the writing ahead, the dynamo in the process. Take the voice away and the writing collapses of its own weight. There is no writing, just words following words. . . . The voice shows how I choose information, organise it, select the words, all in relation to what I want to

say and how I want to say it. The reader says, 'Someone is here. I know that person. I've been there too.'

(Graves 1983: 227)

The predominance of – even insistence upon – the metaphor in these discourses is an interesting one.[1] Why has it come to be so natural to link the production of written texts to a speech metaphor? Why is the concept of voice seen as so 'powerful'? Why is the *reading* of texts seen to be so associated with a writer's 'voice'? What assumptions about the nature of reading and writing are constructed and then supported by the use of such a metaphor?

This chapter will attempt to unravel some of these questions by considering, initially, where the roots of the 'voice' metaphor lie – to trace the discourses to which such roots most comfortably belong. In so doing, it will demonstrate what understandings of writing are promoted through such discursive connections, and what are not. In particular, the argument will be made that the alignment of the teaching of writing to 'voice' metaphors construes writing practices as personal, individualistic and expressive activities, not as socially learned cultural practices. As a result, discourses about the teaching of writing have frequently been able to contribute little to teachers' (or students') understandings of the way that language practices *work*. As Elbow somewhat helplessly claims of 'voice' in the extract quoted earlier, 'I don't know how it works'. The concept of 'voice' will be reframed and conceptualized as a *constructed reading position* within discourse, the recognition of which is dependent upon a number of other discursive factors that popularly predominate in classrooms.

PERSONAL VOICE: 'THE PERSON BEHIND THE TEXT'

The desire by educators to hear and locate a personal voice in a piece of writing can be read as a manifestation of the desire to identify a human presence in the words on the page, to locate a shadowy 'person' standing in the wings behind the text, to be convinced that a human will generated the production of the work in question. As such, this desire is entirely compatible with a number of other preoccupations in western thought which search for human presence, for the essential 'self', for a 'being' and therefore for truth. A critical reading of these preoccupations in western philosophical traditions (see, for instance, Derrida 1976) indicates their reliance on the establishment of dichotomies or polarities, like, for example, man/woman, soul/body, life/death, presence/absence, speech/writing. Such dichotomies are not necessarily 'natural' or internally logical (although they come to seem so with the general 'opacity' discourse assumes in social practice) but their structure operates to privilege the first-named term, and to place the second in a negative or inferior position to the first. For instance, in the case of the opposition of man/woman, woman's position in the opposition places her in an unequal relationship with the concept 'man'. She is constructed as a secondary sex, derived from man, but possessing negative or inferior qualities to man. As a result, woman derives her status through what she is *not*, rather than what she is. Similarly writing, within the binary opposition of speech/ writing, is defined in terms of what it *lacks*, rather than what it has.

And the *lack* is the lack of the human subject: the distance of the 'voice' (of the living breath) from each of the concepts in opposition. Hierarchical oppositions like these inevitably construct a preference for concepts of presence, unity, identity, immediacy, in comparison with concepts of absence, difference, dissimulation or deferral, and it is within this constructed framework that pedagogical fascination with 'personal voice' in writing becomes more intelligible. Because speaker and listener are both present, simultaneously, when language is spoken, speech becomes privileged as the form of language closest to human presence, closest to meaning as the human presence intended, closest to human truth. Writing, on the other hand, separated from its human subject, is forever left to imitate and compensate for the missing qualities of the human voice/speaker/subject, and to remain as a lifeless, alienated form of expression. It draws its status from what it is *not*, rather than from what it is. As a result, writing metaphors frequently draw upon speech and speaking for their construction, with the result that discourses about writing are frequently pro-speech discourses (and therefore pro-person, pro-presence, pro-life), rather than pro-writing discourses, which become, by the forced dichotomies, anti-person, anti-presence, anti-life.

Consider, for example, these statements by teacher-researchers about the nature of writing.

> Writing is not speech written down, but writing which is widely read gives the impression it is spoken.
>
> (Murray 1982: 41)

> authentic writing . . . is a process through which inner speech

. . . is transformed and realised materially in the world. . . .
Such writing clearly and firmly announces the presence of the
writer in the world.

(Cook *et al.* 1980: 5)

The human voice underlies the entire writing process.

(Graves 1983: 162)

The vitality of writing depends intimately on living speech.

(Harrison 1983: 20)

Similarly Macrorie writes that good writing practice lets 'the voices
in their heads speak' (Macrorie 1980: 10), and the title of a very
well-known and respected writing text is *Active Voice* (Moffett
1981).

The argument could be made that this polarization of writing and
speech, and the resultant implicit privileging of spoken discourse
as more honest, truthful, real, sincere and personal, is misleading
and illusory. It cannot be upheld in terms of the *structure* of language, for speech and writing work from the same system of differentiation and deferment in language (see Derrida 1978). While the
conventional features of many spoken and written genres vary (as
do the conventions *within* spoken and written genres), and while
speech and writing draw upon different sets of paralinguistic features to be 'read', the claim can be made that they are different
modes/channels of the same system: that spoken discourse carries
within it the same traces of absence and deferral of meaning as
does written discourse, that they are part of the same language
system, that they could both be included within a general rubric of
'language'. To assume that some texts have greater purchase on
concepts of reality, truth, immediacy, spontaneity or human identity
merely *because they are spoken*, is an illusion. It is also an illusion
to imagine that the effects of reality, truth, immediacy, spontaneity
or human identity cannot be textually produced in any channel of
discourse: iconic, kinetic, oral or printed.

CLASSROOM PRACTICE: READING AND WRITING 'VOICE'

Demonstration of this can be found within the discourses of popular
writing pedagogy, where an array of particular textual conventions
has often been read as evidence of genuine personal engagement
with texts, as the effects of 'personal voice'. In other words, a
school reading practice has developed (and been documented)

which recognizes particular discourse conventions in student texts as indicators of 'personal involvement', 'personal engagement', 'personal revelation'. For instance, consider these statements teachers made about students' responses to literature:

> We find it impossible to believe that Michelle was not deeply moved by Heaney's poem: the way she construes her experience and the form she chooses are eloquent testimony . . .

> [The student] is deeply immersed in imagining this. . . . Teachers we have worked with have been in no doubt about the quality of his imaginative involvement . . .

> The writer is obviously totally involved here . . . he is genuinely thinking about the scene, not merely echoing someone else's opinion.
>
> (Quoted in Gilbert 1987: 241)

While metaphors of voice and presence are closely associated with an orthodox discourse on literature, they are not associated only with 'literary'-style texts in schools, or with writing in response to literature. Whereas the voice metaphor may well be closely aligned to the literary, and to the privileging of the personal that results, it has slipped into general usage as an expectation of 'writing', generally. For instance, position papers on writing often draw firmly upon metaphors of human presence.

> Real authorship, or authentic writing . . . involves the fullest engagement of the writer in the production of meaningful text under pressure of her conscious and unconscious intention. . . . Conceived in this manner, writing involves the most active and direct interplay between thought and language, a transaction which is highly *personalised* and specific to the individual writer. Such writing clearly and firmly announces the presence of the writer in the world. It is a significant act of original and responsible meaning-making, in the best sense.
>
> (Cook *et al.* 1980: 5)

Similarly it is voice metaphors which are often used to describe motivation for writing, and commitment to reworking texts.

> the force of revision, the energy for revision, is rooted in the child's voice, the urge to express. Every teacher has heard the words, 'Do I have to do it over? Why do I have to write?' These

children are saying: 'I don't have a voice. I don't see the sense in what I am doing.'

(Graves 1983: 160)

It is important for many teachers to find evidence of a student's personal involvement in the writing experience, an experience which has hopefully been preceded by a similarly engaging literary experience (see Gilbert 1989). And this is not surprising, given that a reasonably orthodox assumption made of literary discourse – a discourse that holds considerable influence and power in the secondary English classroom – is that it offers readers the chance to share in the universal experience of being human, to enrich and extend readers' perceptions of the human spirit. Literary discourse is thus frequently read in terms of the author's intentions, and evaluated in terms of the quality of the author's perception of the human condition. So if students' 'personal', reflective, imaginative writing – the literature of the classroom – is seen to lie within or be adjacent to public literacy discourse, it, too, may be read from within the same practice.

And this does happen. In many discussions of the writing students complete in English classrooms, it becomes clear that personal writing is recognizable to teachers because it has many of the features typically expected of literature. In fact, personal writing is often described (and discursively constructed by teachers) from within a literary framework. For instance in this discussion of students' written responses to literary texts, Stratta and Dixon (1987) slip easily from the personal subjectivity of the student (the student's *voice*) to the personal subjectivity of the author (the author's *intention*). The 'voice' (what the student really feels or believes) connects with the 'truth' (what the author really intended), and the 'truth' becomes synonymous with the poem.

from her own experience [Fiona] decides the poet is right – this is her positive evaluation of his truthfulness to childhood.

By a strange coincidence, [Michelle] had found a template in the poem to fit something in her own experience, and the way to deal with that was to write her own poem.

(Stratta and Dixon 1987: 186, 187)

Not surprisingly, the poem – *literary* discourse – becomes recognizable and identifiable because it is in opposition to *non-literary* discourse: the binarism again. While the literary is associated with the person, with the emotions and with the human spirit, the non-literary is linked to the public, to rationality and to the mind. It is thus in opposition to the subjectivity/bias/personalism that accrues to the literary, and draws its superiority in several of the oppositions (fact/fiction – reason/emotion – public/private) by its distance from the 'voice'/the person/the human subject. While literature is created, inspired and imagined, philosophy (for instance) is contemplated, intellectualized and reasoned. However, as theories of textuality and critical language studies have now convincingly demonstrated (Foucault 1970; Fairclough 1989), claims for a greater 'purity' of some discourse forms over others, as in, for instance, the constructed opposition between the subjectivity of the literary and the objectivity of the non-literary, are untenable. 'Subjectivity' and 'objectivity' are better understood as particular textual practices: practices significant both in the production ('writing') and the interpretation ('reading') of texts.

Such practices are, ironically, more often recognized by students than by teachers. In work completed with twelfth-grade writing students in an Australian high school (Gilbert 1989), several of the students described the 'reading practices' their teacher seemed to prefer. In interview they remarked:

> I was pleased when she said she enjoyed reading it and that I understood personal voice, because that was what I was trying to achieve. I was trying to show that I understood it. I was happy that she recognised it.

> I tried really hard to make it more personalised and I rigged the whole thing to make it look really personal, whereas all the other ones . . . I hadn't and I had been given really low marks and she gave me a really good mark for it and a good comment.

> Before I do an essay for English, not really any other subject, I think what the teacher would like and the way they dress comes into it even. The way they'd like to see it written. Then I have to go and rewrite what I thought before into what they'd like to see.

> > (Gilbert 1989: 130, 134, 158)

The teacher in this same study similarly sensed the real difficulties associated with the recognition of, and search for, personalism and subjectivity in the classroom, but she was placed in a difficult position as a teacher-reader. While she was able to observe of the students' work that 'They equate personal with "I think", not a style of writing' (Gilbert 1989: 131), she found it difficult to contemplate that personal writing was a conventional form of writing, consisting of a set of stylistic features that were recognizable, repeatable and therefore teachable: 'They don't seem to have that [a style of writing] yet' (131). Similarly she recognized some of the peculiar problems that poetry writing – the form of literary discourse most closely identified with the human subject – introduced into the classroom. Was it to be read through a 'personal voice' frame, or through the more specifically textual frame of poetic discourse?

> Somehow you feel they are much more personally involved with the poetry they write and your criticism of them is somehow more personal when it's about their poetry than when it's about their short stories, especially when you feel that they're trying to express emotions and have failed and then you're criticising them for failing and yet the fact that they tried somehow deserves more credit than writing a short story.
>
> (Gilbert 1989: 154–5)

She recognized, for instance, that she could not read student poetry, in the school site, in the same way that she might read poetry in a public site.

> with Paul, I made a comment there, have you deliberately left out punctuation? It wasn't clear whether it was a deliberate thing in a poem or he hadn't just put it in because he never puts it in.
>
> Fascinating about this. It's the way I read it. When I first read it – terrible punctuation, spelling etc. I first read it and I was really put off. This is hopeless. I don't know why he bothered; he's got the wrong tone . . . then I was starting to go through them again and I said to someone, 'Listen to this'. And I had to read it aloud to them. When I read it aloud I suddenly – it really did have those elements of humour and surprise but because I was so put off with the lack of punctuation when I first started, I hadn't picked them up.
>
> (Gilbert 1989: 152, 151)

In other words, the particular nature of the discursive site of the classroom had prepared her to expect a student voice, not the authoritative voice of an author. The focus on the speech metaphors of 'voice' had again obscured the textuality of the classroom, and made it difficult to unravel the language practices which had both constructed and interpreted the student's text.

DISCOURSE, GENRE, TEXT: WRITING AND READING IN THE ENGLISH CLASSROOM

One way out of the impasse that voice metaphors have constructed is to frame practices in the language classroom through discourse theory: through theories rooted in concepts of language as social practice, rather than theories rooted in concepts of language as personalist expression (see, for instance, Kress 1985; Fairclough 1989). A shift of this nature means that the texts which are produced within the specific situational site of the classroom can then be integrally related to various *social practices* – both writing and reading practices – which operate at the broader institutional levels of the school. In other words, texts that are produced within the classroom site need to be read from within the discursive network that such a site represents.

For instance, when a student constructs a poem in an English classroom, the text that results will seldom be read only in terms of the student's understanding of poetic discourse (however that has been introduced into the classroom site). It will also be read in terms of other discourses that are drawn into the school site. The text that a student attempts to construct, within this discursive network, draws obviously from an identifiable generic form – say the lyric poem – but the *site* means that the production of that genre will vary in significant ways. The classroom site means that the reading of literary genres – their recognition, framing and interpretation – must vary in significant ways from orthodox literary sites, and the teacher's comments quoted earlier indicate some ways in which this happens. Concepts of authorial superiority ('authority') and of intellectual and emotional insight ('poetic vision'), are clearly difficult to attribute to student texts, when the teacher's reading practice is drawn from discourses on learning, on language competence, on adolescent development, on pedagogical practice, on assessment. Rather obviously, a student poem could be placed in a different site (say a recognized poetry magazine), afforded the usual presentational features such a site guarantees, and then be 'read' differently. While most genres rely on particular reading practices for their production, reading practices are, in turn, dependent upon other discursive features as conditions of possibility.

In particular the usual roles and relationships that are

conventionalized within a lyric poem, for instance, become difficult to construct and difficult to interpret at the classroom site. The lyric poem, as is typical of genres of literary discourse, assumes that the writer will take up a powerful and 'authoritative' role, and generically constructs a reading position which defers to the writer and the significance of the literary event. It is a convention of literary discourse to have speaking positions of authority like this, but such a convention is clearly at odds with the speaking positions of authority in a classroom site. Far from taking up a position of authority within discourse, the student is usually the spoken 'other' – the spoken subject of much classroom discourse.

There are few discourses from which students can speak authoritatively in the classroom, and the discourse of 'the person' is really no exception. For even if the person/the individual/the self could be 'known authoritatively' by the student (Henriques *et al.* 1984), ways of writing, talking or constructing such knowing are still limited by available discourses and genres. Personal writing can be recognized when a writing position is taken up from within discourses which conventionalize such a relationship between writer and reader, and literary discourse is clearly one of the best known of these discourses. As a result, narrative and poetic genres – the common genres of literary discourse – have come to be regarded as natural forms of self-expression and of personal voice. The constructed nature of both the genres and their discursive roots is again unnoticed and bypassed in the slippage from voice, to truth, to poem.

The interaction between student-text and teacher-reader thus takes place within a particular – and extremely complex – discursive network. In the school, student writers attempt to construct recognizable social language forms (conventional and cultural generic forms) like letters, news reports, book reviews, short stories, advertisements, arguments, sports commentaries, but without any of the conventional social conditions which made the production (both the construction and interpretation) of such texts possible. As some recognition of this potentially unproductive site for language practice, writing pedagogy has often advised teachers to provide 'real' audiences and 'real' tasks for students (to specify what audience and what purpose the text is to serve), and to write personally, honestly, truthfully – in their own voices. In many ways, 'voice' thus becomes synonymous with 'real': if a student's *voice* can be 'heard' in a text, then it is a 'real' text. Its purpose will be clear. The un-real is seen to be writing that is voiceless – it has no conviction, no personalism, no authenticity. It is removed from the human subject/speaker/voice.

The dynamic features of language as social practice are thus obscured by this stress on reality, honesty, personalism and voice, and, partly as implicit recognition of this, writing pedagogy has instead focused on the creative and expressive potential of language for the individual. The voice takes priority over the text because, in this social site, the text is frequently non-functional.

MOVING FROM VOICE TO TEXTS: THE POSSIBILITIES FOR PRACTICE

The difficulty in relying on a concept of voice to make a text intelligible and readable is that it is both an unhelpful and a misleading explanation of how meaning is produced in discourse. Voice metaphors suggest that finding a personal voice is like 'finding yourself': finding confidence, self-esteem, authority. Most popular writing pedagogy does not address the way in which student texts function in discourse, because it is not based upon theories of language as social practice. However, if writing is conceptualized as a *social* activity, then the conditions of production and the conditions of interpretation of texts can be described as social and cultural practices. Writing/speaking (the production of texts) can then be seen as integrally related to a discursive site: to the generic forms conventionalized through such a site, to specific subject-matter, and, perhaps most importantly for the argument here, to the construction of particular reading positions in texts – to the construction of certain roles and relationships within discourse.

For instance, if 'voice' seems to be something that readers can recognize ('hear'), it is clearly the result of framing (reading) a text in a particular way, or of recognizing certain conventional textual features associated with voice. In other words, once the text is placed within a particular reading practice, the concept of 'personal voice' can be used to describe the construction of a particular *reading position* in that text: a reading position which allows a teacher-reader, in a school site, to recognize an apprentice-writer's attempts to construct a plausible text. It could be argued that the desire to position a student writer in such a personalist mould (to want to see evidence of a personal voice in a student school text) can be understood through a closer consideration of the teacher's position within this particular discursive site.

The English teacher, caught within a number of not entirely

compatible discourses, is urged to maintain an unequal power relationship between teacher and student for school disciplinary (and ultimately political) purposes, and yet to have them write to her as to a trusted adult for writing pedagogical purposes; she is encouraged to disguise the institutional nature of the school site, and yet to assess and grade their written texts; she is urged to have the students write in a variety of forms, for a variety of purposes, yet most student writing is read only by her and has no social purpose outside its school site (see Gilbert 1989). The personal voice metaphor, in such a context, seems to offer something that is real and truthful (the ideal learner) in a site that is otherwise patently un-real and un-truthful.

But language education must be conceived of more broadly than this metaphor will allow – and than much current debate would suggest – if we are to alter classroom practice. The complex discursive positioning of the English teacher has many contradictions and dilemmas, but one dilemma that can be addressed theoretically is that which questions what language knowledge can be taught, and how it might best be taught – although such questions need to be framed carefully within critical discourse theory. For instance, while a dominant current concern is whether an understanding of generic forms might be powerful knowledge to share with students (see, for instance, the debate in Reid 1986), such concerns need to be placed within a broader framework. While an understanding of the generic conventions of a society at a given time is undeniably important social knowledge, such knowledge is only useful if it is *social* knowledge: if it can account for the range of conventions that texts display in social practice, and if it acknowledges the role of reading in the production of various generic designations.

As has been argued earlier, generic forms vary in significant ways depending upon their site. A business letter is not everywhere and always the same, nor is a conversation, a sports commentary, a film review, a quiz programme. The social institutions within which such genres occur, the discourses upon which they have drawn, the writing and reading positions they establish and rely upon, result in the production of a particular text which is recognizable generically, but which relies upon broader social understandings to be unpacked, reworked, repeated. If English education concerns itself with exploring the social dynamics of language in use, and with offering students a rudimentary understanding of discourse theory, then knowledge and competence crucial to both making and remaking of texts become accessible to students. In other words, the way in which language works becomes the classroom focus.

The analysis of texts which occur in a range of different sites, but which exhibit similar generic features, provides an ideal classroom activity for displaying this dynamic nature of language and for emphasizing the importance of *site* – and all that a site entails (see Mellor 1987). Some of the traditional written genres of the English classroom – the poem, the story, the book review, the news item, the essay, the diary – and many of the traditional spoken genres – the debate, the interview, the persuasive speech, the role play, the sales pitch – display dramatic variation of textual convention dependent upon site, and the reason for such variation can become a key research focus for the English classroom. Instead of just asking *how* language works, critical discourse theory pushes questions like *why?* and *where?*

The way in which reading positions are constructed – and recognized – within texts becomes integrally related to such questions. How does a writer produce a plausible and coherent text, and why are some texts more plausible, more coherent, more seemingly 'natural' than others? How important for the recognition of plausibility, coherence and 'naturalness' is the reading frame that the reader adopts to produce the text, and how much freedom do readers have to decide how they will read particular texts?[2] How are writing and reading positions learnt, and what space exists within such positions for resistance, rewriting, remaking? Analysis of a variety of reading positions – again through working with generically similar texts differently sited – demonstrates ways in which readers are coerced and seduced by familiarity and repetition, and ways in which reading positions line up in various reading formations to further entrench the commonsensical nature of reading.[3] In particular, the way in which teachers frame a text to look for evidence of personal voice could become a practice to analyse. What student texts can be read in this way? What textual features key English teachers to such a reading?

The shift suggested in this chapter from voice to text in the English classroom – from speech metaphors to critical discourse analysis – needs to rest firmly on three broad theoretical bases: a base which posits a concept of writing that is not tied to a voice, a presence, or an ultimate meaning; a base which acknowledges the constructed nature of discursive power networks and the way in which such networks organize and systematize social and cultural practice; and a base which accepts that reading is predominantly a social activity which involves learning a set of arbitrary cultural practices which privilege certain meanings. Such a shift, with its emphasis on textuality rather than voice metaphors, would not only demystify many of the confusing and misleading practices that predominate in language classrooms, but it would make the *craft* of writing, and the *practice* of reading, accessible to students (and teachers). In this way critical language study then becomes possible. The way in which language works, and the way in which language can be made to work differently, become the proper focus of language classrooms. And this, I would argue, represents a powerful shift forward in writing pedagogy, and the new direction that writing classrooms should take.

NOTES

A different version of this chapter has been published, in 1991, in volume 23, number 4 of *English Education*.

1 For a fuller discussion of examples of the use of the metaphor of 'voice', see Gilbert (1989; 1991).
2 See Mellor (1987; 1989) for workshop activities for the secondary school on the construction of reading positions and the recognition of different reading practices.
3 The ways in which girls are particularly affected by reading formations, and the possibilities that exist for resistance and re-reading, are discussed in Gilbert and Taylor (1991).

6 Issues of audience: egocentrism revisited

Deborah P. Berrill

This chapter, which deals with argumentative writing of university undergraduates, begins with a conundrum. On the one hand, we generally think of young adults as being relatively sophisticated thinkers who are able to empathize with alternative points of view. Yet, influential voices have identified 'something like cognitive egocentricity' (Hays 1988: 55) in the writing of adolescents and young adults (Bereiter 1980; Kroll 1984; Hays 1988; Hays *et al.* 1988). Bereiter refers to 'egocentric writing in middle childhood and beyond' (Bereiter 1980: 86) and Hays more closely identifies this egocentric writing of undergraduates as being related to the writers' conceptualization of their audiences. She writes, '[This study of undergraduates] suggests something like cognitive egocentricity reflected in papers assessed at the lower and even middle positions of the Perry Scheme [a descriptor of socio-cognitive development]' (Hays 1988: 55). These researchers, then, give testimony to the fact that adolescents and young adults exhibit some sort of egocentrism in their writing.

Yet, as Kroll (1984) indicates, the notion that writers of this age – young adulthood – are egocentric seems to fly in the face of our experience. He writes,

> [An] objection to the social perspective is that the concept of egocentrism cannot be meaningfully applied to college students. While a small number of college-age students may be egocentric in a fundamental way – perhaps even child-like in their assumptions that their readers share their knowledge and perspectives – it seems obvious that the great majority of our students are quite capable of decentering in familiar contexts involving everyday circumstances. If so, then it seems misleading to call these

students 'egocentric', particularly because the label often implies a pervasive deficit in social functioning.

(Kroll 1984: 181–2)

Therefore, we are left with a feeling that there is some kind of egocentricity in the writing of young adults and yet that it is not appropriate or logical to say so.

WHY THE PRESENCE OF EGOCENTRICITY IN ARGUMENTATIVE WRITING MATTERS

Meeting the needs of one's audience has been a concern of those interested in argument since Aristotle. Much of the *Rhetoric* addresses itself to considerations which must be met in order to meet the needs of the audience; and, rhetoricians today remain interested in the same issues. A writer's ability to write for an audience is important, for if the needs of the audience are not met, the argument presented is judged less successful than it would otherwise be. It is less credible, it is deemed less reasonable and it is often judged as being less *reasoned*. We value argument for its inherent reasoning processes, which identify and evaluate alternative positions: therefore, argument which does not recognize the legitimacy of alternative positions fails to satisfy our purposes for engaging in argumentative thinking.

Apparent egocentricity in the writing of post-secondary students is also a concern to us regarding our own instructional practices. From international studies, we know that students at school-leaving age have difficulty writing effective argument (Pringle and Freedman 1985; Applebee *et al.* 1986; Gorman *et al.* 1988). Connor's (1990) recent multiple-regression analysis of the International Study of Written Composition demonstrates that audience concerns, also referred to as socio-cognitive concerns, do contribute to composition quality. Not surprisingly, Connor's analysis shows that the Toulmin measure of reasoning (including criteria of claims, data and warrants) accounts for 48 per cent of the variation in scoring of argumentative texts. In addition, however, effective use of credibility appeal was an important predictor of writing quality. As Connor says, 'In other words, good essays contained the writer's own personal experiences, a good knowledge of the subject, and an awareness of the audience's values' (Connor 1990: 83). If our students' argumentative papers are egocentric, lacking a demonstration of the legitimacy of the audience's values, their papers will not constitute satisfactory argument.

SOCIO-COGNITIVE DEVELOPMENT

Socio-cognitive research is concerned with recognizing the inter-action of social and cognitive aspects of meaning making. This includes awareness of reader needs regarding information process-ing as well as awareness of the legitimacy of alternative points of view. Rubin *et al.* specify some of the dimensions of these socio-cognitive issues to include the following (among others):

- the recognition that the audience may have a different point of view than the writer
- the degree to which the writer is able to construct the audience and their points of view
- the degree to which the writer attempts to use the represen-tation of the audience in selecting writing options
- the degree to which the writer represents the audience's knowledge, values, associations.

(Rubin *et al.* 1984: 299)

The work of Rubin *et al.* confirms that the different social cogni-tive measures they used in assessing papers 'did not exhibit strong interrelatedness among themselves', confirming other research 'which suggests multidimensionality rather than convergence within the construct of social cognition' (Rubin *et al.* 1984: 304–5).

Hays's (1988) work on socio-cognitive aspects of argumentative writing is also helpful in approaching the same issues from a differ-ent perspective. Hays uses the Perry Scheme (Perry 1970) of episte-mic reasoning to analyse socio-cognitive development of secondary school and undergraduate university writers. The Perry Scheme looks at the way adult thinkers make meaning by addressing the writer's acknowledgement of the legitimacies of alternative points of view and the writer's construction of knowledge as either absolute or relative.

Hays's application of the Perry Scheme to argumentative writing is helpful in its different approach to the multidimensional aspects of social cognition. The work that she and her colleagues have done shows that the Perry Scheme 'was a stronger predictor of paper scores [in general argumentative writing performance] than were demographic variables such as grade level, age, major, gender, and so on' (Hays *et al.* 1988: 406). Hays and her colleagues looked closely at the degree to which writers reasonably engaged view-points different from their own and found that most writers omitted 'the statement (implicit or explicit) of reasons for readers' view. Many writers simply articulated readers' positions and then responded to them, often in overfacile ways suggesting that they did not fully understand why their audience might question their points' (Hays 1988: 54). It is apparent from research that socio-cognitive aspects of argumentative writing contribute strongly to the successfulness of the writing. It seems then, that if we are to understand what is happening in the argumentative writing of young adults, we need to have a clearer understanding of the apparent egocentricity in their writing. Let us look at the papers of this study.

DIFFERENCES IN YOUNG ADULTS' ABILITIES TO CONSTRUCT THESES AND TO ACKNOWLEDGE ALTERNATIVE POINTS OF VIEW

This study is concerned primarily with what we might learn from the writing of young adults aged 22+, university undergraduates in their final year of university who show a discrepancy between their abilities to construct theses (a cognitive act) and their abilities to acknowledge the legitimacy of alternative points of view (a socio-cognitive act). Twenty-one undergraduates in their final year of study at a small liberal arts university in Ontario, Canada, volun-teered to take part in the study. Female to male ratio was approxi-mately 4:1; arts candidates made up 90 per cent of the participants and science candidates, 10 per cent. Although this sample might initially seem to be problematic in relation to sex and area of study, there is strong evidence to suggest that the single most important predictor of argumentative writing score is the subject's educational level, even in the presence of other demographic variables of age and sex (Hays *et al.* 1988). All students had a minimum of a B average and there were no students for whom English was a second language.

The prompt given to the writers in this research was: 'Should parents be able to control the lives of their teenage children?' Participants were divided into groups of four to discuss the question for a maximum of two hours before commencing their individual writing in response to the question. Thus, students discussed the topic on one or two days and were given a maximum of two hours, in one- or two-hour time allotments, to write and revise their texts over the next week.

Before evaluation, all papers were typed and identifying information was removed. Three trained raters independently evaluated all essays, using criterion-referenced scales and rating the papers for audience awareness and for thesis development at separate sessions. The audience awareness instrument was based on the Crediton Model of Language Development (Wilkinson *et al.* 1980) and on House's (1980) work on validity.

The audience awareness scale (Figure 6.1) is consistent with other developmental reasoning models such as the Perry Scheme (Perry 1970) and Rubin *et al.*'s (1984) framework for conceptualizing the dimensions of social cognition. However, this scale focuses exclusively on audience issues as they relate to alternative points of view.

The thesis development scale (Figure 6.2) was based on several

Figure 6.1 Audience Awareness Scale

Assumptions: Writers address issues and construct arguments which appeal to particular audiences. The audience may present additional validity complications, whether through the degree of difference of opinion it holds in relation to the writer or through the heterogeneity of its composition wherein there is not only a single different opinion but a number of different opinions.

1 *Egocentric*: Easiest argument to write. The writer assumes that the audience shares the same attitudes and knowledge base. (Some may not recognize this as argument.)

2 *Cursory awareness of alternative point of view*: Argument anticipates an opposing position but does not deal with it.

3 *Acknowledgement of alternative point of view*: Argument recognizes alternative point of view but does not accept the validity of it.

4 *Appreciation of alternative point of view*: Argument recognizes the validity of an alternative point of view and qualifies initial position accordingly.

5 *Accommodation of alternative point of view*: Argument explicitly acknowledges validity of alternative view and incorporates that view in the *structure* of the argument, either through partial support and incorporation of that view or through some degree of refutation of the alternative view which recognizes the validity of the claim but which posits a stronger validity claim to the writer's view.

---

models of language development, especially the Crediton Model (Wilkinson *et al.* 1980) and Vygotksy's (1962) model of concept formation. Models of Moffett (1968), Peel (1971), Britton *et al.* (1975) and Biggs and Collis (1982) also made significant contributions.

Not surprisingly, all papers of the undergraduates in this study display at the least an 'emerging thesis'. It is apparent that people who have had at least three years of university experience have learned how to construct theses and how to provide the evidence supporting the theses.

Figure 6.3 shows that 86 per cent of the papers demonstrate an ability to use a thesis to build an argument and to provide evidence to support that thesis. As well, the development displayed by the results indicates an expected pattern of continuity.

Given the proficiency of thesis construction and support as the

Figure 6.2 Thesis Development Scale

---

1   *No thesis*: Empty assertions; unconnected opinions without developed support.

2   *Loose focus*: Ideas are still essentially independent. There is a general sense that all ideas relate to a topic but most often ideas are linked only to a single other idea in the paper. There is no central thesis.

3   *Emerging thesis*: There is an attempt to prove a thesis and an accompanying attempt to define and support ideas presented. The relationship between ideas is apparent, although sometimes implicit, but the nature of that relationship varies. Items are not parallel in type or in value. Inconsistent.

4   *Restricted thesis*: Explicit statement of thesis which may or may not be an answer to a question at issue. Ideas are adequately defined and supported. The relationship between ideas is apparent with an attempt to maintain consistency in type or value of evidence. There is no attempt to speculate or to apply the thesis to other situations.

5   *Elaborated thesis*: The thesis is a probable answer to a question at issue: this answer largely determines the selection of evidence (content considerations) as well as the structure of the piece as a whole (rhetorical considerations). There may be an attempt to apply the thesis to other situations.

6   *Hypothesizing thesis*: The whole piece is logically linked as for 'elaborated thesis' but now also includes speculation and/or application to other situations as an integral part of the argument.

Figure 6.3 Thesis Development: Papers of Undergraduates (N = 21)

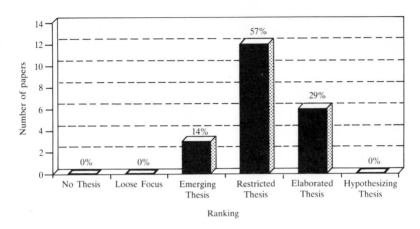

single most telling feature of argumentative reasoning (see Pringle and Freedman 1985 and Connor 1990), what is surprising about these papers is the degree to which the writing does *not* consider points of view which differ from that of the writer. Figure 6.4 shows the distribution of rankings in the audience awareness rating. The fact that 62 per cent of the papers acknowledge, appreciate and accommodate alternative points of view is consistent with the

Figure 6.4 Audience Awareness: Papers of Undergraduates (N = 21

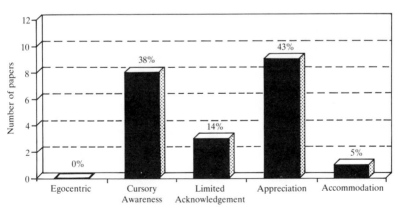

Ranking of degree to which writer considered a point of view which differed from his or her own

generally high level of thesis development. Almost half (48 per cent) of the writers show *appreciation* of an alternative point of view, recognizing the legitimacy of alternative points of view. This corresponds very closely with similar studies using the Perry Scheme (Hays forthcoming).

Yet 38 per cent of the papers in this study demonstrate only a cursory awareness of an alternative point of view, anticipating opposing positions but often not even giving explicit recognition to those positions. Again, this is consistent with results of other studies (Hays 1988; Hays *et al.* 1988). Two things are bewildering about these results. The first is that the development apparent in the results does not indicate the same kind of continuity as that of thesis development. The bi-modal distribution is striking and may indicate different sorts of development from those we have previously considered. The second surprising aspect of these results is that it is not consistent with results from the papers of 16-year-olds who wrote on the same question in a different study (Berrill 1990a).

The papers of the 16-year-olds demonstrate explicit acknowledgement of the legitimacies of at least two points of view, that of the parent and that of the teenager (Berrill 1990a). In fact, the 16-year-olds are at such pains to explain their appreciation of alternative points of view, that they usually do not get to the stage of evaluating the points of view they express: their writing remains expositive, telling 'all about' parental and teenager points of view, rather than being argumentative and evaluating the validities of those points of view. However, it does not seem logical that 16-year-olds write argument that is less egocentric than that of university undergraduates.

EGOCENTRICITY IN THE TEXTS OF UNDERGRADUATES

In order to understand the kinds of egocentricity found in the writing of the undergraduates, let us look at the texts themselves. First we will look at a paper which does accommodate alternative point of view, explicitly acknowledging its validity. Donna's paper demonstrates this.

[1] Whether parents should be able to control the lives of their teenage children is most definitely a controversial issue. The problem I have with this discussion lies in the use of the word 'control'. Parents are definitely faced with many decisions as they raise their children, but I believe the answers to their problems

do not come from controlling the lives of their children. There are a number of important ingredients in the parent-child relationship and if these are considered, I believe that control will not be a necessary factor.

[2] The problem with control is that it stops an action – there is no room for choice or decision. In addition, with control, there is no place for growth. Consequently, it seems far better to allow one to have the choice to make one's own decision. The problem that arises here, though, is whether a teenager has adequate skills to make an appropriate decision. Thus, parents step in and make the decision for the child because they feel they have his/her best interests at heart. The problem is, though, that one day mom and dad will not be there to make the decisions and if a teenager is not given opportunities to make choices when he/she is young, how will he/she know what to do at a later time.

[3] Consequently, I believe that it is important that teenagers make their own decisions. The role of the parents is to supply their children with the necessary tools to make these decisions. Thus, parents should establish rules and set guidelines for their children as they are growing. These rules and guidelines will provide a good basis and background for teenagers to reflect on when they are making decisions.

[4] In addition to setting guidelines, parents must be role models and thus, live what they speak. A growing child will remember the actions of a parent much more than what a parent says. Studies have indicated that when there is conflict between what a parent says and what a parent does, the child will remember what the parent does. Personally, I agree with this philosophy from my own experiences growing up. I do not remember my parents forbidding me to do things – such as smoking or dating boys before a certain age, etc. Instead I feel that this was not necessary because of the role models and home environment provided. I distinctly remember friends of mine smoking and dating boys behind their parents' backs and me feeling how wrong it was. I think my parents had equipped me with information, through my home environment, which helped me realize right from wrong on my own. In addition my mom, being a teacher, always had school work to do and thus she modelled good work habits which became ingrained in me (throughout high school anyway!). Again, my parents never had to decide for me whether I should stay in and study or go to a certain

function. Because of the stable models they provided I was able to decide when I had time to go out and when I had too much work and should stay home. In addition my parents gave me their opinions and advice on what they thought I should do.

[5] In addition to providing models though, it is important for the parents to communicate with their teenagers. They should find out why their children want to do something and listen to their viewpoints and rationale. Communication also entails the parents letting their child know how they feel, their viewpoints. This is how a parent can enable their child to grow. In this way, the parent is outlining how he/she feels giving options, outlining possible outcomes to decisions, reflecting on one's own experience and ultimately giving support. The teenager can then make a decision based on the discussion with the parent and also knowing how the parent feels regarding the issue. The important point is that the decision is the teenager's and that he/she is aware of this fact. This feeling that one has the capabilities to make one's own decisions helps to build self-confidence and self-esteem. Thus, this individual is able to make decisions on one's own – something which is important for a successful, fulfilling life.

[6] Some people may criticize this philosophy by saying that some teenagers are not capable of making their own decisions or that what if a teenager makes a wrong decision which will ruin his/her future. Personally, I still feel that control is not the answer. A parent may be preventing their child from making a mistake that time but what about next time? Making the decision for the teenager will not prepare him/her for the time when he/she will have to make the decision for him/herself. And secondly, what about the resentment that might be building in the child?

[7] Another argument people in favour of control might put forth is that they used control methods on their children and they turned out fine. An interesting point though involves what constitutes 'fine'. Has anyone ever asked their children if they were happy about the controls and limitations placed on them? Have these controls left memories of bitterness and anger which affect their everyday lives and relationships with others? In addition, these same individuals would have probably turned out just as well *without* the control that the parents had over them. Moreover, these individuals may have turned out to be happier feeling that they did it on their own and had the trust and respect of their parents.

[8] In conclusion, I maintain that parents are not expected nor have the right to control their children's lives. They are there to provide guidelines, viewpoints, models of behaviour and advice which will help their children in making decisions throughout life. Parents should trust and respect their teenagers' viewpoints just as teenagers should trust and respect their parents' advice. These mutual feelings will facilitate keeping the lines of communication open between parent and child. Thus, in the end the teenager will make the final decision and is given the room to grow and learn in the process – a necessary ingredient to a meaningful, fulfilling life.

(Donna)

Donna's paper begins with explicit acknowledgement that there is more than one opinion about this topic. Donna establishes her thesis ('There are a number of important ingredients in the parent-child relationship and if these are considered, I believe that control will not be a necessary factor'), defines her use of central terminology ('control') and develops reasons to support her definition ('The problem with control is that it stops an action – there is no room for choice or decision'). The next paragraphs constitute the body of the argument, elaborating the thesis through delineation of responsibilities of parents in teaching teenagers how to make decisions. Each idea in this central section is related both to the initial thesis statement and to adjacent ideas, following classical argumentative structure.

Regarding the legitimacy given to alternative points of view, Donna explicitly states a refutation to her own point of view in the second paragraph. In addition, paragraphs six and seven explicitly state opposing points of view, thereby acknowledging the validity of those views. However, it is not only inclusion of alternative points of view which demonstrates Donna's appreciation of their legitimacy: it is also the language she uses to express those points of view which demonstrates the *reasonableness* of the alternative positions.

Once the plausibility of alternative positions has been presented, Donna goes on to demonstrate why her position has even greater validity, again following classic argumentative strategy. Let us look at the second paragraph to see how she does this. She continues from the above extract, saying,

The problem is, though, that one day mom and dad will not be there to make the decisions and if a teenager is not given opportunities to make choices when he/she is young, how will he/she know what to do at a later time.

Again, not only has Donna made her position and the logic of her position explicit, but she has continued using the same type of language: language which is moderate in tone and reasonable in nature. Not only does Donna exhibit developed 'cognitive' structures, she also exhibits developed socio-cognitive awareness in her explicit reference to alternative points of view and in her use of language which presents the reasonableness of those positions.

In contrast, the papers which scored low on the audience awareness scale showed only cursory awareness of an alternative point of view. Let us look first at John's paper.

[1] 'Should parents be able to control the lives of their teenage children?'

[2] One's point of view towards the above question is influenced greatly by two key words: control and teenager. Dependent on how one cares to define these two words, one's reaction to the question may change greatly. A teenager is any individual between the ages of thirteen to nineteen. With such an age difference, comes differences in maturity, independence, decision making abilities and responsibilities.

[3] The word 'control' provides the largest degree of controversy surrounding the question. If you attach a literal meaning to control (i.e. oppressing, domineering, limiting, restrictive . . ., etc.), I feel the answer to the question is a categorical *NO*. If on the other hand you see control as meaning influencing in a positive way, the question becomes much more easier to defend. The argument concerned with here is not whether parents should or should not exert control but how is control defined.

[4] Control is not a realistic term, one person cannot 'control' another if they are to maintain a well balanced relationship. You do not control the people around you, you merely influence them. You cannot control an individual, you can manipulate the circumstances or conditions they encounter. If you have control of a person's life they are no longer an individual. The concept of control may work initially on a child but inevitably it is doomed to failure. If control is gained through punishment, removal of privilege and threat eventually the child will ignore the parents and rebel to gain freedom for themselves. Fighting for control sets up a power struggle between parent and child

that neither wins. A healthy relationship is one of give and take not domination and submission.

(John)

John's paper expresses ideas with considerable potential, but the lack of elaboration and explanation of his generalizations reveal a lack of awareness of the reader's needs even from an informational point of view. John has placed the initial question in a larger framework, but he has failed to explain that framework sufficiently. As readers, we need to understand the differences the writer intends between the words 'control', 'influence' and 'manipulate'. As well, the short, terse style and the hammering repetition of the word 'control' renders the statements assertive. The lack of elaboration combines with this assertive tone to make the sentences didactic. In addition, however, the writing is dogmatic due to the actual language used, such as when John writes, 'The concept of control may work initially on a child but inevitably it is doomed to failure.' The words, 'inevitably . . . doomed' are highly charged and insistent, negating the legitimacy of any other conclusion.

Another example which shows a different sort of assertion and lack of awareness of reader needs is found in the following extract from Judy's paper:

> I would hope that 'control' would never be an issue, for control is to me a form of manipulation and not a form of guidance, and therefore diametrically opposed to the concept of love. Love recognizes basic human dignity – manipulation does not. Love respects and honours – manipulation cannot. Love when faced with fear remembers that fear can restrict if not discussed. Control and manipulation thrive on unexplained fears.

(Judy)

It is interesting to see writing which uses sophisticated stylistic structures of repetition and varied metre still lacking in attention to readers' other needs of explanation of terms which are highly connotative, such as 'manipulation' and 'fear'. As a reader, one wonders whether manipulation and control are interchangeable. Judy implies that any use of control negates human dignity: yet many parents would argue that dignity has nothing to do with decisions which are made on the basis of safety. In fact, one assumes that Judy did not necessarily intend such interpretation. But, without additional explanation of terms which are themselves dogmatic, it is very difficult to determine to what extent the writer appreciates the point of view of parents who do use varying degrees of control with their teenagers. It is the apparent dismissal of alternatives and the incontrovertible nature of the assertions, regardless of the degree to which the position is elaborated, that makes these papers seem egocentric.

EGOCENTRICITY IN THE TEXTS OF 11-YEAR-OLDS

In order to clarify what we mean by egocentricity of young adults, it is enlightening to look at the kind of egocentricity found in papers of pre-adolescent writers. Eleven-year-olds who participated in another study (Berrill 1990b) wrote texts on the same topic that more closely approximate classical Piagetian egocentrism than do the texts of the undergraduates. Jeremy writes as follows:

> [1] Yes I think the parents should have some control over them but not every thing.
>
> [2] For instinse the parents should have control over what you do and what time you go to bed and what cloths you should get but the kid should have a choce to and the kids should have the choce of his or her friends.
>
> *Dating*
> [3] I think that the kid has a choce who he or she dates but the first thing the kid should is to interduce them to her parents and they will tell what they think of them, and then give her advise like if he drinks and he ask you if you say no same with smoking and drugs and tell you what time you should be in.
>
> *Bed Time*
> [4] I think when your thirteen you should go to bed when your told because you are growing and need a lot of rest to keep hethy.
>
> *Work around the house*
> [5] I thing the kid should do some kind of work around the house like the dishes, babysit clean the table off, but he or she should not be exspected to do all these all the time, because it is a lot of work and he or she has homework to do and should have some time to do stuff with her friends.
>
> (Jeremy)

In this paper, Jeremy generates particular examples of situations which might arise within the framework of parental-teenager conflict and he has given opinions about what the correct response should be within those situations. Yet, he gives no indication that any other viewpoint even exists. Similarly, Chad's paper focuses on some powerful specifics but does not acknowledge the validity of any other position than his own.

> The parents should let us have our say in some things but when it comes to a job the parent should deside if you should take the job or not. Some people who have a paper route. When they go out every day after school to deliver them. Then on Thursday when they hafto go to get the money. They should be able to spend the money. I think a teenage should be able to make most of his desion because it's his live. The teenage child should know the rights of taking drugs. Parent like to pick out our cloths, but some parent are out of styal the same with hair cut I mite won't to get my head shaved down with a number on the side. But most parent won't let you because it look dum but you say it's in styal.
>
> (Chad)

Chad and Jeremy's papers are compelling in their focus on the particular. Yet, that focus is the drawback as well, for the texts rarely go beyond a narrow focus on the particular. The young writers make lists of 'shalls and shall nots' in relation to particular items. Ideas are expanded only to give more precise instructions rather than to widen the focus of the ideas. The narrow focus on the particular combines with unsupported assertion of correctness with regard to each particular sample to render these papers egocentric in a classic sense. Few papers of these young writers put the question into a larger context of either human development or human relationship (as do the papers of the undergraduates). These papers focus on individual issues that spring to mind in relation to the topic and the arguments remain in the realm of the particular. In contrast, the papers of the undergraduates focus on larger issues embedded in the particular question. The texts themselves reveal a different way of thinking about the topic which seems to involve different social awareness.

DIFFERENT UNDERSTANDINGS OF EGOCENTRICITY

We identify these papers of 11-year-olds and of the university undergraduates as being *egocentric*. Yet it becomes apparent when we look at the texts that we are using the term 'egocentric' in different ways. When we speak of writing as egocentric, we are primarily using a Piagetian notion of cognitive development, which posits egocentricity as a feature of early development. This understanding of egocentricity thus carries with it connotations of lack of development. Therefore, reference to the egocentricity of adolescents or young adults carries negative connotations, whether we are conscious of this or not. Before we continue, let us briefly review Piaget's notion of egocentricity.

It is helpful to remember that Piaget's model of cognitive development is built on the premise that 'knowledge is actively constructed and reconstructed over time by human beings' (Basseches 1984: 33). This assumption of personal construction of knowledge continues to be a primary assumption in much language research today. In relation to egocentricity, Piaget's development of thought is a gradual socialization of non-verbal autistic thought wherein children are egocentric, blinkered creatures who, in Donaldson's summary of Piaget,

> look out on the world from one's own position in it, literally or metaphorically, and fail to realize how the same world seen from a different stance, would appear – or what meaning the same words, heard and interpreted by a different brain with a different store of previous knowledge and experience would carry.
>
> (Donaldson 1978: 10)

According to Piaget, individuals slowly shed egocentrism as they become socialized. As Flavell defines the state of egocentrism, the egocentric individual 'sees the world from a single point of view only – his own – but without the knowledge of the existence of other viewpoints or perspectives and . . . without awareness that he is the prisoner of his own' (Flavell 1963: 10). For Piaget, socialization provides a mechanism for cognitive growth as contrary points of view introduce individuals to alternatives they may not have previously considered. This awareness of alternatives provides opportunities for individuals to use reason in assessing alternative positions as well as their own stances. Thus, according to Piaget, individuals move from egocentric, narrowly focused thought and feeling to social, outward and broadly oriented thought and feeling, with an orientation of self to the larger human condition. Much research on audience awareness in writing, in particular in relation to argumentative writing, follows the assumptions of Piaget's model.

In contrast to Piaget, Vygotsky's (1962) model of development of thought and language is built on a premise of social interaction. Vygotsky writes, 'In our conception, the true direction of the development of thinking is not from the individual to the socialized, but from the social to the individual' (Vygotsky 1962: 20). Vygotsky formulates the development of the child as evolving from an identification of self with others to *an increasing differentiation of oneself from others*. Altogether, the egocentrism of which Piaget speaks in negative terms is seen in positive light by Vygotsky, who declares that '[Egocentric speech] does not merely accompany the child's activity; it serves mental orientation, conscious understanding; it helps in overcoming difficulties; it is speech for oneself, intimately and usefully connected with . . . thinking' (Vygotsky 1962: 133).

According to Vygotsky, one differentiates oneself from others and, in so doing, defines oneself. Egocentric speech arises from this awareness of oneself as being different from others and develops into inner speech, a positive 'new faculty' which one uses as an adult to make sense of the world.

We thus have two very different models of development and two different interpretations of egocentricity. Certainly, our assessment of argumentative writing will always include a factor which relates to the degree to which the writer accommodates alternative points of view. However, our interpretation of development in texts which do not exhibit accommodation of alternative points of view will vary depending on the underlying assumptions we hold about the nature of egocentricity. For instance, a teacher acting from a Piagetian basis would endeavour to focus on the 'other': on somehow teaching the writer about the legitimacy of alternative points of view and, possibly, on strategies to incorporate those points of view. A teacher acting from a Vygotskian basis, on the other hand, would focus on helping the individual to differentiate her or his *own* position from that of others. This process might well include delineation of other points of view, as in the Piagetian approach, but it would focus on the writer rather than on the audience.

Close reading of the texts of the undergraduates reveals that the assertiveness in their papers seems to be qualitatively different from that of pre-adolescents. The younger writers' texts are concerned with delineating particular correct responses in relation to particular instances of the question. Their ideas are not elaborated upon even when contradictions are stated, and the writing seems to reflect a stance that the writer's view is so obvious that all readers will agree with it. This 'classic' egocentrism carries with it pejorative connotations relating to the inability to go beyond an absorption with the self to a recognition of oneself as part of a large and varied human community.

However, the papers of the undergraduates reveal an

egocentricity of a different nature. The undergraduates do frame their texts in a larger framework, recognizing that the question relating to parents and teenagers relates to wider issues of human development and human relationships. However, the generalizations are often not thoroughly explained and the writing is assertive and egocentric due to language which seems to dismiss alternatives through its use of imperatives and its connotative word choice.

IDENTITY DEVELOPMENT OF YOUNG ADULTS

It is interesting to speculate on the reasons for the dogmatic tone in the writing of undergraduates. Although it might seem that the need for egocentric language should no longer exist by young adulthood, it may be that there is a much more complex questioning of identity and self which emerges at this stage of life and possibly remains for a number of years. Ritchie (1989) corroborates this idea in her study of first-year university students who are becoming aware both of their own histories and of the values inherent in those personal histories. She writes,

> The personal, educational, and linguistic histories students bring to our classes contribute to the rich texture of possibilities for writing, thinking, and for negotiating personal identity. They also contribute to the confusion and anxiety many students experience.
>
> (Ritchie 1989: 157)

Ritchie stresses that undergraduate writers 'view the ongoing scene from their own shifting perspective within it, as they negotiate their identities amid the cacophony of voices and social roles around them' (Ritchie 1989: 153). It may be that the differentiation of self from others (as Vygotsky would say), the reconstruction of the self in new social situations, is achieved through a thought/language process which is perceived as egocentric by others.

Berkenkotter's (1981) study of expert writers' awareness of audience illustrates this point of egocentric thought in re-identifying one's position in relation to new social situations. The thinking-aloud protocols used in her study reveal a strong egocentrism operating with expert writers in the process of reconciling self-identity with that of an audience whose alternative point of view was recognized as legitimate. One English professor's thoughts included the following:

What in the hell can I tell them about my career? I mean how am I supposed to tell these people who are in the midst of a technological revolution, dioxiden poisoning, gas shortages, energy blackouts that somehow my career as an English teacher is rewarding, which I think it is. O.K. What I think I'll emphasize is that my career allows flexibility and change.

(Berkenkotter 1981: 391)

Essentially, this expert writer is redefining himself, renegotiating his identity, in relation to this social community of secondary school students. It may be that a similar reconstruction of identity has been prompted by the argumentative question of this study.

Therefore, one possible reason for the apparent egocentricity of 38 per cent of the undergraduates may relate to a redefinition of self which is occurring during university years as individuals become more aware of the legitimacy of alternative points of view and less certain about who they are in the light of compelling aspects of alternative positions. My own experience with undergraduates points to a deep self-questioning of identity. As undergraduates recognize that they seem to hold contrary points of view, they often question whether they have any core to their beliefs, to their persons. They often wonder if they have begun to believe everything they read and in these cases they wish to stop reading secondary sources and alternative points of view.

Oftentimes, undergraduates have not thoroughly analysed alternative points of view to discover with which parts of a position they agree and with which parts they disagree. Especially pertinent is the fact that they have not synthesized those different facets into a cohesive whole which reflects their own view, their present self. And, most importantly to teachers of writing and thinking, we do not teach them how to do this.

As Lamb writes, before one can connect with the other, 'it is critical that one already has and retains a sense of one's self' (Lamb 1991: 16). The papers in this study may be particularly egocentric due to the unfinished attempts of the writers to define their identities in the midst of a myriad new ways of understanding the world. If they are forced to assume a single position, as they are in argumentative writing, they may feel pressure to counter alternative points of view even if they have not yet determined why their own point of view has greater validity than opposing views, or how to incorporate aspects of seemingly opposing views which they recognize as being legitimate into a single synthesized viewpoint. This could well result in the type of writing we see here, in which the single position is explained but in which alternative points of view are summarily dismissed rather than evaluated.

It may be that it is not just a matter of not understanding alternative points of view; but that it also concerns an inability to disentangle one's own emerging position from opposing positions, to specify what aspects of an opposing position have greater validity and which aspects have less validity. Certainly, if a writer finds it difficult to evaluate properly alternative positions, one writing strategy is to explain fully one viewpoint and to ignore the others. The difficulty is that this results in writing which appears egocentric and is not as fully reasoned as it might be. However, this may be precisely what some of the undergraduates are doing.

It may also be that our present methods of teaching argumentative writing inadvertently encourage writing which is more egocentric and monological than it might otherwise be (see Ritchie 1989 and Lamb 1991). Many of us still frame argument in the metaphor of war (Lakoff and Johnson 1980; Berrill 1991), where the opposition is silenced rather than explored. The underlying assumptions which accompany this metaphor include writer-as-combatant whose mission is to obliterate the opposition. The difficulty with this position is that it may discourage dialectic exploration of the truthfulness of alternative positions and instead result in entrenchment of one's own position.

CONCLUSION

Writing of undergraduates in their final year of university has been found by this and other studies to be surprisingly egocentric. However, exploration of the egocentricity shows it to be of a different nature from that found in young writers. Where the young writers concentrate on the particular and on the listing of 'right' action in relation to a specific instance, the undergraduates write about larger issues embedded in the particular question and attempt to discuss those issues. The egocentric papers of the undergraduates, however, are characterized by an assertiveness which seems to dismiss alternatives through use of imperatives and connotative word choice.

If, as it is speculated, young adults are in the midst of reconstruction of their own identities, instruction in argumentative processes may well enhance their abilities to analyse and synthesize their own ideas, helping them to form their own new identities which accommodate recognized legitimacies of alternative positions. Possible areas for further inquiry include (1) reframing the term 'egocen-tricity' from a Piagetian sense to a Vygotksian sense to see it as a positive term which denotes metacognitive reassessment of oneself in different social situations and (2) reframing argument from a war metaphor, which is monological and seeks to destroy opposing viewpoints, to a different metaphor, which encourages a dialectical exploration of the truths offered by alternative points of view.

The egocentrism noted in the writing of the undergraduates shows us that we need to help them learn to synthesize, to put themselves together, to reconstruct new identities. At a recent workshop, Donald Murray (1991) said, 'I have been lost . . . and found . . . in this writing.' Similarly, these young adults may be showing us that they need help in reconstructing themselves. The process of argument is one of the best ways of doing this if we, as teachers, help our students to analyse and synthesize. If this happens, it may then be that final products can reflect stronger awareness of the legitimacies of alternative positions, for writers will have stronger awareness of themselves.

7 On teaching non-fiction

Carla Asher

About a year ago a colleague and I were asked to conduct an evaluation of the language arts programme of a school district I shall call Woodward, a small suburban town just north of New York City. I was intrigued by the opportunity. My own work is largely in the New York City schools, the largest school system in the United States, and one faced with a host of urban ills. In fact, I am a graduate of that system, having attended elementary, middle and high schools in New York City. I knew little about suburban schools, except that they had few of the problems of city schools. The town of Woodward was an affluent one and had only three schools, an elementary school, a middle school and a high school. Classes were small, buildings new, supplies abundant. Hundreds of teachers applied for each job opening. What, I wondered, did the teaching of writing and reading look like in such an ideal setting?

Much of the news was good. At the elementary school, teachers read to children daily; beginning in kindergarten, children had opportunities to compose their own stories; classroom libraries were filled with fine children's literature; even very young children had access to typewriters and computers; parent volunteers ran a publishing room in which they bound the books of student writers.

But all was not perfect. Although Woodward children at all ages were routinely expected to draft stories, poems and personal narratives freely and get responses to their drafts from peers and teachers before revising them, exposition was taught through formulas. Beginning in elementary school, students followed pre-structured formats to produce most essays. For example, a middle-school assignment sheet for a book report instructed students to structure their first paragraph as follows: 'Give the title and author of the book along with a brief summary of the book. State the purpose of the essay.' In paragraph two they were instructed to

'State the trait [of a character in the book] in the topic sentence. Give incidents from the book which illustrate that trait. Use a concluding sentence to sum up the paragraph.' Paragraphs three and four were similar: 'State another trait in the topic sentence but introduce it with a transition.' In paragraph five they were to 'Summarize what you have written.'

By high school, writing in English classes focused almost exclusively on the writing of essays about literature. Before beginning to write their essays, students were required to prepare notecards following a single format and these were collected and graded before the writers could proceed. Students were told what information should be included in each paragraph of their essays and how many paragraphs an essay should contain. The children of Woodward wrote lively and inventive poems, plays and stories, most frequently in elementary and middle school, but on occasion in high school too. But their essays and reports, even in the primary grades, were stilted and dull. The unique, personal voices that emerged in their 'creative' writing were almost entirely absent from their non-fiction.

This contrast between students' fiction and non-fiction writing was echoed in students' reading. In elementary school students were exposed to very little non-fiction except in textbooks. The books they read and which were read to them were generally fiction, plays and poetry. By high school, when story writing had largely been replaced by essay writing, students still read very little non-fiction in English classes. They read novels, plays and poetry and then wrote about what they read, but they almost never read published writing about literature.

I was dismayed, but not really surprised, by what the teaching of non-fiction looked like in Woodward. I had seen similar practices many times in city schools. The existence of a formulaic and rote approach to the teaching of expository writing in the Woodward schools, which were enlightened and forward-looking in so many other respects, simply emphasized for me the extent of the problem. It seemed to me that schools and teachers had lost sight of what non-fiction is, that schools were teaching a kind of writing that did not exist outside their walls.

Expository writing in many American schools has become a genre unto itself. Students are routinely required to construct essays which have no more than five paragraphs, the first baldly stating a 'main idea', and the next three backing up the main idea or thesis with 'reasons', one reason to a paragraph. The fifth paragraph states the conclusion. For the most part, these essays are impersonal in tone and content; the word 'I' is rarely to be found. The personal voice, the wit, the style, the digressions, the use of narrative, and the accounts of the development of the writer's thinking which characterize much non-fiction are rarely part of the recipe. Indeed, they are frequently forbidden.

Further, the broad range of non-fiction that exists outside school rarely gets inside. High-school English departments, in particular, often take it as their mission to train students to become junior literary critics, teaching them to write essays about required texts (essays which bear little resemblance to the way people actually write about books in English) to the exclusion of most other kinds of non-fiction. The world of non-fiction – letters, memos, reports, critiques, case studies – which students are more likely to encounter in their working lives, is almost entirely absent from most classrooms. In history and science classes the situation is no better. Students most typically do their essay writing on tests. These short 'essays' are written in one draft under tight time constraints and are generally graded on the extent to which the writer demonstrates that he has retained information presented in class. Reports in history and science are usually library exercises in which students paraphrase information gleaned from books and encyclopedias. The writer's opinion may be ventured in a final sentence, after all of her information has been presented.

Non-fiction writing has been reduced to a formulaic exercise in many American schools in large part because of its prevalence on standardized tests. In New York State, for example, students are required to take 'competency' examinations and 'Regents' examinations which require the writing of exposition. These required essays have led, in many cases, to teachers teaching to the test, training students to write essays which will minimally satisfy test requirements. The writing of non-fiction that is unrelated to examination questions has fallen by the wayside in many classrooms.

In addition to what I saw in schools and heard about from teachers, my concern about the teaching of non-fiction writing was fuelled by a change in my own relation to non-fiction. I have always been an avid reader of fiction, but in recent years, I have begun to seek out more history, sociology, anthropology and biography. Consequently, I have become much more aware of the qualities I admire in non-fiction. Over the last few years I have also done a good deal of writing of non-fiction. As part of my work I write grant proposals, memos and letters, case studies of schools and programmes, and articles for professional journals. I have become increasingly troubled by the contrasts between the non-fiction I read and write and the non-fiction students read and write in schools.

When I had the chance to teach an advanced summer course for high-school teachers through the New York City Writing Project, I seized the opportunity to develop and try out some ideas about how to change the way non-fiction is taught. I had three notions that I wanted to try out. The first was that in order for teachers to change the way they teach exposition, they need to immerse themselves in reading it. We need to remind ourselves of what we like and enjoy in non-fiction writing and what we don't like. We also need to remember how many and diverse are the forms non-fiction comes in. My second notion was that in order to change the way they teach exposition, teachers need to write non-fiction themselves and to examine the process by which they do so. In looking at *how* we write non-fiction, we can discover what kinds of preparation, support and structure non-fiction writers need as they compose texts. My third notion came from my own experience as a writer of non-fiction. Much of the non-fiction writing I have done has been collaborative. I have worked with a research assistant, writing partly from her notes; I have worked collaboratively with other writers, each of us writing part of a text and then working together to weave our words together; I have composed parts of texts aloud with colleagues with one of us serving as scribe. Although my own experience has been that, in the workplace, people frequently work together to create non-fiction texts, I have seen little recognition of that in schools. It seemed important that as part of their course work, teachers have the experience of collaborating on the composition of a text. This experience might encourage them to engage their students in collaborative writing projects, a kind of writing experience students might well encounter in their working lives.

With these notions in mind, my colleague Gail Kleiner, a high-school English teacher, and I set out to design a course which would meet for five hours a day for twelve days. Our twelve participants were experienced New York City high-school teachers who had previously taken New York City Writing Project courses in the teaching of writing. Nine were English teachers, one taught English as a second language, two were Spanish teachers (in New York City Spanish teachers frequently teach native speakers), and one was a social studies teacher. In a letter to the group, we asked that they collect examples of non-fiction that they admired and bring them to class on the first day.

We began our first morning together by writing about an

experience each of us had had with writing non-fiction and an experience with reading non-fiction. Volunteers read their writing aloud and we looked at what our experiences had in common and the relationship between our reading and writing of non-fiction. The discussion was animated. Some group members recounted negative experiences with non-fiction writing in school. We heard stories of assigned topics which the writer had little investment in, of reports copied from encyclopedias, of writers feeling overwhelmed by the task of organizing and synthesizing their research to produce a coherent text. But some class members told of experiences where they had become fascinated by a topic and enjoyed writing about it. Our experiences with reading non-fiction were similarly diverse. Many of us associated non-fiction with texts we were required to read in college. Fiction was pleasure reading; non-fiction was work. As soon as you got out of school you stopped doing it. Others of us told of particular books or subjects which had intrigued and involved us, of authors whose work we had sought out. We discovered that non-fiction reading and writing were more closely associated with school for many of us than were other kinds of reading and writing.

In the afternoon, we asked the group to consider the examples of non-fiction they had brought with them. We asked the teachers to write for a few minutes about what their choices indicated about what they liked in non-fiction. Next we asked the teachers to focus on one piece, writing about what they liked about it, and what they noticed about how it was written. We also asked that everyone bracket a paragraph from one of the pieces they had brought that they especially liked. We then divided into small groups, reading to each other what we had written and talking about the non-fiction we had selected.

When we gathered back together as a whole group, we talked about what we admired and responded to in non-fiction writing. We mentioned, among other things, an inventive use of language, a distinct personal voice, humour, primary research and the making of connections to other disciplines or to personal experiences. Next we read our bracketed paragraphs aloud in turn, without comment. It was a powerful experience. We heard the words of fourteen writers, some famous, some not, but almost all eloquent, reminding us of what non-fiction could be. We listed the forms of non-fiction we had heard and the forms we had not heard. It was a long list. Already we were asking ourselves, do I teach my students to write the kind of non-fiction I admire? How broad a range of non-fiction do my students write and read? Do my students, like the writers we heard, write on subjects they are interested in and knowledgeable about? Do I give them enough time and opportunity to become knowledgeable?

We ended the day by arranging for oral readings: each day, one of us would read aloud an excerpt from a piece of non-fiction. We also invited the group to continue to bring in non-fiction that they liked. We would set up a table in the room where copies of this writing would be available. Finally, we gave a homework assignment: to read a chapter from *The Power Broker* (1974), Robert Caro's book about Robert Moses, the builder of most of New York's roads, bridges and parks. We asked the group to underline parts that were particularly striking to them. The oral readings, the non-fiction table, and the assigned chapter were all part of the plan to immerse ourselves in non-fiction. Without this immersion, we might find ourselves writing the same stilted, voiceless prose that our students frequently produced.

Our second day began with an oral reading. After Mary Carter, a high-school English teacher, read to us from an essay by Virginia Woolf, we wrote in our journals in response to what we had heard. Volunteers read their entries aloud and we talked about our responses. We talked not only about the content of the essay but about what we responded to in the writing. Once again, the issue of personal voice arose. We liked Woolf's wry commentary on her subject and were glad that we were offered more than an assemblage of facts. On other days, we heard excerpts from writing by Joan Didion, Alan Bloom, Richard Rodriguez and Russell Baker, among others. This sequence of oral reading, journal writing, and discussion of the text and our responses to it began each of the days that followed. Our intention was to make our group sensitive to their responses to non-fiction, aware of what they wanted to emulate as writers and what they wanted to avoid.

After the oral reading and discussion, we began our experiment with collaborative writing. Gail and I had decided that in the first week of our course we would involve the class in working together to produce reports based on primary research. We hoped that this activity would not only expand the teachers' thinking about how exposition is written, but also about what constitutes research. We thought that writing from data they had gathered through interviews and observations would expand the teachers' notions of what research is and how it is integrated into writing.

We told the group that over the next few days we would be

working in small groups to research and write reports on questions or topics related to expository writing. Groups would gather information by talking to people, possibly observing, collecting samples of writing, and through reading. The group would decide together how to divide responsibility in both the research and writing phases. We told them that all of their data collection would have to be done on the college campus where we were meeting. We spent some time brainstorming possible questions or issues that could be reported on within the constraints we had outlined. We agreed on three general topics: 'Students' and teachers' views of non-fiction reading', 'The expository writing assignments that teachers give', and 'The newspaper-reading habits of adults and teenagers'. Everyone signed up for one of the three groups. We told the teachers that they would have the morning of the next day to collect their data and that their groups would meet to pool information in the afternoon. The following morning groups would meet to organize and begin to write up their reports. In the afternoon they would meet to respond to the writing of the others in their group and to make decisions about revision. Over the weekend they would rewrite and revise, meeting once more on Monday morning. It was an extremely tight time-frame and Gail and I had our doubts about whether it would work.

Our participants were willing to go along with us, and before lunch they met in their groups to narrow their questions and decide what their sources of information would be and what each group member would do to gather information. Since there were many courses in session on the campus, some for teachers, some for undergraduates, and one for high-school students, there was a ready source of informants. Before breaking for lunch we met again as a whole to hear what each group had planned. One group was constructing a questionnaire; the other two were planning interviews. Despite the contrived nature of the assignment, the teachers' excitement was palpable. They were enjoying working in teams and looked forward to bringing the data they collected back to their groups. There was relief that they would not be individually responsible for a final product.

After lunch we switched gears. We asked the teachers to turn to the Caro chapter. The chapter we had selected is called 'One mile' and it tells the story of how Robert Moses overrode community objections and destroyed neighbourhoods to build the Cross-Bronx Expressway. It begins: 'Robert Moses built 627 miles of roads in and around New York City. This is the story of one of those miles.'

We began by asking everyone to read the lines they had marked. We went around in our circle, reading in turn without interruption. Interestingly, from a very long chapter, several people had chosen the same lines. We invited the group to talk about the chapter, first about their response to its content. Our group of New Yorkers had strong reactions. Some drove regularly on the Cross-Bronx Expressway; some remembered Robert Moses; some knew the neighbourhoods mentioned in the chapter or ones like them. We asked the group to consider how Caro had crafted the chapter. How had he achieved the desired effect? We noticed a number of things. First was the strong sense of narrative and storytelling, starting from the first words of the chapter. Then there was the use of suspense. Could the people of East Tremont triumph over the forces that would destroy their neighbourhood? And there was generous use of the voices of the people involved. And a conscious use of such stylistic devices as repetition. We asked the group to imagine the process that Robert Caro had gone through to research and write the chapter. We listed possible steps on the board. Finally, we wrote down events in our communities that we would be interested in writing histories of and the steps we would need to take to write these histories. Gail imagined herself writing the story of several generations of an extended immigrant family who lived in her apartment building and Sheila Lesser considered writing about a controversial water-main replacement project in her neigh-bourhood.

We followed this same process each time we read a text. First, we read aloud underlined passages in order to bring the writer's voice into the room. Then we talked about our responses to the text and the writer's craft in producing those responses. Finally, we generated topics or short pieces of writing inspired by the text we had read.

In our end-of-day reflections, writing that we each did in our journals at the end of the day and then read aloud if we wished, several people remarked on what they had learned from reading Robert Caro. They noted that what they liked in non-fiction writing was not that different from what they liked in fiction – lively descrip-tion, narrative drive, an artful use of language, and the voices of the different characters in a drama. One teacher remarked on how different Caro's writing was from the writing she asked her students to do; others noted how much research must have preceded the writing and how often they asked their students to write essays based on almost no research. We were on our way.

In the days that followed our group continued to listen to, read and discuss a varied collection of non-fiction. Our reading included Gore Vidal on Somerset Maugham, Stephen J. Gould on forced sterilization, James Baldwin on race, Primo Levi and George Orwell on fascism, Rebecca West on the Nuremberg trials, Arnold Rampersad on the life of Langston Hughes, as well as letters, grant proposals and reports. Our discussions focused on our responses to what we had read and an investigation of how each writer had shaped our responses. We learned, thanks to Gore Vidal, that literary criticism doesn't have to be dull. Stephen J. Gould showed us that science writing can be passionate and deeply humanistic. James Baldwin gave us a powerful demonstration of how personal experience can be wed to an examination of a social issue. And Arnold Rampersad taught us that a biographer needs a point of view. We encouraged the group to try out techniques that they liked in their own writing.

At the same time that we were reading and discussing non-fiction, we were composing it. Our report groups met daily throughout the first week of the course and into the second. After each group meeting or writing session, we asked teachers to make an entry in their notebooks, recording and examining the process of working on their reports. These 'process journal' entries were read and discussed in the large group as we attempted to discover how non-fiction is written.

For the most part, the report groups went very well. Most of the teachers had never before had the experience of working collaboratively on a piece of writing and they found they enjoyed it. We discovered through our process journal discussions that each group was working differently. One group pooled their data, organized it thematically and then assigned each group member to write a section of the final report. A second group decided that each group member would write up the data he or she had collected. The third group composed most of their report aloud together with one member recording the words they decided on. All the groups found that they needed to work together to construct their final product, deciding on an order to the report and writing transitions from one part to another.

In our second week a different group presented its report each day, distributing copies for us to read and then listening to and responding to our reactions. Many group members mentioned ways that our readings had influenced them. One report began with a quote from an informant, and the writers remarked that it would not have occurred to them to use direct quotations throughout their report had they not read Robert Caro. Another group, noting that many of the writers we had read had not hidden from the reader their own reactions to what they reported, felt free to include in their report the story of what it had been like to conduct their research.

Once the reports were complete, we felt it was time to try some individual writing of non-fiction. We invited the group to review the list of non-fiction forms we had compiled on our first day and the writing we had read, and to decide on a piece of writing that they needed or wanted to do. We assigned class members to small writing-response groups that would meet regularly to respond to this writing. At a first meeting, we asked group members to talk with the group about what they were thinking of writing. As we had done with the collaborative reports, we asked all the teachers to keep journals recording their writing processes. These journal entries became the focus of many class discussions. Through discussion of the journals, we were able to examine such issues as whether writers choose form first and then content, or the reverse (they do both) and the differences between writing for an external requirement and an internal one. The group's writing spanned a wide range of non-fiction, including a dissertation proposal, a memoir, a grant proposal, an article about portfolio assessment of student writing, an essay on bilingual education and a history of the suburban county in which one course member lived. Here, too, we saw the influence of our readings. Encouraged by James Baldwin's 'Notes of a Native Son', in which he weaves the story of his relationship with his father into an examination of race relations in the United States, Gilda Tesser experimented with combining personal history and an exploration of the effects of the Nazi holocaust on the children of survivors. Spurred by Robert Caro, Sheila Lesser conducted a series of interviews in order to write a critique of a mentoring programme in her school. And influenced perhaps by George Orwell's 'Such, such were the joys . . .', Chico Chichester wrote a powerful account of his early life in Guyana. We discovered that our writing processes are as diverse when we write non-fiction as when we write poetry and fiction. Now it was time to look at our teaching more directly.

On the next-to-last day of the course, Gail and I asked the group to consider two pieces of literary criticism written by students. The first, by a Woodward student, was an essay on Oscar Wilde's *The Picture of Dorian Gray*. It begins this way:

The Picture of Dorian Gray written by Oscar Wilde, concerns a young man who lives in England in Victorian times. Dorian Gray is a young man who starts out innocent and wholesome and becomes corrupted by internal and external influences. Dorian Gray has many different qualities which will be discussed in this essay.

One of Dorian Gray's traits was self indulgence. He fulfilled all his whims and desires. One incident which shows this is when he passes through the library to the door of his decorated room. . . . He decorates his room just to be luxurious.

Four pages later it concludes:

Dorian Gray was certainly an unusual character with many different traits. Three of his most prominent traits were self indulgence, being influenced easily, and immorality. *The Picture of Dorian Gray* was a difficult book, but it was a good experience for me. This story was unusual and had a twist to it.

The second, written by a New York City high-school student who had participated in our High School Students Writing Project, was about Alice Walker's *The Color Purple*. It begins this way:

When I first read in The Color Purple that Shug and Celie was loving one another in bed as a man and woman do, I wanted to put the book down. I had no interest knowing about their 'lesbian' relationship. Even though you can't cut any corners on that, Shug and Celie did have a lesbian relationship, their relationship together was and had much more to do with something else other than sex.

Let's examine the facts. Celie was raped by her stepfather Alphonso. She was practically sold to the man she married. This was only to take care of his children which treat Celie like dirt. The only person who's judgement she valued was a person who thought she was somebody, her sister, Nettie. Once Nettie was gone, Celie felt that emptiness of not being anybody. Then came Shug Avery. But what was Shug to Celie? Shug represented everything Celie wanted to possess. She stood up for what she believed and more importantly, Shug could love.

It concludes:

The 'big' sister and mother image was what Celie saw in Shug and that's what their relationship consisted of. Sex only touched the surface of what was already there. Their love for one another.

I feel what Alice Walker was trying to convey to the reader was to get him/her to understand the feelings which can lead two people into sharing everything they had to offer.

What, Gail and I wondered, would our city teachers make of these essays? The first, written to a formula, showed a firm command of the conventions of standard written English. It was also, to our eyes, stilted, voiceless and largely empty of anything to say. The second, while less firmly in command of standard English, was passionate, personal, and showed the writer struggling to come to terms with an aspect of *The Color Purple* that troubled her. Would our teachers, who rarely saw students like the ones in Woodward, forget the last couple of weeks and vote for that one?

We need not have worried. Mary Carter, who characterized herself as a traditional teacher of literature, broke the silence. 'You win,' she said.

Rather than focusing on how to get the city student to write like the surburban one, our group began to wonder what sort of essays Woodward students might write were they granted the freedom to write honestly and personally about their responses to their reading and exposed to the work of writers who had done the same.

On our last morning we gave our group one last writing assignment. We asked them to imagine that they had been asked to evaluate a school district's expository writing programme. Against what criteria would they measure the programme? We asked the teachers to work in groups to develop a list of principles for teaching expository writing. After pooling our lists, we had sixteen principles to guide our teaching. They are as follows:

1 Students should be encouraged to read a range of expository writing, selected by both teachers and students, and to examine the craft of these selections in order to explore what makes for effective expository writing.
2 Students' ideas, interests and concerns should play a major role in the expositions they read and write.
3 Students should have opportunities to undertake writing assignments that arise from a coherent, planned curriculum.
4 Students should have opportunities to talk and write informally about the content of their expository writing.
5 Students should be encouraged to draft their expository writing without fear of error.
6 Students should be encouraged to use their own voices in their expository writing.

7 Students should have opportunities to write exposition independently and in collaboration with others.

8 Students should be encouraged to write for a variety of purposes and audiences and in a variety of forms of exposition, as they exist in the real world.

9 Students should be encouraged to write exposition in all disciplines.

10 Students should have opportunities to receive feedback on and to revise their expository writing.

11 Students should learn expository writing skills and the conventions of standard English in the context of meaningful reading and writing, as the need arises.

12 Students should be encouraged to talk and write reflectively about the varied processes they use in writing exposition.

13 Students should have opportunities to see their teachers as active participants in the writing process.

14 Students' expository writing should be valued and respected through public display and publication.

15 Students should be aware of the criteria by which their expository writing will be judged.

16 Teachers should distinguish between test preparation and writing instruction; the teaching of exposition should not be driven by test preparation.

In the afternoon we celebrated ourselves as writers, reading aloud from the writing we had done during the course. We also wrote and read from final journal entries. One teacher wrote:

> Before I came to the course I had a very narrow view of exposition. In fact, I had difficulty choosing pieces to bring because I thought of exposition in its narrowest terms. I'd look at a piece of writing and say that it was narrative or descriptive rather than expository. The Robert Caro piece destroyed that myth right away.

Another commented:

> My perception of expository writing before this course was narrowly confined to test tasks. I also, God help me, would have discouraged the inclusion of personal experiences in essays if I had found them there which I never did. I had vague notions of the 'correct,' 'academic' approach to be taught.

And another:

> It's important for me to note that the collaboration and group time we all shared provided the best of the class for me. Actually enjoying working with my group threw my ideas about the naturalness of the solitary writing experience out the window.

Clearly, we had achieved many of our goals for the course. Our participants were returning to their classrooms motivated to approach the teaching of non-fiction in new ways. But there would be many obstacles to their implementing the principles they had developed – the tests they had to prepare their students for, their students' expectations of how teachers wanted essays to be written, the books that were available for use in class, their own previous practice in teaching exposition, and the practice of their colleagues. We could only hope that their experiences in our course would serve as touchstones, that in remembering what it was like for them to read and write non-fiction they would be inspired to recreate those experiences with their students.

8   Narrative, argument and rhetoric

Richard Andrews

When I reflect on narrative and its place in my reading and teaching, it is the dislocations to expected narrative pattern that have excited the children I have taught and myself as a teacher and reader. They have made me more aware of narrative and what it can do. Take the passage in Kurt Vonnegut's *Slaughterhouse Five*, for instance, in which Billy Pilgrim imagines the war running backwards, like a film running backwards before his eyes; or Pinter's *Betrayal*, Kunert's 'Film Put in Backwards' or Ian Seraillier's backwards fairy-tale. Running narrative backwards makes you much more aware of how the sequence is constructed forwards, and what its constituent parts are.

There is no shortage of literature on how stories are constructed, but it tends to be a critical account of how existing texts are constructed. Barthes's (1966) 'Introduction to the structural analysis of narratives' was seminal, but there were other seeds germinating in 1966 and before: Booth (1961), Propp (1968), Bremond (1973) and others.

Another strand of story analysis is that in which Bartlett's work on memory in the 1930s is looked to as a foundation. The work of Rumelhart (1975), Mandler and Johnson (1977), Johnson and Mandler (1980), Stein and Glenn (1979) and others focuses on story structure, but again we are dealing with minimal stories, analysed within a syntactic paradigm, and via their retention and comprehension. Yet another strand is the ethnographic and sociolinguistic, characterized in the work by Labov and others (e.g. Labov and Waletsky 1967) on naturally occurring oral narrative.

Any teacher knows that the description of the construction of an existing narrative is no guide to the composition of narrative. There is no neat formula to translate reception into production, though of course what we read and hear must have a connection to what we write and can write. There are guides on how to write a story, but only Mills & Boon hopefuls take them seriously.

This lack of understanding of how children compose narratives (and other modes of writing) prompted me to try to devise ways of getting inside that process. My focus was on structure and arrangement, not on drafting or any of the other more organic aspects of writing. I was interested in the routes taken by writers in the very act of composing; not in any rules for the conduct of the journey, but in the split-second decisions that are made to take a story one way rather than another.

What I devised was an instrument based on the filmic principle of putting one image alongside another. Working with 150 year 8 pupils in the three comprehensive schools in Beverley, I gave each pupil a set of seven photographs. I asked them to compose (literally!) a narrative, using any number of the photos in the series, and arranging them in any order. I had two sets so that students sitting next to each other would not be affected by the choices of their neighbours.

What happened was that only two students in my sample came up with the same structural sequence. Most of the stories were different, and no doubt would have been even if the sequences of photographs had been the same. Here is an example of one of the stories, generated from two photographs in a set:

Revenge of the killer kippers
Deep in the sea some herrings were thinking of a way to get back at humans because they were smoking them then eating them. So they formed an air force of flying fish and set out to smoke and eat humans! They flew out of the water of the flying fish and attacked! The gun on the port wall started shooting them but they kept on coming and eventually wiped out the inhabitants of the village and had smoked humans for tea.

Nine months later, all England is ruled by kippers except for one town – Beverley – where Iain Norman was keeping the kippers at bay with fish mongers. So all the kippers in the land attacked Beverley and the fish mongers attacked the fish, and we all had smoked kippers for tea and the reign of the kippers was over.

Pedagogically, these were a success. I've yet to come across a child who cannot use these to generate a told or written story. The sample covered a wide range of ability, including a semi-paralysed child in a wheelchair who composed a story half in words and half in pictures. But that is not the point. What did they tell me about the structure of the stories and the ways in which those structures were produced?

I used Van Dijk's term 'episode' to describe the units of narrative discourse, preferring it to 'narreme'. My analysis is one level 'higher' in the linguistic scale than that at which the 'narreme' operates. An overall term to describe the units of narrative and argumentative discourse I have been looking at is 'stage' – that way, a setting or an opening proposition in argument can be seen as stages rather than as 'episodes' or 'points'.

Iain's story can be analysed as consisting of five episodes: the setting ('Deep in the sea . . .'), a 'then' episode ('They flew out of the water . . .'), another 'then' episode ('Nine months later . . .'), a 'cause' episode ('So all the kippers in the land attacked Beverley . . .') and a resolution ('. . . and we all had smoked kippers for tea and the reign of the kippers was over'). But it could equally be analysed as consisting of seven, if we took each sentence as an episode and the last one as two episodes. As a principle, I have looked for larger structural units in the stories.

The average number of episodes per story was 7.9. Almost all these stories began with a setting of some kind: 98.6 per cent of the total sample. The exceptions might be considered to have the function of settings, even if they did not actually set the scene, giving the reader a glimpse of action from the middle of the narrative. The sample as a whole ranged from stories with three episodes to one with seventeen. Only two structures were alike. In terms of form, there were stories within stories, stories purely in dialogue, stories as letters, picaresque structures, stories from different points of view, stories in the present tense – and combinations of these.

As an example of the variety of structures evidenced in the sample, here are the structures of the six stories that took a three-part structure:

Kelly Sheepwash	In media res (a rumour) + narrator tells story which itself has six subsections + resolution
June Robinson	Setting + event (then) + event (then) – abrupt ending
Nicola Hastings	Setting + event (and) + event (and)
Simon Davidson	Setting (long) + event (then) + event (resolution)
Fergus Whinham	Setting + event (dialogue) + event (resolution)
Paul Ramsay	Setting + event (cause) + event (then) – incomplete

What was particularly striking was that, when asked whether they could envisage a rearrangement of the basic structures of the stories without affecting the nature of the stories, only 26.45 per cent of the sample said that they could. This compares with 62.16 per cent who could envisage a similar change in their arguments – more on which later. Only two students in the whole sample could envisage complete flexibility of order. Of those who could envisage some change (only one-quarter of the sample, remember) most envisaged just one change to the original order of their story.

I felt it important to pursue this question because, as Pringle and Freedman (1985) had reported on their research in Ottawa in the early 1980s, very little revision goes on above the level of the sentence in schools, despite the facilities offered by word-processors. I am not surprised by that, because of the history of 'marking' in English teaching and also because computer monitors are not generally big enough to enable writers to see the whole text at once.

Let us return for a moment to the beginnings of the students' work on the narratives. I made planning – on paper that is – optional; 49 per cent took up this option. Of this 49 per cent, the majority (70 per cent) did not plan in the conventional sense of that term. That is to say, they did not map out the whole story before they began to write/transcribe it. Most of these plans were drafts of the beginning of the story; they were foundations from which the story might be built, first attempts to get started.

The number of stages in the plans did not always correspond to the number of photographs chosen, and in turn the final stories did not always correspond to the plans. This is very different from what happens in the composition of argument. It appears that each stage of planning in the composition of narrative acts as a springboard to the next stage. Each stage in the process supersedes and jettisons the previous one. As teachers of writing, we probably need to be aware of the different compositional processes involved in different types of writing. Certainly, the imposition of drafting for every type of writing would be, from this point of view, a mistake.

Here are some of the statements made about the process of writing narrative by the students in the research sample. I took a 12.5 per cent sub-sample to interview: in effect, three students from each of the six classes I worked with. The three were selected on the following basis: one who said they could change the order of their narrative but not of their argument; one who could change the argument but not the narrative; and one who could envisage changing both. Apart from that, selection was random.

> I quite often change my plans in narrative. I add things but don't change the order much. In argument I add things and rearrange things.
>
> (Emma)

> I think writing narrative is difficult for the same reason as having a bath is difficult: the hardest part is actually getting in.
>
> (Philippe)

> *Q*: What is it like being in the middle of a story?
> *A*: It's like going into a series of caverns.

> The ending could be considered to be the most important part because everything has been brought together for an actual final countdown to a closure, and everything is then falling into place . . . like a jigsaw.
>
> (Simon)

Any research in this field throws up more questions than it can answer. If you move above the level of the sentence, not only in trying to find ways of helping students to play with their writing – to revise, to rethink at the 'macro-level' – but also in simply trying to define what the units of composition are, you run into difficulty. The analysis of the structures of narrative is more complicated than that of the structure of arguments. Conventionally, argument is more subject to division, categorization and logic than narrative. I used the Stein and Glenn taxonomy, applying the 'then', 'and' and 'cause' categories to the story as a whole. I had to use a range of determinants to define the narrative units:

paragraphs (where they existed – and of course they did not always correspond to shifts in the narrative when they did)
textual markers, like 'then', 'so', 'After a few years', 'suddenly', 'in the end', and so on
introduction of new characters or settings
spaces in the text, indicating a shift of perspective or time
shifts of tense
the introduction of chunks of dialogue (a difficult one).

What about argument? First, there is no doubt that it is important and pervasive, and that considering the modes of discourse is part of our business.

My second observation rests on the work of Fox (1989a,b, 1990), Wilkinson (1989, 1990), Wilkinson *et al.* (1990) and others, and it is this: argument starts early, much earlier than is recognized in the National Curriculum for English. Fox has indicated, in a series of papers on the stories told by 4-, 5- and 6-year-olds, how many of the rhetorical devices of argument are embedded in their narratives. Wilkinson's chapters in *Spoken English Illuminated*: 'Our first great conversationalists', 'Homemade argument' and 'Primary acts of mind', and two articles published recently in *English in Education* argue for our recognition of the presence of argument in the first discourses of pre-school children.

Third, what is argument? A brief look at the *OED* reveals three strands, strands that are there in the Latin *arguere*, meaning (i) to show, to make clear; (ii) to assert, to prove; and, as part of a legal process or as dialogue, (iii) to accuse, to blame. Translate those through the centuries, and you get a range of meanings from the narrowly logical (e.g. in astronomy and mathematics, 'the angle, arc or other mathematical quantity from which another required quantity may be deduced') to 'a connected series of statements or reasons intended to establish a position; a process of reasoning; argumentation', that is, both the product (argument) and the process (argumentation). You also get some interesting peripheral definitions, like 'the subject-matter of discussion or discourse in speech or writing; theme, subject' and one that is close to narrative, 'the summary or abstract of the subject-matter of a book; a syllabus; the contents'. It is as though the function of argument is to move one step beyond the present state, both in the sense of moving 'up' a level in terms of abstraction and exposition, and in the sense of taking a position that will move things 'on'.

But of course, if you presented these definitions to a child or, for that matter, almost anyone, they would point out that there is a huge dimension of argument missing. Indeed, the first thing most of us probably think of when we hear the term 'argument' is a row, a tiff, a barney, an argy-bargy, a squabble, a ding-dong, a good shouting match, a set-to, a spat, a difference of opinion, a μεγαλω ψυσσερια (*mighalo fusseria*). Reason hardly comes into it, sometimes. These encounters are often driven by passion and feeling.

My point here is that to see argument as merely 'a connected series of statements or reasons intended to establish a position' and to limit its expression to the written essay – a form that gained prominence in the Renaissance and now maintains a stranglehold on much of education from about age 15 or 16 upwards – is to

narrow the possibilities of expression. It has been notoriously difficult to teach, and I think only now are we beginning to look
seriously again at ways of making it accessible to all children and
students. The difficulties were outlined by Clarke (1984) and by
Freedman and Pringle (1984). The APU surveys (Gorman *et al.*
1988) between 1979 and 1983 (not fully published until 1988) pin-
pointed argument as one of the areas in which 11- and 15-year-olds
had trouble, and several of the researchers published independently,
expressing their concern about this. Meanwhile, Dixon and Stratta
(1986a,b) were carrying out inductive research for the Southern
Regional Examining Board (as it was then) and publishing their
findings in small pamphlets. Some of these findings and meditations
were collected in two publications in 1986: *Writing Narrative – and
Beyond* and *The Writing of Writing*. Among others, I want to add
the name of Deborah Berrill (1990a; see also Wilkinson *et al.* 1990),
whose work adds a great deal to our understanding of how teenagers compose argument, and especially to the difference between
exposition and argument.

Recently my own focus has been on the *difference* between narrative and argument. Before I present my findings from the study on
the composition of argument I would like to address the distinction
between narrative and argument made by Kress (1989) in the collection *Narrative and Argument*. This distinction has not been without
controversy. Kress suggests that narrative and argument are two
very different modes of organizing verbal or visual text. Although
both aim to handle difference in a culture, argument 'provides the
means for bringing difference into existence' while narrative, as a
textual form, 'provides means of resolution of difference in an
uncontentious mode'. So argument is a progressive cultural form in
that it is an agent of change; narrative is conservative in that the
closure comes from within. When closure takes place in argument,
it is imposed from without.

There seems to have been some misunderstanding of the application of this distinction. Kress is not saying here that narrative
is an inferior cultural form to argument (though conventionally
argumentative forms have been privileged over narrative forms like
'anecdote' and 'tale'). On the contrary, the suggestion is that critical
awareness of these two modes of expression enables us to free
narrative from such a position. Elsewhere in his chapter, Kress is
at pains to point out that he does not accept the view that sees
narrative as the vehicle and argument as the tenor of expression.

The distinction is worth further debate. At least it is clear from

Kress's work that narrative and argument are modes of organization, operating at a more general level than genres or forms. It is at this point we can return to the study.

The same sample of 150 12/13-year-olds in the three comprehensive schools in Beverley wrote arguments. They had completely free choice as to topic, some of which were:

It is wrong that first years get to lunch first
It is wrong that girls are treated differently
We should play football in school time
There should be more dinner ladies [*sic*]

It is wrong to have to go to school
What good does war do?
There's too much violence on TV
Using animals in experiments is wrong

Birds should not be allowed to live on the earth
Koala bears should wear climbing gear
Lightning should not be allowed to strike in the same place
'I think sheep should not be air hostesses'

Candy is brill

More central to my own concerns, however, was arrangement. I deliberately limited the range of argumentative forms so that I could make a reasonable comparison between the essays, and between them and the narratives written in the same week by the same children. Most of the children wrote what tends to be called a 'discursive essay'. Not all. Here is an example of one child's work. It takes the form of Socratic dialogue but then seems to move into a report of the proceedings of a meeting:

Should fleas wear protective clothing and helmets?
'I think they should because they are always flying into walls and hurting themselves and getting bruised and falling to the floor, what a torture.'

'How do you think we could supply every flea with 50p worth of gear? How do you think we could afford all that?'

After further to-ing and fro-ing, the argument ends:

Chairman: The votes follow like this *For*: 42 *Against*: 20
So fleas will wear protective clothes.

In this research the approach is one of aiming at the heart of the problem in argumentative writing: the essay. I use this term to mean a sustained piece of writing that puts over a point of view or argues a case, as in the John Gross (1991) collection *The Oxford Book of Essays*.

All the students wrote plans for their essays, though only 2 per cent of these were in the 'for and against' pattern that is often taught. Ten per cent of them took the form of drafts, rather like the majority of the plans for narrative. The rest consisted of a combination of spider diagrams, lists and points in the order that the writer was going to make them.

There is a major difference between narrative and argument in the relationship of the plans to the final written pieces. Despite the artificial context I had provided for the students, with planning optional for the narrative and compulsory for the argument, students reported in a questionnaire and in interviews that they would usually plan for argument but not for narrative. I have already mentioned the function of planning in narrative. In argument the student is much more likely to 'stick to the plan'; he or she may rearrange it or add to it, but the additions are adjustments, embellishments and so on *within* the structure mapped out in the plan.

The average number of stages in the arguments written in this study was 6.1, compared to the 7.9 I have mentioned as the average for the narratives. Those figures may or may not be significant. It might be simply a matter of length (though students had the same amount of time to write each piece); it may be something to do with the additive nature of composition in narrative; it may be that the six-stage argument corresponds closely to the Aristotelian six-part oration. These questions still have to be resolved, but I can say from analysing the arguments that hardly any follow the Aristotelian six-part pattern. I shall return to Aristotle in a moment.

As with the narratives, we can look at a manageable number of structures. Unlike narrative, it is possible to compose two-part structures (basically statement and proof) but again I have chosen those compositions which took a three-part structure. There were seven in all:

Paul Ramsay	Statement + 'nevertheless' + 'on the other hand'
Malcolm Spencer	Statement + reason + expression of opinion
Philip Ashby	Statement + reason + 'when' (instance)
Stephen Spivey	Supposition ('if') + example + example
Kathryn Pengilly	Statement + credo + anti-credo ('I don't think')

Melanie Wright   Statement + reason + statement
Sarah Pelham   Example + example + example

A general point first: most of these (and indeed 86.2 per cent of the total sample) take the 'statement + proof' shape. The two that do not fit the pattern begin 'If people keep killing whales, there won't be any whales left in the world' (Stephen Spivey) and, in an essay entitled 'Murder in our homes and streets', 'I have nothing against London, but I just decided to use it as an example. London, especially East, is a main drug area' (Sarah Pelham). The others in the total sample that do not fit the basic pattern begin with exordia, examples (in the form of micro-stories), suppositions, definitions, reasons, larger stories and a setting.

More specifically, what seems to me to be striking is the variety of sequence and strategy evident in these seven structures. No two essay structures are alike in the whole sample. I find that heartening. But not only is there variety. As I reported earlier, 62 per cent of the students in the sample felt that they could rearrange the order of their arguments. Of these, 26.6 per cent could envisage their same essay in any order; the rest suggested specific changes. For many of these, 'the first point has to come first' – but not for all.

What do the students themselves say about argument? One mentioned the importance of the voice in argument:

> I think that voice has a lot to do with how good your argument is. You can use your voice like plasticine: you can mould it into the argument, bringing your voice high and then letting it drop down.

Another talked about the construction of the different parts of an argument:

> I tried to fit the different rail tracks together so that they'd fix up so that one would lead to another, which is quite hard to do.

And another talked about different ways he might approach the writing of argument:

> I could then do it the other way round: put the less important first and build up to a climax if you like, where the importance really wants coming out; or you could do it another way. You could put the middle ones first as a taster, build up to a climax and then go down again. What I usually do is to do it in my own style, which is to build right up to a climax.

It is the flexibility on the part of the students, their willingness to play with the structures of argument, their experimentation, their personal imprint (and, by the way, many of them see argument as more personal than narrative) that seem to me to be some of the outcomes of this relatively small-scale research. I find it particularly interesting to look at statements and suggestions from classical rhetoric about the construction of arguments alongside the structures generated by the students. These are from Aristotle (1926) and the author of the Roman *Ad Herennium* (1954), and they focus on the aspect of composition with which I am concerned here, namely *dispositio* or arrangement. From Aristotle,

> A speech has two parts. It is necessary to state the subject, and then to prove it.
>
> at most the parts are four in number: exordium, statement, proof, epilogue.
>
> (III, 13, 19)

though 'statement' might be divided into 'narrative' and 'division', and a refutation might be added to make a six-part oration. From the *Ad Herennium*,

> The most complete and perfect argument, then, is that which is comprised of [*sic*] five parts: the Proposition, the Reason, the Proof of the Reason, the Embellishment and the Resumé.
>
> The fullest argument is fivefold, the briefest threefold [without the last two parts] and the mean fourfold, lacking either the Embellishment or the Resumé.
>
> (107, 113)

Compare these with the rather crude formulae we have come down to, like 'A good essay must have an introduction, a development and a conclusion' or the equivalent for narrative, 'a beginning, middle and an end'. Or even worse, 'First say what you are going to say, then say it, and then say what you've just said'. And compare these formulaic approaches to the teaching and learning of writing with the actual practice of these students, even under artificially tight conditions. Furthermore, how much do our students 'know about language' at the level of discourse? On the evidence of the eighteen students I interviewed, quite a lot. Not only do they know about the nature of language forms but also about appropriateness, that much-vaunted and, as Harold Rosen has pointed out, dangerously loaded word in the National Curriculum.

But they also know how to subvert propriety, and by subverting, dislocating and rearranging, they make their own marks and learn a great deal more at the same time about themselves, about their audience, about their subject-matter and about language. There is also a lot of humour to be had in inappropriateness, incongruity, dislocation – humour that children and adolescents enjoy.

To summarize some of the points made so far:

The arrangements of narratives and arguments are not fixed. There are general formulae which we can apply after the event of composing, but in the middle of the act of composing, they are not much help. We need a theory of writing in which process and the possibilities of product are interrelated. We need to be able to account for the speed at which the mind chooses to take this route rather than that.

It may be that in a particular context a certain genre will suggest itself. This does not mean that we have to accept this genre whole-sale. For example, if we have to make a funeral oration or speech, or, more informally, say a few words about someone who has died, we can – as a friend of mine did recently – tell the story of someone's life backwards, from death to birth. There is a kind of hopefulness about that approach.

The process involved in composing narrative is different from that involved in composing argument.

Children know more about language at the discourse level than might be imagined, but the National Curriculum in English does not reflect this.

Children can argue from an early age. The assumption that narra-tive precedes argument in learning should be looked at critically.

Narrative and argument might be separate rhetorical categories of mode, but they need not be polarized; there can be narrative in argument and, looking at it at a different level, narratives argue.

There is much to be done to liberate argument for pupils in school and students in colleges and universities, right across the curriculum.

Questions of narrative and argument are concerned with rhetoric, in the best sense of that word. In the Library of Congress classifi-cation of the book *Narrative and Argument* (Andrews 1989), 'rhet-oric' appears in brackets after both 'narrative' and 'argument'. What rhetoric can offer is an overview of the relationship between speaker/writer, audience, subject-matter and text or utterance. This theoretical perspective, like all good theory, suggests possibilities and alternatives – the kind of alternative explored by 12/13-year-olds in the research reported here. It's indubitably creative and imaginative. Perhaps as a term, it should still remain in parentheses? On the other hand, perhaps those brackets now need to come off.

9 Intertext or inner text? How children learn to read and talk together

James McGonigal

Taking the kids to school, we travel through the intertextual city. Some of us feel more at ease than others here, but all find our gaze attracted to the big picture-books of billboards that we pass. They are the 'real books' in our urban home. Like any books, these giant interactive texts teach their readers as much about form as content (their content, after all, changes with the months and seasons). There is a deep knowledge about typography and language choice to be gleaned there that is only rarely explored or articulated in the classrooms which wait at the end of our daily journey.

These advertisements are *interactive* texts because, like any beginning readers, we find our minds involved in actively helping to construct the meanings that flash past us: we create what we half-miss, or live with that puzzlement till the next big page appears with the same picture. And they are *intertextual* because their messages often depend on knowledge of other texts in any particular series of a developing advertising campaign, or of an opposing campaign created by a different team of writers. Discourse and image complement or compete with others further along the road, or vanished (never quite beyond recall) miles and years back.

An example, before we get down to the serious business of reading; and since we are driving through, let us focus on car adverts. This one is designed for a diptych of twin hoardings that comment on or complete each other's sense. In the first, in sepia tones, two cloche-hatted and demure women stand beside an old Vauxhall sports car (late 1920s or 1930s? The decade, and the fashion of the women, is difficult to judge: pre-Second World War, anyway). The setting appears to be a gravelled driveway, and the motto 'Vauxhalls have often inspired love and affection' creates a nostalgic sense of leafy ease and moneyed innocence. This might be Ethel and friend, while William and his Outlaws are plotting mischief in the bushes behind them.

The complementary picture framed in the neighbouring billboard is a powerful counter to this fabled past. Sleek, black and potent against a storm-lit desert landscape, the new sporting Vauxhall saloon makes its statement: 'Enter desire.' From family album snap with Edenic echoes of loyalty and innocent pleasure to subtle icon of an acquisitive age in one change of glance that driving past achieves for us. The point of the twin display is that each text exists in interrelationship, here extended on the hoarding to the relationship between owner and machine: we used to live like that, now we live like this.

The two posters of this campaign are sometimes seen apart, but each then serves to stir the memory of the other half of the message: the intertext is reconstructed from memory, as when, encountering a snatch of text from a well-loved story, we often recall the illustration that accompanied it. The interaction between reader and text then takes place at a level of inner mind rather than outer stimulus: such intimacy of text and meaning, or product and desired response, may be the real point – a form of persuasion or acquiescence which we internalize in passing. This city street is the forum we move through to have heads and hearts stirred by the silver arts of a commercial rhetoric, which works upon us through structures and conventions of which we may be barely aware.

Where is this journey taking us except back to school? I am concerned here to explore what happens to young children's minds as they read, and what we can do as they grow to help them become more explicitly aware of the interplay of meanings in the texts they are exposed to. The progress extends from what Young and Tyre (1989: 163) call 'lap learning' (the rhymes, jingles, songs, stories listened to in the security of parent's lap or knee) to early 'incidental reading' (of street signs, posters and environmental print which often exploit rhyme, jingles and story in the sorts of ways explored above) and stretches to the demands of national examinations that, ten or so years later, expect our young readers to have become articulate in exploring the emotional and linguistic impact of print and other media in their lives, and to be able to communicate such insights within forms of discourse which have their own conventional structures. Confident control of the conventions, of course, is also very much part of the exercise.

How is the full agenda to be covered? In a sense, we need to alter the title of Meek's (1988) influential essay 'How texts teach what readers learn' to 'How readers learn to share what texts are saying'. As usual, such rephrasing has an inherent heaviness, but this may echo the longer time-scale of reading development envisaged here, and the more public and dialogic emphasis which is demanded as young readers move beyond the personal experiencing of story to articulate in the arena of classroom or examination hall a sense of their own sophisticated interaction with a range of texts.

Even the earliest experience of text is dialogic, of course. Wells has recorded some lovely examples of the four-way interaction between child, parent, text and world that takes place whenever young children are read to:

David: 'The Giant Sandwich'.
   [*Four-second pause.*]
Mother: Who's this here on the first page?
David: The wasps.
Mother: The wasps are coming. [*Turns the page.*] Here's some
   more, look. Wow! [*Reads.*]
   One hot summer in Itching Down
   Four million wasps flew into town.
David: I don't like wasps . . . flying into town.
Mother: Why's that?
David: Because they sting me.
Mother: Do they?
David: Mm. I don't like them.
Mother: They'll only sting you if they get angry. If you leave
   them alone they won't sting you. But four million would be
   rather a lot, wouldn't it? They'd get rather in the way. [*Reads.*]
   They drove the picknickers away . . .
David: Mm.
Mother [*continuing to read*]:
   They chased the farmers from their hay.
   They stung Lord Swell [*chuckles*] *on his fat bald –*
David: Pate.
Mother: Do you know what a pate is?
David: What?
Mother: What do you think it is?
David: Hair.
Mother: Well – yes. It's where his hair *should* be. It's his head
   – look, his *bald* head. All his hair's gone.

(Wells 1989: 152–3)

What seems to be happening here, which becomes highly

influential on the child's future success in school, is the ability of story to generate a particular sort of thinking about words and the world, for 'the child is beginning to discover the symbolic potential of language: its power to create possible and imaginary worlds through words – by representing experience in symbols that are independent of the objects, events, and relationships symbolised, and that can be interpreted in contexts other than those in which the experience originally occurred, if indeed it ever occurred at all' (Wells 1989: 156)

Meek and others have pointed out too how young readers learn through story not only to move between the outer and inner realities of world and imagination, but also to master the lessons of narration, the manifold ways in which skilled writers for children actually teach their young readers how to read:

> Children quickly learn the rules for 'how things work around here'. Having done so, in behaviour and language, they know that the rules can be broken, by parody, for example. There are alternative versions of nursery rhymes, Christmas carols, national hymns which never find their way into books, all of which show that, when they have learned the rules, children learn how to subvert them. A joke is often the best reading test.
>
> (Meek 1988: 91)

All of which also suggests that even the best reading test is something of a joke if it neglects, as it probably always must, these crucial aspects of intertextuality. Skilled readers meet and can quite quickly learn to recognize in a given text references, echoes, parodies and plot unfoldings: text recognition rather than word recognition. This is why some young readers become hooked on books and others fail to find a way in:

> Children enter the intertext of literature, oral and written, very early; as soon as they know some nursery rhymes, in fact, and later, when they have amassed the lore of the school playground, they are able to recognise in their reading what has been in their memories for some time.
>
> (Meek 1988: 94)

The pleasure and power of story in creating this confident awareness in young readers has frequently been commented upon. There is a jigsaw attraction of whole texts being built up in the reading, and a human desire for resolution of whatever problem lies at the heart of the story. Thus we can sometimes forget how much children still puzzle over the individual *bits* of language which life presents them with: rhythms, usages, patterns of words, part messages of the whole code.

As parents we are often kept too busy finding answers to their questions to see where their minds are tending; and as teachers we are often intent on socializing children into the school culture of answering our questions rather than asking their own. I am not attaching particular blame here. Both sets of adults are just trying to survive the onslaught of children's minds. But it does mean that we often fail to recognize, let alone build upon, the inner dialogue with language that goes on (the inner or interim text, rather than the intertext) because as yet the structures are only coming into shape.

Often it is only in the retrospect of autobiography that we can regain access to this inner dialogue with text. Here is someone from the same background as Meek describes for herself, learning to read in a Scottish village primary school:

> One school book had a passage on the common house fly by T H Huxley, who described the insect as 'washing its hands with invisible soap and imperceptible water'. That made me look more closely at my mother's pet aversion! The words had a fine sound and were a joy to repeat as were passages about ants from the *Book of Proverbs*:
>
>> Go to the ant, thou sluggard! Consider her ways and be wise; which although she hath no guide, nor master, nor captain, provideth her meat for herself in the summer and gathereth her food in the harvest . . .
>
> Verse became one of our keen interests about the same time, an interest awakened first by the metrical psalms. Although songs were also in the air they did not register as powerfully as the psalms, as word patterns. At some point between the ages of six and eight David and I made the great discovery that metre and rhyme were something we might be able to handle. It was a wet and windy day and our noses were pressed to the window pane when a seagull swooped past blasting a large white dropping against the glass. 'Scorrie's scoot on the window pane' one of us cried. A few seconds later, 'He's done it once and he'll do it again!' continued the other, and we chanted our couplet again and again triumphantly.

(Ross 1989: 27–8)

This sudden movement from inner text to intertext is part of the charm and unpredictability of children's language, both spoken and written, where sheer enjoyment of the sound and colour of words suddenly shapes itself round a complete parody text of impolite content. Children can live with the hesitancy and indeterminacy of the inner text, but only so long as there is pleasure rather than frustration in process:

> Neither at school nor at Sunday School was there any real discussion of these subjects; not that it worried me at the time since questions could always be asked at home, and in any case they were not very pressing. Years later I would hear T S Eliot advise an audience to *listen* first to his poems, without searching for *meaning* in the lines. The important thing was to admit the impact of sound and imagery, to allow the poetry to communicate in its own way before attempting to analyse it and identify it. That was how we received the Bible.
>
> (Ross 1989: 30)

The world has changed since Margaret Meek and Anthony Ross went to school, and the reading curriculum has too, but anyone who observed young children's response to the mysterious language of sound and imagery of Raphael, Michelangelo, Donatello and Leonardo during the recent Mutant Ninja Turtles craze will realize that essentially the same sorts of learning and enjoyment are still going on. We may regret the commercialism that attends this exploitation of children's fascination with word play; or feel that its transitory passage through their consciousness does little lasting damage (for even as I write, the Turtles are being replaced by repeats of a rival, though still intertextual, cartoon hero: Count Duckula). But our work as teachers should surely explore and exploit in less commercial ways the same sorts of aspects of the attractive rhetoric of texts.

We have a wealth of excellent writing to start from. The first step is for the teacher to sense what is happening at the levels of language *below* the narrative in well-loved books for beginning readers. The language course for primary teachers with which I am most familiar[1] includes a student survey of the language patterns and effects of a range of early texts, and an exploration of the way these patterns, and their interplay with illustration and layout, both create the meaning for young readers and support them in their quest for the further meaning to be found when the page turns. At the same time, the text is instructing them in the rhetorical patterns of attraction and repulsion through which conflict and character operate in the discourse of story.

As a contrast to the Turtles, take a few traditional teddy bear stories as examples. *Teddy Bears 1 to 10* by Susanna Gretz (1986) can be seen to exploit variations in the patterns of the noun group:

> 1 teddy bear. 2 old teddy bears. 3 dirty old teddy bears. 4 teddy bears in the wash. 5 teddy bears on the clothes line. 6 teddy bears on the radiator. 7 teddy bears at the cleaners. 8 teddy bears at the dyers. 9 teddy bears in the bus. 10 teddy bears home for tea.

Of course there is a plot-line here, and the whole text may explore something of the childish psycho-drama of being dirty and getting clean. Yet it is in the playful building up of the word groups that the real attraction is to be found, as well as in the detailed and delightful support of meaning in the accompanying pictures.

This is the Bear by Sarah Hayes and Helen Craig (1989) works on the repetition and development of a two-clause sentence pattern, with strong similarity in the sound effects of rhythm and rhyme: 'This is the *bear* / who fell in the *bin*. This is the *dog* / who pushed him *in*.' Or 'This is the man / in an awful *grump* / who *searched* / and *searched* / and *searched* the *dump*', where the repetition contributes rhetorically to the creation of the desired effect of exasperation.

In *My Brown Bear Barney* by Dorothy Butler (1991) the young reader's quest for meaning is supported by a narrative which depends on a repeated sentence pattern, namely 'When I go to X, I take my $A+B+C$ – and my brown bear Barney.' The illustrations meanwhile strongly assist the child's efforts to read the variations which occur in the pattern, as the heroine moves between different social settings before arriving (minus Barney) as a big girl now in Primary One.

The range of rhetorical patterns in children's books is wide, and their exploration has its own fascination. Patterns of question and answer, so central to children's language development, are used in *Brown Bear, Brown Bear, What Do You See?* by Bill Martin Jr (1986) and *Burnie's Hill* by Eric Blegvad (1978). Sentence patterns signalling cause and effect are often found. In *Oh Dear* by Rod Campbell (1989), Buster's search for eggs for his Grandma takes him on a syntactic journey round the farm: 'So he went to the X and asked the Y, but . . .' until he finally finds the hen house. The basic sentence pattern recurs, with all its variations again being supported and clarified by illustrations.

Many effects are possible. The humour in similarities of sound and onomatopoeic resonance is delightfully exploited by Pat Hutchins in *Don't Forget the Bacon* (1976) and *Goodnight Owl!* (1973). Further creative play with language choice is explored by Taylor (1991) in his 'Books in the classroom and "knowledge about language" ', where he considers lists, direct speech, tense forms and figurative language.

Where does such exploration lead us in the classroom? First, it informs our own reading aloud to children, enabling us to stress the language patterns and so emphasize both meaning and involvement. At the same moment, we are helping to create the echoes referred to earlier in the memories of beginning readers. We are investing in their intertextual account, so to speak: imaginative writing, as has been recognized at least since classical times, is both pleasurable and profitable, *dulce* and *utile*.

Second, by helping children to learn to read like writers, with deeper appreciation and enjoyment of the intended effects (even at a level as yet unarticulated) we are setting them on the true road to becoming writers themselves. Student teachers can learn a good deal by attempting similar literary/linguistic effects, and so can their pupils.

The *Foundations of Writing* project by Michael and Jackson (1990), and its further development by Michael and Michael (1990), creates frameworks of illustration and sentence patterning which enable young children to produce their own unfolding 'little books'. What is unfolding, of course, has as much to do with cognitive as with aesthetic pleasure: or rather, the two are so intertwined as to bring about a changed perspective on writing and reading both for the children and for their readership (which will include other children as well as teachers and parents, of course).

A natural development of this approach is the involvement of upper primary and lower secondary school children in what could be called 'paired reading/paired writing' projects with beginning or struggling readers. Here the older children first revisit the language worlds created by professional writers for children, in terms of the sorts of patterns, repetition and variation referred to above. For some of the older children, of course, this may be in effect their first visit, and a new world of discourse is being opened up to them at a stage of awareness at which they can begin to sense the usefulness of such techniques for their own writing purposes.

The young authors now create their own books on those models, with advice and guidance from teachers, from peers and, importantly, from the response of their intended readership when these carefully crafted products are finally tried out with younger children. The effect of such projects is not only evident in the commitment shown and attention paid to linking text and illustrations. Gains are evident at the level of sentence structure and cohesion, particularly where a cartoon format and basic limitation of character and setting are suggested as framing devices:

> The least able pupils probably derived the greatest benefit. Whether it was the use of drawing, the basic simplicity of the plot, or the high level of interest, or whatever, their stories all showed some mastery of structure. The story ingredients did converge to produce logical and sensible plots. During the course of the redrafting there was an obvious attempt to organise the material into as clear a form as possible, making evident the connections between the various separate events. Often what had been two disconnected events or pieces of information:

> *It was raining*
> *John and Mary went to the park*

became a logically connected and closely related sequence

> *Even though it was raining John and Mary went to the park*

Similarly

> *It was a very rainy and dull day and puddles were all about the park when Harry and Donna were on the swings.*

became

> *It was a very rainy and dull day but nothing could keep Harry and Donna out of the park. Even the puddles that were everywhere did not stop them swinging high up on the swings.*
>
> (Gormley 1990: 6)

The frequent use of connectives is found even in the work of those pupils who would not normally use such words or phrases. One used the following in a ten-drawing story: 'next . . . both . . . when . . . just . . . then . . . as . . . luckily . . . as . . . when . . . in no time at all . . . even more quickly . . . later . . . when . . . right away . . . as . . . this meant'. These were indications that the pupils were seriously attempting to structure the story at the level below overall narrative.

There are other sorts of metacognitive gains also, difficult to quantify, which are likely to be helpful when these youngsters, as the next generation of parents, begin to release afresh the power of language through introducing their own offspring to the surfaces and depths of story. But before reaching that stage, of course, they have to undergo modern society's strange initiation rituals of National Curriculum and assessment.

It is here that a conscious awareness of how language works in a variety of genres and contexts can be developed. Recent attempts to create programmes of study incorporating knowledge about language at key stage 3 of the National Curriculum have reminded us of the range of potential starting points for exploring language as text and as behaviour: the speech of young children, investigating reading aloud, speech forms in novels, language styles in media presenters and texts, learning to read the illustrations in books, analysing and transforming genres – these activities and many others (see Keith 1991) enable upper-school students to build consciously upon the insights and experiences gained from the classroom activities mentioned above.

Something more is needed, though, and that is an awareness on our part that the forms of classroom organization may well need to shift slightly to accommodate this new reflectiveness about language, and also to allow the support for (and assessment of) talk in the classroom. How are youngsters to learn to approach such sophisticated procedures as using language to talk about language, or engage in the teasing out of the tangled intertextual constructions of the linguistic world(s) they inhabit unless the forms of their own group processes for selecting, developing and communicating ideas to audiences both formal and informal, immediate and distant, can be made explicit?

Two approaches have appealed to me recently here. In *Talk About Poetry*, Ovens (1989) consciously builds into her range of classroom approaches for exploring specific features of poems and also whole texts (such as finding odd poems in a trio, reconstructing poems, evaluating statements about a text, anticipating context or symbol for a theme, setting questions for the writer, making up rules for types of poems – some twenty-five approaches in all) an explicit use of varied classroom groupings and a highlighting of talk criteria. So that, for example, the required discourse for describing personal experience to a partner, or when reporting to a group, or to the whole class, or when discussing in a group, is displayed using an overhead projector and focused upon explicitly either before or after performance.

This sounds mechanical, and yet there is a real sense in which if we fail to make such features of the language of persuasion or conviction clear to our classes, we actively prevent many of them from gaining a sense of how their language alters in response to context and purpose. And we leave them unprepared to respond with a lively critical awareness, therefore, to the rhetorical powers of political and media voices that surround them in the world, as well as to the language of learning itself.

Douglas Barnes has recently reminded us[2] that while misunderstandings in conversation are always open to the possibility of repair, in typical school dialogue the pupils are either not sufficiently self-aware or are not really encouraged to be in a position to check or challenge understanding. Hence the 'ground-rules' of dominant literacy practices in schools – ways of thinking and ways of expressing – remain unformulated in their minds.

Or worse, in their action: for the danger of teaching children genre forms or mechanical modes of discourse, rather than ways of acting in the world, can be that it traps them in limited thinking instead of releasing them into action or negotiation. That danger may be inherent even in the approach to group talk sketched out above.

A further and more active development of the pupils' awareness of group language and processes is the recent Canadian focus on co-operative small-group learning, where a variety of groupings (informal groups, base groups, combined, reconstituted or representative groups) are deployed according to the given task, with time spent in evaluating the process and performance, and a clear sense of the roles to be performed by different members.[3] Some might sense the danger here of a subtext which aims at creating an executive class able to move from school to corporate identity without a hitch. Yet experience of trying such approaches in school and college courses suggests that they do in fact release a creative force and sense of organization in spoken language which as English teachers we are more accustomed to aiming for in written work. And when they are employed with a clear focus on the exploration or reworking of a story or poem, then a powerful engagement of minds can take place.

It seems to me that it is only by some such focus on the arts of language, as they are employed in the group and whole-class contexts in which young people in schools are learning to negotiate their own (tentative) views of reality and text, and the interplay between these, that we can fully prepare them to read the world that opens for them again at the end of the school day.

We may feel it is a jungle out there, but it is salutary to remember that folk-tales and sagas were born of our ancestral forest world. Through exploring the paths of story and the language that carries it, by revisiting the half-remembered haunts of intertext and inner text, youngsters can learn to assume some control of the language of the tribe, and responsibility also for passing on to a new generation its almost magical powers to challenge and persuade.

NOTES

1 The BEd Literacy and Oracy course in St Andrew's College of Education, Glasgow. I owe the examples and insights below to Bernard Flood, Head of Language and Literature there.
2 At the International Convention on Language and Literacy held at the University of East Anglia, April 1991.
3 Information is available on these approaches from the Co-operative Resources Centre in the Ontario Institute for Studies in Education, Toronto. Group roles include reader (of task material), recorder (of best answers), discussion leader, encourager (of quieter members), checker (who asks for explanation or summary of points made), praiser and grouper (who ensure that members feel good about their work and keep to task) and timekeeper (to ensure completion).

10 A rhetoric of reading

James E. Seitz

I

One of the most salient advances of contemporary theory lies in its recognition of the rhetoricity in all *writing*, even fiction – but to what extent have theorists speculated on a rhetoric of *reading*? The question may at first seem strange, since rhetoric, understood as the art of persuasion, appears naturally to align itself with that which does the persuading – the writer or the text. But a model which grants all activity to the text and reduces the reader to mere passivity does a serious injustice to the actual shaping of meaning which occurs in the dramatic exchange that constitutes reading. Whether or not we go as far as Stanley Fish, who claims that the reader creates *everything* in the textual encounter, most of us now recognize that 'the role of the reader' – the reader's *participation* in the creation of meaning – cannot be ignored. Therefore, the time appears ripe for a model of reading that would conceive of the reader not only as receiver but as producer of what we commonly call 'rhetorical stance'.

In *The Rhetoric of Fiction*, Booth contends that all fictional texts suggest an 'implied author' with whom the reader connects in the course of reading:

> the implied author of each novel is someone with whose beliefs on all subjects I must largely agree if I am to enjoy his work. Of course, the same distinction must be made between myself as reader and the very different self who goes about paying bills, repairing leaky faucets, and failing in generosity and wisdom. It is only as I read that I become the self whose beliefs must coincide with the author's.

(Booth 1961: 137–8)

One advantage to Booth's view of reading is its conception of both author and reader as inhabited by multiple selves or roles which are called into play as the occasion demands. The 'implied author', an author who possesses a system of values indicated by the text, addresses the 'implied reader', a reader whom the text needs to hold (at least temporarily) those same values and thereby 'see eye to eye' with the implied author. Readers who are unable, for whatever reasons, to assume the values of the implied author will find the text less satisfactory than they would otherwise. Concerning this phenomenon, Booth quotes Walker Gibson, who claims that texts we reject are often those whose 'mock reader we refuse to become, a mask we refuse to put on, a role we will not play' (Gibson 1950: 268). A text whose values we cannot accept we *evaluate* negatively.

What this version of reading offers, then, is a reader as embedded in rhetorical stance as the author or text. Readers, after all, approach texts with their own sets of values that condition their experience of those texts, values that limit or qualify the kinds of mock readers they can become. Booth claims that this is in fact the case with his own disregard for Lawrence's *Lady Chatterley's Lover*, a book whose belief in sex as the key to salvation he cannot accept. As he candidly comments:

> Whether I should blame myself or Lawrence for this, I can never be quite sure. Perhaps we are both partly at fault. Even if I cannot resist blaming him, at least a little, it is difficult to know whether his failure to carry me along is a failure of craftsmanship or a fundamental incompatibility that no amount of craftsmanship could overcome.
>
> (Booth 1961: 138–9)

It appears that readers serve not only as addressees, but that readers themselves address the text through their dispositions towards the mock or implied readers they are asked to enact. If rhetoric is defined broadly as the relationship one assumes between oneself and the addressed, then the reader's *response* to the text constitutes a rhetorical act – an inscription, as it were, of the reading. Readers attempt to convince the text (and themselves) that it has presented itself in the very way they have read it.

My suggestion that readers contribute their own implicit rhetoric goes a step further than Booth does in his essentially modest description of the rhetorical situation.[1] But my proposal is not intended to be an echo of recent claims that the reader alone writes the text, for I wish to respect the sense in which the text arrives before the reader already written; otherwise, there would be nothing to read. Nevertheless, writing is always in some sense provisional, always in need of reading; and my point is that reading requires a rhetorical positioning similar to that assumed in conversation. Reading, like dialogue, constitutes a form of social engagement which consists of both reception and participation – a notion for which Pratt convincingly argues in her description of 'the literary speech situation', wherein both writer and reader rely on an established role structure commonly understood to be in force (Pratt 1977: 100–51). Readers, for instance, accept the imposition of 'giving up the floor' (as an audience does for a speaker), with the understanding that they have the right to interpret, respond and evaluate. In other words, it is not only writers but also readers who eventually have their 'turn', their reactions, their opportunity to speak. In this turn – which interestingly echoes the 'turn' of tropes and figures – lies what I want to recognize as a rhetoric of reading.

But before considering the rhetorical predicament of the reader, we must examine how the rhetoric of the *writer* is already a reading.

II

While most reader-oriented studies in recent literary theory insist on attempting painstaking delineations of an epistemology rather than a rhetoric of reading,[2] a refreshing exception, one that has implications for rhetoric even though its explicit concern is semiotics, can be found in Eco's (1979) *The Role of the Reader* – a book whose very title indicates recognition of a strategic element in reading. Eco's concern is with the ways in which writing itself is a reading, for the writer's success depends upon the social intuitions through which he reads his own text and thereby plays the role of the reader even as he writes. Reversing the habit of theorists who seek to describe how readers create their own texts, Eco explores the many ways in which texts create their own readers. Eco acknowledges that readers can convert their reading into anything they please by regarding the text as 'an uncommitted stimulus for a personal hallucinatory experience'; but such irresponsibility is not the kind of reading he wishes to elucidate. His interest lies instead in the way a text is 'realized' through its reading, which the text itself activates. In other words, as every writer knows, a good piece of writing must anticipate its reading.

Eco demonstrates the textual presence of this anticipation, this awareness that the reader must perform certain acts, through a close analysis of Alphonse Allais's short story 'A most Parisian incident' (1890). The story concerns a jealous couple, Raoul and Marguerite, who both receive messages that the other can be found 'in a good mood' at a masked ball that week. Raoul is told that Marguerite will be disguised as a Congolese Dugout, and Marguerite is told that Raoul will be disguised as a Knight Templar. When the Dugout and the Templar finally meet at the ball and later unmask themselves, Allais writes:

> Both at the same instant cried out in astonishment, neither one recognizing the other.
> *He* was not Raoul.
> *She* was not Marguerite.
> They apologized to each other and were not long in making acquaintance on the occasion of an excellent supper, need I say more.
>
> (Eco 1979: 266; trans. Fredric Jameson)

What has happened here? Suddenly, all the reader has expected collapses, for the characters presumed to be Raoul and Marguerite turn out to be others – characters whom the reader does not know and who do not know each other. As Eco explains, the text has never said that Raoul or Marguerite plan to go to the ball, and it never says outright that the Templar and the Dugout at the ball are in fact Raoul and Marguerite; furthermore, it never claims that Raoul and Marguerite have lovers. Rather, it is the *reader* who assumes that such things are the case; it is the reader who jumps to conclusions about the adulterous intentions of Raoul and Marguerite. But, as Eco goes on to indicate, this apparently foolish reader has been authorized by the text to make the very assumptions that eventually get the reader into such trouble: 'the text postulates the presumptuous reader as one of its constitutive elements: if not, why is it said . . . that the two masks cried out in astonishment, neither one recognizing the other?' (Eco 1979: 206). The astonishment, of course, should belong to the reader alone, for the Dugout and the Templar have no knowledge of Marguerite and Raoul. Since the text openly inscribes the reader's perplexity, one can only conclude that Allais generated his story from a set of predictable readerly gestures.

What this duping of the reader makes evident is that texts rely on a series of expectations by the reader which fill out, so to speak, the rather incomplete information provided by the text. Eco maps a number of ways in which this happens. Through what he calls 'stylistic overencoding', for instance, when Allais says that Raoul and Marguerite are 'married', we take this to mean that they are *married to each other* (Eco 1979: 20). Or, to give an example of inferences based on a social store of what Eco calls 'common frames': when Raoul raises his hand during an argument with Marguerite, we apply the frame 'violent altercation' and assume that he intends to strike her, even though the text does not explicitly say that this is the case (Eco 1979: 21). Similarly, we anticipate an adulterous frame when each spouse receives a message about the other's disguise at the ball. Later, our 'mistake' revealed as the masks are withdrawn, it becomes clear that Allais has anticipated his readers' anticipations. All of these instances parallel what Grice calls 'implicature' in ordinary conversation: the dependence of a great deal of our utterances on not what is said but what is *implicated* (Grice 1975: 41–58).

What, then, does the story mean? Eco makes an insightful reply:

> The implicit lesson of *Drame* [an abbreviation of the French title] is, in fact, coherently contradictory: Allais is telling us that not only *Drame* but every text is made of two components: the information provided by the author and that added by the Model Reader, the latter being determined by the former – with various rates of freedom and necessity. But, in order to demonstrate this textual theorem, Allais has led the reader to fill up the text with contradictory information, thus cooperating in setting up a story that cannot stand up. The failure of the apparent story of *Drame* is the success of Allais' theoretical assumption and the triumph of his metatextual demonstration.
>
> (Eco 1979: 206)

On one level, the 'metatextual demonstration' illustrates nothing more than what common sense already tells us: the text forms the site of an interaction between writer and reader. But on another level it specifies this interaction as something not so much located *in* the text as provoked *by* the text. Eco's 'Model Reader' – a term that I find somewhat unfortunate – is effectively the 'implied reader' described by Booth: the reader whom the text gives evidence it expects or desires.

Writers, therefore, in their concern for rhetorically positioning their texts in ways that will somehow appeal to readers, must in effect write those readers into being. In other words, playing 'the role of the reader' is an inevitable part of the rhetorical act. But to claim that rhetoric requires an act of reading is not the same as claiming that the act of reading requires rhetoric. In order to assert the latter, we must turn from writers to readers themselves, whose motives may come to seem less receptive than they at first appear.

III

Let us begin by noting that the issue of terminology about reading is crucial. Eco's 'Model Reader' has the drawback of suggesting an *ideal* reader – one who performs the reading merely as responses to a series of instructions provided by the text. This is surely a *part* of reading, but a rather limited definition for the comprehensive act, and one that does not allow for sufficient variance in reading experience. Another problem lies in the potential connections between Eco's 'Model Reader' and Culler's 'competent reader' (Culler 1975: 113–30). Culler's notion of 'literary competence' has taken severe criticism for its misappropriation of Chomsky's concept of linguistic competence. Both Kintgen (1983) and Smith (1978) point out that for Chomsky 'competence' is innate and universal, while for Culler it is learned by those who study literature. Furthermore, as Smith notes, to pursue the notion of Chomsky's idealized native speaker-listener in the realm of literature would be to posit an idealized writer-reader; but a skilled reader is not necessarily a skilled writer. With this critique in mind, I would prefer to speak of an implied reader who is *capable* rather than competent, for capability denotes someone having traits *conducive* to a particular activity – without locking our theoretical reader into a behaviour that might not pertain to various actual readers.

What, then, constitutes a capable reader? Paradoxically, a capable reader is one who not only has the ability to 'follow' the text but also the ability to jump *ahead* of it – to make what Eco calls 'inferential walks'. Eco notes that during the course of a narrative, the reader is required to make 'forecasts about the forthcoming state of affairs', for the text 'elicits expectations' which function as hypotheses about the propositional content of the story (Eco 1979: 32). In other words, while we read we not only keep track of specific events but also imagine what these events might mean in terms of the story as a whole; only a reader who is in some sense dysfunctional would wait until the narrative were completed before attempting a guess at the author's intentions. The act of forecasting, which generally comes into play from the text's opening lines, clearly forms an important part of how capable readers orient themselves in relation to the unfoldings of the text. Eco contends that forecasts are made possible by reference to 'intertextual frames', frames like 'the adulterine triangle' which help us to situate events even as they are being uncovered: 'To identify these frames the reader [has] to "walk," so to speak, outside the text, in order to gather intertextual support. . . . I call these interpretive moves *inferential walks*' (Eco 1979: 32). In other words, the text prompts its own reading, but it does so by leading the reader beyond itself to other already established 'texts' or cultural paradigms which help the reader to make the inferences necessary for reading. We cannot read the text without in some sense 'walking' ahead of it.

Inferring, forecasting and expecting are all terms that describe a process by which readers create a rhetorical interaction with the text – for these acts necessitate that readers interject their own 'stance', their own values, hopes and imagination, into the textual exchange. If persuasion in the broad sense forms one of the goals of any text, then the achievement of that goal will depend on the relations with a text that the reader is capable of establishing. In other words, a text that persuades the reader is one that provides the conditions whereby readers *persuade themselves* that a particular interpretation of the text is preferable to others. Interested readers – that is, readers who know how to make texts interesting – tend to play not one but several readerly roles in the course of reading a single text. The study of rhetoric must examine not only the relations between text and reader but also the relations between what I will call various 'virtual' readers which struggle for position during the reading.

Earlier I discussed Booth's notion of an 'implied reader' whom the text would like the actual reader to become. But one does not assume the values and attitudes of the implied reader unproblematically; reading in fact sets in motion a process of negotiation which consists of at least the following moments:

A attempting to determine what kind of implied reader the text intends

B the struggle of 'virtual readers' to assume the dominant reading

C an evaluation of the text as a result of the (however temporary) dominant reading.[3]

I am contending that reading provokes an internal dialogue that might best be described as polyphony – derived from the Greek *polyphonos*, having many voices. Vygotsky informs us that, contrary to what we might assume, the origins of social interaction lie not in inner speech, but precisely the opposite: inner speech is the transfer of 'social, collaborative forms of behavior to the sphere of inner-personal psychic functions' (Vygotsky 1986: 35). In other words, the forms of language at play in our inner speech or 'stream of consciousness' have been internalized from the language at play in the social roles we observe around us. This is how we come to 'talk to ourselves' in voices which approximate various figures from our experience: parents, teachers, friends, enemies and so on. Similarly, reading brings not only an encounter with the discourse of the text, but also the discourse of the reader's inner speech – any number of internal voices contending for the most persuasive account of what the author intends and how one should respond.

The rhetoric of reading, then, consists of the relationships that readers create between themselves and the emerging possibilities which they anticipate in the text. In Allais's 'A most Parisian incident', for example, the actual reader may assume several competing readerly roles in the course of reading. At the end of a brief first chapter, we are told of Raoul and Marguerite:

> They would have been the happiest of all couples, except for their awful personalities.
>
> At the slightest provocation, pow! a broken plate, a slap, a kick in the ass.
>
> At such sounds, Love fled in tears, to await, in the neighborhood of a great park, the always imminent hour of reconciliation.
>
> O then, kisses without number, infinite caresses, tender and knowing, ardors as burning as hell itself.
>
> You would have thought that the two of them – pigs that they were! – had fights only so they could make up again.
>
> (263)

We must first confront the issue of what reader this text would have us become. The opening sentence of this passage, for instance, might be read as a straightforward expression of the characters' failure – but it is rather obvious that such a reading would be naive. The narrator alerts us to his ironic stance through the extremity and simplicity of his description: 'awful personalities' registers as a joke, an unexpected summation of those who would otherwise be 'the happiest of couples'. Other jokes follow – 'a kick in the ass', 'as burning as hell itself', 'pigs that they were!' – so that by the end of the passage the reader may be fairly certain that the text anticipates a reader who shares the narrator's cynical amusement with lovers who continually feud only to re-enact their passion.

To establish a sense of the reader that the text implies, however, is not necessarily to decide that the implied reader is the reader whom one wishes to become. 'Virtual' readers of all sorts may call for attention if one feels in any way resistant to the values of the implied reader. It might be, for instance, that one finds the narrator's irony at the expense of lovers in 'A most Parisian incident' a kind of affront, a sign of insensitivity to the difficulties of human relationships; or one might simply feel that the narrator is being too clever, thereby setting a tone from which the reader is unlikely to profit. Whatever the particularities of response, resistance results in an internal dialogue or polyphony in which virtual readers compete for dominance. The competition is rhetorical – that is, virtual readers attempt to persuade the actual reading subject why they should provide the reading that he or she enacts. While one virtual reader argues for a reading that would condemn Allais's text as frivolous, another insists that the 'metatextual demonstration' is interesting but empty of the emotional power which characterizes the most impressive literature. And so the reader oscillates between positions until one reading overpowers another.

This view of reading suggests a conception of rhetoric as not only a strategy of persuasion but also as an *orientation* towards the other, an attitudinal 'stance' based on what we value at the time. A rhetoric of reading, in other words, includes the reader's *ethos*, which we might begin to locate along a continuum of submission and resistance. When a text 'works' as intended, one submits or yields to its authority, gives oneself over to the perspective of the implied reader. We speak in these cases of what a poem or book *did* to us, as if we were helpless in the face of its powerful design. When, on the other hand, one resists to whatever degree and for whatever reasons the apparent intentions of the text, readings which the text does not seem to anticipate arrive on the scene, murmuring (or sometimes shouting) their objections. A rhetoric of writing now confronts a rhetoric of reading.

The outcome depends on the persuasiveness of the virtual readings on the actual reader, who must finally decide which reading to employ. On no account do I mean that the reader must adopt a single orientation towards the text as a whole; I mean only that at any time in the course of reading – perhaps for as long as a chapter or as short as a phrase – a *dominant* reading must assert itself in order that the text be read.[4] This is simply to assert that perspective is a requirement in reading, something that we cannot avoid, even though we may assume a different perspective upon re-reading a passage. It is not that perspective precedes reading, but that perspective and reading, as Fish says of identifying context and comprehending utterances, 'occur simultaneously' (Fish 1980: 313). To 'assume' or 'take on' a perspective in relation to a text *is* to read it, to submit to or resist it, to evaluate it.

In his theory of literary influence, Bloom similarly implies a rhetoric of reading through his equation of reading with writing: 'strong' readings, in Bloom's view, are necessarily *mis*readings that generate a space for writing (Bloom 1975: 3). Misreadings are essentially resistant readings, revisions that are produced by the belatedness from which all reading suffers. For Bloom, the scene of reading is a struggle for power not unlike the one I have described between implied and virtual readers. But in Bloom's scene, the price of submission is high, even fatal: 'If we have been ravished by a poem, it will cost us our own poem' (18). Strong reading, in this view, must reject the implied reading in favour of a virtual reading, a misreading, that comes to be *written*. Bloom's study is that of the 'relationships *between* texts' (3), how texts misread their predecessors in order to create space for their own writing.

But what of readings that never become actual texts, neither works of literature nor criticism? Is a reading that submits to the apparent will of the text a 'weak' reading, one that has lost the struggle for power and control? I think not, on two counts. First, the 'will of the text' is always a fiction, an interpretation of how the text asks to be read. Interpretations are surely based on 'evidence' of some sort, but the complexity of most texts provides a good deal of latitude in judgement, as we see when two differing but equally compelling interpretations are offered of the same text. Even the 'submissive' reading, then, forms a creative act, the composition and enactment of an implied reader. Second, if the authority of the virtual readers constitutes a rhetoric of reading, then the authority of the implied reader constitutes an *aesthetics* of reading, a *coming under the influence* of the text. When the rhetoric of the text has done its work, when we are persuaded to read as the text appears to desire that we read – that is, when we can no longer anticipate and thereby dull the influence of what the text anticipates in us – then we have found our way to what Barthes has called the 'pleasure of the text', which is the pleasure of reading (Barthes 1975). If submission to the text 'costs us our own poem', it does not cost us the poem we have read.

Of course, 'submission' and 'resistance' are metaphors for ways of reading, and it would be wrong to suggest that the reader ever stands entirely on one side or the other. To completely submit to a text would in one regard represent the death of one's ego; to completely resist is to close the book permanently. Surely any reading is composed of various submissions and resistances, the recollection of which would tell the crucial story of rhetorical and aesthetic influence in the textual encounter. The issue here becomes the degree to which reading can be recovered, the possibility of accounting for the 'effect' of design, of figurality, through rhetorical awareness. We turn, then, to the pedagogical opportunities created by the concept of reading as a rhetorical act.

IV

What do our students think of rhetoric? What role does rhetoric play in their own conceptions of their reading? In New York, the first-year college students that I teach appear to be caught in the conventional notion of rhetoric as some kind of dirty trick with words, most often employed by politicians and advertisers. Their only encounters with the term seem to be limited to its appearance in the media – generally when someone *accuses* another of rhetoric: 'Let's have more substance, less rhetoric!' Certainly their secondary-school teachers have abandoned the term in all but pejorative uses; still committed to the view of literary language as divorced from social concerns, most of these teachers confine their students to traditional questions of theme, character and symbol in discussions of their reading. Consequently, when first-year college students enter my own classroom, they are often surprised to hear me use the word 'rhetoric' approvingly – as an act they *should* not avoid – and ubiquitously – as an act they *cannot* avoid.

But the place to begin with our students is not a series of lectures on the history of the misunderstanding of rhetoric. We must instead begin by engaging them in rhetorical acts that they do not even recognize as rhetorical; afterwards, issues of terminology and definition will be fairly simple to resolve. If the rhetoric of reading involves a struggle between conflicting interpretations – what I have called virtual readers within the actual reading subject – then it becomes clear that we might initiate discussion simply by asking our students to relate the *story* of their reading. All readings are themselves narratives, consisting of characters (that is, virtual readers) who work to persuade the reader that the text should be read in the light of a particular value or set of values. As Culler writes: 'reading is divided and heterogenous, useful as a point of reference only when composed into a story, when construed or constructed as a narrative' (Culler 1982: 69). Another way of stating this is to say that during the course of a single reading we generally play the role of any number of readers. Paradoxically, mature reading is a form of rehearsal: we do not simply 'read', as a child might, trapped by the single desire to move forward – but rather, we 'try on' readings, envision the text through the eyes of various masks, all the while attempting to forecast what it proposes, 'what it all adds up to'. We wonder which mask will provide the most convincing reading – the reading we ultimately choose to believe.

Our initial task, then, is to get our students to understand that '[t]o read is to operate with the hypothesis of a reader, and there is always a gap or division within reading' (Culler 1982: 67). What most entry-level students do not yet recognize is that is that the most exciting possibilities for reading lie not in the earnest attempt to wrench from the text what the author supposedly 'put' there, but in the ability to play a whole repertoire of readerly roles whose engagement with the text will produce various results. When we ask them to account for the stories of their reading, to describe their encounters, hesitations and discoveries, they begin to see that their stories are really quite different from one another and that they might indeed attempt to read under any number of guises. They often find, in fact, that they are already reading like others – perhaps like some particularly charismatic English teachers who have taught them during their formative years to read as those teachers read, with their habits of mind, biases and proclivities. Comparing and contrasting their stories of reading, students come to see that their progress through a text is marked by all manner of response which conditions their interpretation of what follows. For instance, if one reads Book 1 of *The Odyssey* with the sense that Telemakhos would prefer to confirm that his father is dead rather than discover he is alive, then one interprets the son's journey for information in a different light. In this sense, readers actually *compose* the story even as they read it.

Once students realize that the story of their reading is a story of various shifts between roles – between, for example, roles of innocence and scepticism in regard to Telemakhos' motives – they now have the foundation for beginning to examine the rhetorical element of reading. Rhetoric, as we know, is the art of promoting certain values, and as readers we are more or less adept at negotiating our values with those of the text. What our students need is to comprehend how their stories of reading reflect their own values and their ability to interact with the values of others: reading can only proceed through a framework of *assumptions*, and it is precisely their assumptions, their forms of positioning themselves before the text, that students must come to recognize. As Pavel notes, the journey of the imagination required by reading is not simply 'neutrally beheld but . . . vividly bear[s] on the beholder's world' (Pavel 1986: 145). In other words, our response to texts is characterized by our commitment to our own world, to the world of possibilities we bring with us and explore in our reading.

As I have already mentioned *The Odyssey*, I would like to relate a story of reading that occurred when one of my classes read Homer in the autumn of 1990. After my students completed the book, I asked them to describe how they felt when reading about Odysseus' revenge in Book 22, 'Death in the Great Hall'. Not surprisingly, they spoke of how much they enjoyed Odysseus' triumphant defeat of those who had pursued his wife and had attempted to humiliate him while he was disguised as a beggar. The turning point in this conventional response, however, came when I read aloud a passage depicting the execution of female servants who had slept with the suitors. Odysseus has first ordered these women to dispose of the slain bodies of their lovers and to wash their blood from the floors and walls. Then, once the great hall has been thoroughly cleaned, Odysseus has the servants taken outside so that they can watch Telemakhos as he prepares the ropes for their hanging:

> They would be hung like doves
> or larks in springes triggered in a thicket,
> where the birds think to rest – a cruel nesting.
> So now in turn each woman thrust her head
> into a noose and swung, yanked high in air,
> to perish there most piteously.
> Their feet danced for a little, but not long.
>
> (Homer 1963: 424)

My students were momentarily silent, but for some nervous laughter. There appears to be something in these lines that qualified their initially unbridled enthusiasm for Odysseus' retaliation. Some of them began to speak their hesitancy: 'It seems like he's going a bit too far here'; 'Why does he have to kill *them*, too?' and so on. These pieces of resistance intensified when I went on to read aloud the passage which immediately follows the slaying of the servant girls, when a traitor, Melanthios, receives his punishment from Telemakhos and Eumaios:

> From the storeroom to the court they brought Melanthios,
> chopped with swords to cut his nose and ears off,
> pulled off his genitals to feed the dogs
> and raging hacked his hands and feet away.
> As their own hands and feet called for a washing,
> they went indoors to Odysseus again.
> Their work was done.

(424)

There are few who can re-read and ponder such a passage, regardless of the respect for Odysseus and allowance for the practices of
'that day and age', without pausing to consider whether this form
of revenge is ultimately too excessive. And it is important to
remember that Odysseus does not stop here. The final act of the
poem consists of Athena staying Odysseus' hand from further violence, for the hero is bent on the death of the suitors' fathers and
brothers as well. Even the gods balk at the scope of Odysseus'
rage.

The questions in my classroom were these: how did we allow
ourselves, the first time through, to read these passages without
pause? What led us to acquiesce in the face of violence that we
would ordinarily find repulsive? Why did we submit to Odysseus'
values rather than question them? Of course, there are many possibilities. Odysseus' values may be more in accord with our own
values than we would like to admit: everyone, at some time or
another, desires revenge, and in those moments we may feel what
Claudius says while plotting with Laertes: 'Revenge should have no
bounds.' But it is also possible that the rhetorical force of Homer's
narrative is so effective that we find ourselves playing a readerly
role that in retrospect we might see, from a certain ethical perspective, as more or less regrettable. In other words, the position of
the implied reader in Homer's text is voiced so artfully and
seductively that other readings – that is, other potential relationships to the text posed by what I have called 'virtual readers' – are
silenced. Only upon second glance, lingering over the images of
slavery, torture and execution, did my students begin to entertain
alternative roles for their reading, roles that questioned the necess-
ity of submitting to Odysseus' values.

This, then, is a rhetoric of reading in an educational setting:
students exploring the persuasive force of the readers whom they
may choose to become. Ultimately, the spectrum of possibilities is
much more intricate and various than a simple binary of 'submissive'

and 'resistant' readings. The metaphor of submission is too self-effacing for what occurs when we encounter textual power, even of Homer's magnitude. I would like to suggest that good readers do not 'submit', like the vanquished, to a particular reading; but rather, they *respect* it – which means, etymologically, *to look* at it. Experienced, agile readers use the text to envision themselves as readers they had not anticipated becoming. Thus, a rhetoric of reading hardly means that everything is in the readers' control, but that they must listen to the voices of all the readers within themselves that a single text might engender. Reading, like writing, is an invigorating, dialogic, imaginative act of composition.

NOTES

1 Booth's discussion of rhetoric is 'modest' in that he adheres to a traditional view of the rhetorical scene: the text wields the rhetoric which the reader merely receives, however positively or negatively. I do not wish to suggest, however, that there is anything 'modest' in Booth's pioneering labour to unveil the rhetorical layers of prose fiction.
2 See, for example, Iser's (1978) *The Act of Reading*. Iser is one of the most perceptive of reader-oriented theorists – but it is his very perception of duality in the production of meaning that earns him so much resistance among fellow theorists, many of whom accuse him of trying to have it both ways (that is, allowing *both* text and reader to create meaning). Yet this same dual participation which appears so inconsistent on an epistemological plane makes perfect sense on a rhetorical plane, where a dialogical exchange may be taken for granted.
3 I do not conceive these 'moments' as ordered stages. We bring, for instance, some sort of evaluation with us to our reading – be it based on our knowledge of the author, a review we have read, our attraction to the title, etc.; in this sense, evaluation can hardly be described as the last step we take. I would prefer, then, to envision these 'moments' as rapidly alternating or even as concurrent.
4 The term 'dominant' in this regard derives from Jakobson's notion of a 'dominant function' in any discourse. Jakobson notes that while any of the six possible functions he postulates for language use (emotive, referential, poetic, phatic, metalingual and conative) may be present in a verbal message, *one* of these functions will dominate – that is, serve as the primary focus and thus characterize the message. Likewise, I am contending that at any one time in the reading, one of the virtual readings will be chosen over the others.

11 Shakespeare's rhetoric in action

Rex Gibson

There is no more powerful vehicle for teaching language than Shakespeare's plays. They are filled with argumentative human voices that plead, cajole, reason, threaten and debate. In a huge variety of ways Shakespeare's voices contend, dispute and enjoin as they seek to influence, convince or spur to action. All are examples of rhetoric in action: the persuasive use of language.

Obvious illustrations of that persuasive use of language spring instantly to mind. The Forum speeches of Brutus and Antony are classic instances: politicians at work, swaying an audience. Henry V seeks to rouse his soldiers with 'Once more unto the breach' and to reassure and inspirit them with his St Crispian's Day speech. Iago utters devious asides ('I like not that') and spins a malicious web of false evidence as he entraps and poisons Othello's mind. Cleopatra's infinite variety of language tricks keep Antony in thrall. Shakespearean persuasion can also be inner-directed, most notably in Hamlet's constantly self-questioning soliloquies. He seeks meaning in his fractured, dangerous world through those probing conversations he conducts with himself.

It is one thing to notice how inventively Shakespeare draws on rhetoric to create his unparalleled dramatic worlds. It is a far more difficult task to seek to enable school students to develop insight into Shakespeare's creativity in order to resource their own. But there is no doubt that school students can study and use rhetoric in ways which help them explore, order and extend their imaginative, intellectual and emotional lives. In what follows (and always remembering there is no one single way to teach Shakespeare), I draw upon the research evidence of the Shakespeare and Schools Project (Gibson 1986–92).

Any school study of Shakespeare's rhetoric should not confine itself to the identification and analysis of rhetorical devices and figures. The remarkably systematic and comprehensive approach exemplified in Sister Miriam Joseph's classic text (Joseph 1947) has very little appeal for most school pupils. In the 1990s very few pupils gain satisfaction (or much real understanding) from teasing out the four types of puns: antanaclasis, syllepsis, paronomasia, asteismus. Rather they enjoy, have facility in and learn from making up puns in a variety of ways. They readily appreciate the mordant humour of Mercutio's dying words 'Send for me tomorrow and you will find me a grave man', and are quick to respond successfully to the imaginative challenge to invent their own puns. Similarly, it is difficult to make the argument that most pupils will profit from learning the names of the figures of vehemence (exuscitato, aposiopesis, ecphonesis, thaumasmus, etc). What the research evidence shows is that real learning takes place when the students speak, enact and parody such exclamations as:

O tiger's heart wrapped in a player's hide

I will do such things . . .

O Antony, Antony, Antony . . .

O you gods!

An older tradition of teaching approached the Forum speeches in *Julius Caesar* by asking students to analyse them into the classical divisions of rhetoric:

exordium (introduction: gaining the attention and approval of the hearers)
narratio (development: stating the matter or aim of the argument)
confirmatio (reasons, proofs, arguments)
confutatio (answering likely objections)
conclusio (brief summing up or recapitulation)

For many students such an analytic task is formal and uncongenial. It is further handicapped by Shakespeare himself who very rarely, even in his early years, slavishly followed any given rules. Shakespeare drew on rhetorical devices to suit his particular dramatic purposes, and was never afraid to amend or adapt. Mechanical rule-following or neatness of fit did not appeal to him. At the Grammar School in Stratford Shakespeare received a thorough grounding in rhetoric. He drew on that schooling to great effect as a playwright. But he wore his learning very lightly, and always used it flexibly. He broke the rules cheerfully and to masterful effect. Shakespeare's purpose was not to *teach* rhetoric. His task lay elsewhere, drawing on his learning and his natural talent to present a story in dramatic form on stage.

Students find that in practice the classical model does not quite work in the analysis of the Forum speeches. This is not to reject the value of the structure that traditional rhetoric offers. Students can (and do) construct their own speeches using the five categories. But rather than have students work on an analytical exercise that frustrates success, we have found that more active, re-creative approaches enable them to grasp the structure of the speeches:

1 Echo certain key words of Antony (e.g. 'ambition', 'honourable') and identify the effects of such repetition.
2 Make up your own 'Tips for public speakers' based on the two speeches.
3 Write and deliver a speech that Shakespeare did not write: e.g. Cassius' Forum speech. How does he open and close his speech? How is it like and unlike that of Brutus?
4 Imagine the First Plebeian is your father and you were with him in the Forum. You heard his shouts ('This Caesar was a tyrant!' etc.). Explain to a friend (who was not present) what provoked each comment.

Most students gain more from imaginative enactment of the rhetorical figures than from literary analysis. Such analysis should of course be part of school Shakespeare, but every teacher has to make subtle judgements as to its form and range. In certain plays, rhetorical devices necessarily require conscious identification and discussion. But it must always be remembered that Shakespeare did not use them as sterile figures to be imposed, but as integral to his story, characters and themes. The oxymorons in *Romeo and Juliet* become meaningful to school students when they physically enact them as tableaux ('loving hate', 'fiend angelical') and recognize how such oppositions represent a major structural theme of the play (Gibson 1992). The very language echoes the violent conflicts of the Montagues and Capulets, the tensions between youth and age, the contrasts of night and day, death and life. Oxymorons were not just 'tacked on' by Shakespeare, but used because they are deeply organic to the whole play, expressive of its deepest preoccupations. Similarly the use of hendiadys in *Hamlet* is utterly consonant with the theme of delay. The persistent 'ands' prolong and reinforce, draw out and deepen each speaker's meaning ('an auspicious and dropping eye', 'post-haste and rummage', 'rank and gross').

All our research evidence points to the insights achieved when students actively and collaboratively explore Shakespeare's language. For most students individual analytic work comes after and as a result of active, shared dramatic experience. These joint explorations acknowledge that Shakespeare's language is a script, written for theatrical enactment: a drama acted out on stage before an audience. Shakespeare uses rhetoric frequently but for his own dramatic purposes to create atmosphere, to enable his characters to seek their own objectives, and to tell his story in a way that will fully engage his audience. Shakespeare's language is accompanied on stage by other signs (movement, costume, set, etc.) that influence the audience's reception of and reaction to the words. The only Shakespearean intention of which we can be quite sure is that he intended his language to be bodied forth in the total context of theatre. Three questions arise from that total context. Each identifies a way in which Shakespeare uses language to persuade: how does Shakespeare persuade his audience? How do characters persuade others? How do characters persuade themselves? These three questions serve to introduce work that has been successfully undertaken on *Macbeth* with school-age students.

PERSUADING THE AUDIENCE

Shakespeare faced the eternal problem of every dramatist: how to persuade the audience to enter the imaginative world of the play? Like all playwrights (*pace* Brecht) he wanted each audience willingly to suspend disbelief as they sat or stood through the performance, watching and listening with close attention. Any modern staging of Shakespeare brings into play a huge variety of theatrically persuasive devices. The language is spoken within a rich and complex physical setting: faces, bodies, movement, gestures, properties, costume, set, lighting, sound. All are part of the modern rhetoric of theatre, devices to create and sustain interest. They contribute hugely to the audience's desire to know what happens next.

But spectacle is insufficient in Shakespeare. At the very centre is language, the script itself, the words that each performance (or each classroom reading) attempts to bring to imaginative life in vivid, particular contexts. It is the words that bear the weight of creating atmosphere. The audience, whether silently in the theatre, or actively and vocally in classrooms, is persuaded through language. Such persuasion is vividly evident in *Macbeth*.

Macbeth is one of the shortest of Shakespeare's plays. Its language, highly compressed and ambiguous, reflects that brevity in the intensity and energy of its powerful narrative drive. Short scene succeeds short scene, displaying a wide range of distinctive linguistic forms. The opening catapults the audience into the dark world of the supernatural. The ritualistic incantatory rhythm of 'When shall we three meet again?' immediately establishes the mood. Its brooding, malign pulsation is fully but succinctly realized in the menacing 'fair is foul and foul is fair'. The ominous story of the master of the *Tiger*, elliptical and mysterious, is followed by the all-hailing of Macbeth and Banquo. The standby of all school Shakespeare, the cauldron scene, is compulsive in its invocations. Mutilated ingredients are dropped in to the same four-beat rhythm: 'Eye of newt and toe of frog.' The hypnotic throbbing of the language is powerfully persuasive in gaining and keeping attention. For school students it rarely fails to ensure animated and imaginative participation.

The Witches' language is only one of Shakespeare's methods to engage the audience. Many of the familiar devices of rhetoric are used frequently to striking effect: repetition ('O horror! horror! horror!'); memorable accumulation ('dwindle, peak and pine'); long listing ('bloody, luxurious, avaricious, false, deceitful, sudden, malicious, smacking of every sin that has a name'); antithesis ('fair is foul and foul is fair'). Often, in this play of contrasts, Shakespeare packs vivid antitheses into brief space ('Who can be wise, amazed, temperate and furious, loyal and neutral, in a moment?').

Vocabulary contributes potently, creating the atmosphere of a cruel world of violence, darkness and evil. 'Blood' occurs over one hundred times in the play. Everywhere, Shakespeare increases linguistic density so as to draw the audience into the conflicting worlds he creates. In only seven lines, as Macbeth moves towards the sleeping Duncan, he speaks of 'dead . . . wicked . . . abuse . . . witchcraft . . . withered murder . . . alarumed . . . wolf . . . howl . . . stealthy. . . ravishing . . . ghost'. But Shakespeare balances his dark, murderous story with strong reminders of the better society that opposes Macbeth's tyranny. In this searching exploration of the struggle between evil and good, the language of health, promise and benevolent rule is insistently present. In just six lines Duncan uses words of kindness and harvest: 'welcome . . . plant . . . growing . . . noble . . . deserved . . . infold . . . heart'.

The cosmic imagery of the play further heightens audience involvement. 'Pity, like a naked new-born babe striding the blast' is a linguistic invitation to the imagination. Elsewhere images of sleep, clothes, disease, feasting, light and dark, enrich emotional and intellectual response, as do the frequent recurrence of bird and animal images: raven, crow and the dark agents of night. All these reinforce and deepen another linguistic device by which Shakespeare secures involvement: the subtle and ironic use of the language of equivocation. Double meaning is one of the central themes of the play and hence equivocations recur with insistent and compelling force. Macbeth and his wife follow their own advice: 'Look like the innocent flower, but be the serpent under it.' As Lady Macbeth welcomes Duncan to Inverness, or as Macbeth greets Banquo with 'A friend', the chilling irony of saying one thing but meaning another engages audience and reader alike in fascinated, absorbed attention. In classrooms, this equivocal language provides rich opportunities for practical work in tableaux, alter egos, and good and bad angel activities.

PERSUADING OTHER CHARACTERS

The use of language to persuade others is the most obvious use of rhetoric. *Macbeth* contains many examples where, in very different ways, one character seeks to persuade another to his/her point of view, or to move them to a course of action. The bleeding Captain informs and persuades Duncan of Macbeth's bravery and prowess. The Witches' incantatory predictions ('Hail, King of Scotland') are magnetically tempting to a warrior of Macbeth's ambitious disposition. They provide the motive power to fuel his murderous aspirations.

Other characters attempt to sway their hearers to their points of view: the Porter jokes with Macduff on the equivocation of drink; Macduff's son reasons with childish logic as he questions his mother about traitors; Lennox obliquely tests the loyalty of the anonymous Lord. When Lady Macbeth attempts to reassure the Thanes at the Banquet, she manages to pack five reasons and three commands into only six lines. She has already shown herself the mistress of the fulsome language of hypocrisy as she welcomes Duncan to Inverness ('All our service'). Yet she succeeds fully in encouraging his view of her as sincere and trustworthy ('our honoured hostess').

Macbeth also draws on the rhetorical insincerity of public utterance. He greets Duncan with elaborate courtesy: 'The rest is labour, which is not used for you.' He uses a mixture of lies, insults and bullying to persuade the murderers of Banquo to their task. The conversation with the murderers presents a superb opportunity for school students to write the persuasions of that absent scene when he set out the wrongs that Banquo had done to them ('This I made good to you in our past conference').

Detailed examination of two examples show how school students respond to Shakespeare's use of rhetoric to convince others. First Macbeth. When challenged by Macduff about his murder of Duncan's grooms ('Wherefore did you so?') he falls back on a sequence of reasons that are virtually textbook examples of the language of persuasion.

> Who can be wise, amazed, temperate and furious,
> Loyal and neutral, in a moment? No man.
> The expedition of my violent love
> Outrun the pauser reason. Here lay Duncan,
> His silver skin laced with his golden blood,
> And his gashed stabs looked like a breach in nature
> For ruin's wasteful entrance; there the murderers,
> Steeped in the colours of their trade, their daggers
> Unmannerly breeched with gore. Who could refrain,
> That had a heart to love, and in that heart
> Courage to make's love known?

These lines evoke a wide range of responses in school students. Some argue they are patently insincere, others maintain that they carry, in context, powerful conviction. Macbeth begins with three densely packed antitheses expressing the conflicting emotions of the loyal subject. But he does not simply list those oppositions; he sets them out as a challenge. His initial 'Who' defies denial. It states that the answer is obvious. Sure enough, Macbeth follows his question with the emphatic 'No man'. Nobody could experience those wildly swinging emotions without being impelled to violent action. To experience the force of Macbeth's challenge, students attempt to answer his question physically. They prepare tableaux of the six adjectives, and then try to show them 'in a moment'. The resulting tableaux are not only intellectually insightful, they contain movement, the violent switching between moods that generate a mobilizing energy to action. One student remarked, 'He's right! No man – nor woman – nobody can be in those states all at once.' Physical enactment by the students reinforced their understanding of the linguistic powers of Macbeth's appeal.

Macbeth expands the antitheses into a persuasively inevitable explanation: 'The expedition of my violent love / Outrun the pauser reason.' Another student commented 'He can't help himself, and it sounds very convincing up to here. But from now on it's downhill all the way. He goes over the top with all that stuff, so theatrical, with "Here lay" and "silver skin" and "golden blood." He just sounds insincere because he piles it on too deep.'

The logical, evidence-based structure of Macbeth's rhetoric is clear as he moves from 'Here lay Duncan' through 'there the murderers', to the concluding 'Who could refrain . . .?' Students grasp the structure fairly easily. They physically point as they follow the steps in Macbeth's reasoning ('Here', 'there', 'Who'). Although they feel uneasy about the hyperbole with which Macbeth loads his appeal, they do find Macbeth's final appeal to 'Courage' convincing: 'It echoes the manliness theme that is so appealing to these Scottish warriors.' Few students place much stress on a point many editors emphasize: 'Unmannerly breeched with gore.' Students are generally content to accept this as 'bloodstained'. They appear little impressed with the technical explanation based on the incongruities of 'breeched'. Somewhat similarly, many students do not immediately identify Lady Macbeth's swoon that follows Macbeth's speech ('Help me hence, ho!') as showing that she does not think he is being convincing. But when this interpretation is made, students report they find it adds to their sense of the insincerity of Macbeth's eleven lines.

Our second example is that arch-persuader in the first half of the play: Lady Macbeth. How she persuades Macbeth to kill Duncan after he has decided to abandon the plan ('We will proceed no further in this business') illustrates vividly how emotional force and rhetoric overcome logic and human sympathy. She mixes commands and advice as she prepares her husband for the murder ('look like the innocent flower'; 'Leave all the rest to me'). She assaults him with a barrage of accusing questions and taunts. It is argument by battering ram; an onslaught on male self-esteem.

> Was the hope drunk
> Wherein you dressed yourself? Hath it slept since?
> And wakes it now to look so green and pale
> At what it did so freely? From this time
> Such I account thy love. Art thou afeared
> To be the same in thine own act and valour,
> As thou art in desire? Wouldst thou have that

Which thou esteem'st the ornament of life,
And live a coward in thine own esteem,
Letting 'I dare not' wait upon 'I would',
Like the poor cat i'the adage?

Lady Macbeth hammers home her taunts like nails. Students respond powerfully when invited to enact the speech imaginatively rather than to engage in passive analysis. With a volunteer Macbeth in the centre and the rest of the group around in a circle, the speech is rich in choral speaking possibilities. The sentences are shared out among the students who then hurl them in turn at the hapless Macbeth from all angles. 'The poor sod doesn't know which way to turn with all that coming at him,' said a sixth-former. Group echoing of a word (that each student chooses independently) from each line, brings out the barbed force of 'drunk', 'slept', 'green and pale', 'freely', 'love' or 'afeared', 'valour', 'desire', 'ornament', 'coward', 'dare not', 'cat'. After this experience a fifth-former commented, 'It's like a bull in the ring with all those darts in him.'

Macbeth does try to rally:

Prithee peace.
I dare do all that may become a man;
Who dares do more, is none.

His reply only brings down a greater storm of invective on his head. First a torrent of abuse about his manhood, then the terrifying image of a mother killing her baby:

What beast was't then
That made you break this enterprise to me?
When you durst do it, then you were a man;
And, to be more than what you were, you would
Be so much more the man. Nor time, nor place,
Did then adhere, and yet you would make both:
They have made themselves, and that their fitness now
Does unmake you. I have given suck, and know
How tender 'tis to love the babe that milks me:
I would while it was smiling in my face,
Have plucked my nipple from his boneless gums,
And dashed the brains out, had I so sworn
As you have done to this.

The conventional persuasion categories: thesis, argument, evidence, proof, rebuttals, conclusion, pale before this tirade. The words produce their own powerful energies as students, in pairs, whisper, hiss or shout the phrases or sentences at each other. Persuasion is made palpable, and Macbeth's querulous reply shows the impact of her words on his faltering decision: 'If we should fail?' Lady Macbeth's two-word reply 'We fail!' always produces heated student discussion over its delivery. Is it spoken flatly or incredulously? Stressed on the first or second word? Her final lines complete his downfall as she outlines her plan. They have the outward form of logic in their hideousness as they move from exhortation and assurance:

> But screw your courage to the sticking place,
> And we'll not fail.

through calculating inference of the effects of the King's arduous travels:

> When Duncan is asleep
> (Whereto the rather shall his day's hard journey
> Soundly invite him),

to the cunningly convincing proposal to drug Duncan's attendants into insensibility:

> his two chamberlains
> Will I with wine and wassail so convince,
> That memory, the warder of the brain,
> Shall be afume, and the receipt of reason
> A limbeck only:

There is a challenging and triumphant QED in the conclusion:

> when in swinish sleep
> Their drenched natures lie, as in a death,
> What cannot you and I perform upon
> The unguarded Duncan?

Assurance is made double sure as Lady Macbeth proposes how the blame can so easily be fixed on the King's attendants:

> what not put upon
> His spongy officers, who shall bear the guilt
> Of our great quell?

Macbeth needs no further persuasion. Her words have done their poisonous work. His response is all of a piece with what he has heard: 'Bring forth men-children only!' The student who commented 'Bloody sexist!' went on to argue that the values of Lady Macbeth's speeches are utterly congruent with the male warrior society of Duncan's Scotland. 'She caught him on his rawest spot: his macho feelings. That's what's important in that society. Even the saintly King Duncan responds to the account of Macbeth's savagery in battle with "O valiant cousin! Worthy gentleman!" '

The persuasions of Lady Macbeth are precisely fitted to their hearer, Macbeth. They touch the already over-exaggerated chords of courage, soldierliness, manhood and ambition. The reality, the callous murder of a defenceless, sleeping old man, goes unregarded. It is both overwhelmed and obscured by the passionate, point by point appeal, not to logic, but to warped desire, fuelled by a distorted value system. As one sixth-former put it: 'You don't have to be reasonable to persuade. People will listen to what they want to hear and if you are in that frame of mind, it's not the reasons that count, but the sheer force and power of the emotional appeal. Lady Macbeth knows her husband of old and knows she can always win by putting in needles or swords at his vulnerable emotional parts.'

THE LANGUAGE OF SELF-PERSUASION

Rhetoric is not simply used to persuade others. It is a powerful means of self-persuasion. In *Macbeth* the two main characters often express their private thoughts. On these occasions the strongest impression is that they are speaking to themselves: persuading themselves to a course of action, or confirming their beliefs or suspicions, or exploring what obsesses them.

Lady Macbeth's two initial soliloquies in act I, scene 5, 'Glamis thou art' and 'The raven himself is hoarse', offer magnificent opportunities to explore the structure of argument where passionate intensity overpowers any possibility of reasoned, moral objections. Her second soliloquy is rich in the language of command. Students enjoy and learn from the emotion-packed progress of her injunctions: 'Come . . . unsex me . . . And fill me . . . make thick . . . stop up . . . nor keep peace . . . Come . . . and take . . . Come . . . And pall . . . see not . . . Nor heaven peep . . . Hold! Hold!' The atmospheric impact is increased as she thickens her invocations with the dark images of the play: 'raven . . . fatal spirits . . . direst cruelty . . . blood . . . remorse . . . nature . . . fell purpose . . . gall . . . murdering ministers . . . sightless substances . . . nature's mischief . . . thick night . . . pall . . . dunnest smoke . . . hell . . .

keen knife . . . wound . . . blanket of the dark.' As one student put it: 'She's driving herself into being a psychopath. The sheer force of her words show what she is, but it makes her that too. It's very private, but it's like a public speech to someone else you want to make evil.'

The words that Shakespeare puts into Macbeth's mouth provide striking examples of self-persuasion. Much of what he says to other characters can be interpreted as conversation with himself. All his soliloquies can similarly be seen as internal argument. An obvious example of such self-address is when he questions himself continually after the murder of Duncan: 'But wherefore could I not say Amen?' So too, his comments at the Banquet: 'Blood hath been shed' and 'It will have blood', have that same reflexive quality as his bloody determination after seeing the Apparitions. In the cauldron scene, Macbeth's interpretations of the Apparitions are self-persuasions. He seeks to put the best light on the ambiguous pronouncements he hears. Successively, he acknowledges Macduff as an enemy, is cheered by 'none of woman born', and takes heart from Birnam Wood's apparent fixity. The show of kings urges him to declare his bloody intentions ('the castle of Macduff I will surprise . . .').

Macbeth is a compulsive reasoner and imager. He reveals his inner life in ways that no other character except Hamlet does. Every one of his soliloquies can be explored actively by students. These explorations seek the purposes, meanings and imaginative reasoning of Macbeth's language and thought. In his first long soliloquy self-persuasion is patently evident:

> If it were done, when 'tis done, then 'twere well
> It were done quickly: if the assassination
> Could trammel up the consequence, and catch
> With his surcease success; that but this blow
> Might be the be-all and the end-all! – here,
> But here, upon this bank and shoal of time,
> We'd jump the life to come. – But in these cases,
> We still have judgement here; that we but teach
> Bloody instructions, which, being taught, return
> To plague the inventor: this even-handed Justice
> Commends the ingredience of our poisoned chalice
> To our lips. He's here in double trust:
> First, as I am his kinsman and his subject,
> Strong both against the deed; then, as his host,

Who should against his murderer shut the door,
Not bear the knife myself. Besides, this Duncan
Hath borne his faculties so meek, hath been
So clear in his great office, that his virtues
Will plead like angels, trumpet-tongued, against
The deep damnation of his taking-off;
And Pity, like a naked new-born babe,
Striding the blast, or heaven's Cherubins, horsed
Upon the sightless curriers of the air,
Shall blow the horrid deed in every eye,
That tears shall drown the wind. – I have no spur
To prick the sides of my intent, but only
Vaulting ambition, which o'erleaps itself
And falls on the other.

The Shakespeare and Schools Project has developed very successful active approaches which bring out the power of the argumentative structure in this soliloquy. One of the most effective methods is to have students in pairs or threes reading the speech as if it were being argued by several persons. Each student reads, in turn, a short section. This gives an understanding of the way in which the argument builds up. The sections can be up to a punctuation mark or in short 'sense units' determined by the students. When the students sit closely together, speaking their short sections to each other, the sense of step-by-step progression comes through strongly:

First student: If it were done when 'tis done,
Second student: Then 'twere well it were done quickly.

First student: If the assassination could trammel up the conse-
                   quence,
Second student: and catch with his surcease success

First student: that but this blow might be the be-all and the
                   end-all!
Second student: here,

First student: But here,

Students grasp the feeling of growing urgency. Sharing out the language enables them to grasp how the see-sawing movement of the verse embodies the conflicting feelings of Macbeth's internal debate. Some students choose very short speech units indeed ('If it were done / when 'tis done . . . surcease / success'). The internal debate can also be felt by physically expressing the mobile alternations of Macbeth's thoughts. Students join hands and gently push or pull as they read. This movement catches the rhythms of each phrase, line or sentence. Students who find difficulty with meaning can often feel the rhythmic flow of the language as Macbeth mentally weighs the possibilities and opportunities, the dangers and evils of his intentions. Such physical response is productive in unlocking meaning.

Other rhetorical features of the soliloquy can be explored in similarly active manner. Macbeth avoids directly naming the reality of what preoccupies him. The closest he gets is 'assassination'. Elsewhere he uses a series of euphemisms for the killing: 'it', 'deed', 'taking-off', 'intent', etc. Students gain extra insight into language by working in pairs with one reading the speech aloud and the other challenging each euphemism with 'Kill Duncan!' Subsequent discussion is sharply revealing of the language of tyrants.

Students also work on the soliloquy as Macbeth talking himself out of the murder. His self-persuasion begins with a series of hopeful hypotheses ('If . . . If . . . that but'). He wishes the killing of Duncan held no consequences for him on earth or the after-life. Then Macbeth's reasoning imagination comes into play with the 'But' which begins a series of accumulating reasons. One group of students tackled the developing argument by listing those reasons:

Reason 1 But in these cases . . .
Reason 2 This even-handed justice . . .
Reason 3 He's here . . .
Reason 4 First . . .
Reason 5 then . . .
Reason 6 Besides . . .
Reason 7 that his virtues . . .
Reason 8 And Pity . . .
Reason 9 I have no spur . . .
Reason 10 but only . . .

The students prepared a mini-lecture accompanied by actions. One student delivered each point as a lecturer might, the others mimed actions for each reason. Again, the physical representation of the language helped students grasp the structure of the soliloquy and understand the flow of the argument.

Like all Shakespeare's characters, Macbeth uses arguments that are never simply the reasonings and evidence of a philosopher. Shakespeare employs the passionate imagination of a dramatist as he fuels Macbeth's exhortations, arguments, urgings and incitings.

Macbeth's language of persuasion is uttered in the open-ended world of the stage. That world is, of its essence, one of multiple possibilities. It provides teachers with both the justifications and the methods for active, collaborative and imaginative opportunities in teaching rhetoric. Those methods are far removed from the tedium of artificial grammatical analyses. They embody intellectual integrity and creative vigour in ways that are inspiriting for students and organic to Shakespeare's humanizing imagination.

'RHETORIC': A LOST CAUSE?

My purpose in this chapter has been to show how Shakespeare provides the English teacher with unparalleled rich resources for teaching language. But I must close by noting a problem that necessarily besets any teacher who seeks to restore rhetoric to the curriculum: the problem of the word 'rhetoric' itself.

'Rhetoric' traditionally meant those devices and skills that enable speakers and writers to make their language more memorable, effective and impressive. But rhetoric is almost invariably used today to refer to speech or writing that is pretentious, over-ornate, insincere, ostentatious. The problem for teachers is that 'rhetoric' or 'rhetorical' has acquired pejorative overtones of insincerity and untruthfulness. The roots of this go back at least to the Elizabethan period when the most approved language was the most artificial language.

The aim of Elizabethan rhetorical manuals was to help writers write persuasively and elegantly. George Puttenham's *The Arte of English Poesie* (1589) and Abraham Fraunce's *Arcadian Rhetorike* (1588) enjoyed great popularity. In practice, this meant that poets and dramatists endeavoured to achieve an ornate, obscure vocabulary. Rhetoric was affected, high-sounding, bombastic, hyperbolic, rich in conceits, puns and word play. Shakespeare often took this verbal over-ornateness as a target for ridicule. 'More matter, with less art', snaps Gertrude to the rhetorical pedantry of Polonius. Hamlet parodies Osric, Falstaff mocks 'King Cambyses vein', and Pistol is the repository of all braggart excess.

I take rhetoric to be the use of language to create atmosphere, and to persuade people, move them to action, seek to change them. My own diffident redefinition is one that shakes free from the formal, rigid, historical legacy. It is 'all the ways in which a speaker or writer seeks to persuade listeners or readers, by appealing to their reason, their emotions, their imagination and their confidence

in the speaker or writer'. Within this definition of rhetoric, Shakespeare is the writer who provides us, as teachers, with the most
varied, compelling and vivid examples to empower our students'
linguistic development.

12 Reading across media: the case of *Wuthering Heights*

Patsy Stoneman

Wuthering Heights is one of the most famous novels in the world. In Britain it is so well known that a mass audience can be relied on to recognize allusions like the 'Monty Python's Flying Circus' semaphore version, in which Heathcliff and Catherine stand on opposite hill-tops with semaphore flags, sending messages as follows:

> Oh Catherine!
> Heathcliffe! [*sic*]
> Oh! Oh! Catherine!
> Oh! Oh! Heathcliffe!

and so on (Chapman *et al.* 1989: 199). Some essential features of the novel are encapsulated by this minimal rendering: the hill-top setting, two separated lovers and an expression of their need for one another. The *Guardian* cartoonist Steve Bell also assumed that his audience would recognize his quarter-page drawing of Catherine and Heathcliff on a hill-top (Figure 12.1), even though both of them have the face of Sam Goldwyn, who produced the famous 1939 film of *Wuthering Heights*.

Wuthering Heights has been disseminated into the general culture by repeated reproductions in a variety of media from the date of its first publication to the present day, and few of these reproductions are simple facsimiles of the original written text. Academic criticism and the education system present the novel embedded in scholarly discourse in the form of introductions, notes, critical essays, biographical sketches and so on. But there are also editions with illustrations, stage, film and television adaptations, musical, operatic and ballet versions, picture-book and 'comic' versions and,

Figure 12.1 Cartoon by Steve Bell of Sam Goldwyn as Catherine and
Heathcliff, *Guardian*, 21 September 1989. Reproduced by courtesy of
Steve Bell.

most interesting of all, a variety of 'reworkings' of the famous text by subsequent creative writers. These later reproductions, moreover, are not limited to Britain or even to the English-speaking world; a comic-book version of *Wuthering Heights* was published in Japan in 1989.

Kristeva has argued that all literature is 'intertextual' in that 'any text is constructed as a mosaic of quotations; any text is the absorption and transformation of another' (Moi 1986: 37). Famous texts which are repeatedly 'plundered', like *Wuthering Heights*, however, acquire 'mythological' status, rather like that of a fairy-tale, which depends partly on some inherent significance in the original text, but partly also on the process of reiteration itself. Eco speculates that 'in order to transform a work into a cult object one must be able to break, dislocate, unhinge it so that one can remember only parts of it, irrespective of their original relationship with the whole' (Eco 1984: 447). Similarly, in his book on *Frankenstein*, Baldick defines such cult texts as 'modern myths', which 'prolong their lives not by being retold at great length, but by being alluded to. . . . This process . . . reduc[es] them to the simplest memorable patterns' (Baldick 1987: 3).

There are two interesting questions that we can ask ourselves about such 'modern myths'. One is: what is it in the original story which gives it such enduring interest? Another question, however, is: how has the original text been transformed in the course of its reproduction, and what relationship do these transformations have to the societies that made them? Kuhn argues that 'a society's representations of itself . . . may be seen as a vital, pervasive and active element in the constitution of social structures and formations' and that 'interventions within culture have some independent potential to transform' them (Kuhn 1982: 5, 6). I too shall argue that myths are not 'changeless' but are transformed by the real history which they also help to construct.

Because versions of the same myth share elements such as characters and incident, any comparative study throws emphasis on their formal differences, both of medium (novel to film or picture) and of signifying structures ('plot' and 'style'). Although, therefore, I could use this whole chapter to describe the great variety of transformations of *Wuthering Heights*,[1] I shall, in fact, deal with only a few examples so that I can look in detail at how our reading of different versions of the same original text is conditioned by formal changes, both of medium and of internal rhetoric. Following Eagleton I see rhetoric as the study of discursive practices: 'the way specific discourses are constituted and the manner in which they compete in the construction of cultural meaning' (Hawkes 1983; see also Eagleton 1983: 205–10). Like Baldick's approach (Baldick 1987, 1983), and Kuhn's (Kuhn 1982: 43), this concept of rhetoric assumes that 'discourses . . . shape forms of consciousness and unconsciousness, which are closely related to the maintenance or transformation of our existing systems of power' (Eagleton 1983: 210).

In order to bring together a manageable collection of examples, I shall focus on representations of Catherine and Heathcliff out of doors. We have seen, in the 'Monty Python' and Sam Goldwyn examples, how the hill-top is a part of the essential mythology, transmitted in the simplest allusions. There is, however, very little description of them out of doors in *Wuthering Heights*. There are only two direct references. The first, from chapter 3 (Brontë 1965: 64), is simply two sentences from Catherine's diary, written as a child, describing how her 'companion' – presumably Heathcliff – is impatient for 'a scamper on the moors' since they 'cannot be damper, or colder, in the rain than we are here' and they will, moreover, escape from the house and the 'surly old man' (Joseph, the servant). The second passage (Brontë 1965: 88–9) is part of Nelly's narrative in chapter 6, describing how the two children 'promised fair to grow up rude as savages' because Catherine's brother Hindley did not take proper care of them. Her description includes some of Heathcliff's direct speech, describing how he and Catherine 'escaped from the wash-house to have a ramble at liberty' and how they 'ran from the top of the Heights to the park, without stopping – Catherine completely beaten in the race, because she was barefoot'.[2]

We might notice three things about these passages. First, although they are very brief, they include less about Catherine and Heathcliff on the hill-tops than about what they have left behind – the 'surly old man', the curate who 'reprimanded' them for not going to church, the 'young master' who would order 'Heathcliff a flogging, and Catherine a fast', Nelly herself, who 'cried to [her]self to watch them growing more reckless daily', and the Linton children in their drawing-room. Second, both passages refer to the period of childhood; there is not even an indirect reference to Catherine and Heathcliff out of doors together as adults. Third, neither of these episodes is recounted directly to the reader. Catherine's diary is reported to us by Mr Lockwood and Heathcliff's story is related by Nelly, together with her own feelings, to Mr Lockwood. This means that the image of Catherine and Heathcliff 'scampering on the moors' is 'framed' for us by the judgements of Joseph, Hindley, the curate and Nelly, who find the children 'savage', 'naughty' and 'reckless', as well as 'unfriended'. These formal characteristics of the original text may help us to identify the later transformations.

The caricature of Sam Goldwyn as Catherine and Heathcliff is, of course, a reference to the Metro-Goldwyn-Meyer film of *Wuthering Heights* directed by William Wyler, with Laurence Olivier as Heathcliff and Merle Oberon as Catherine which appeared in 1939. More precisely, it is a reference to the still photograph from the film showing Catherine and Heathcliff, as adults, alone on Penistone Crag (Figure 12.2). This image, which becomes a repeated motif in the film, was also widely used as a publicity still, and seems to conform to what Eco describes as an 'intertextual archetype', in that it has the 'magic' quality of a frame which, when separated from the whole, transforms the movie into a cult object (Eco 1984: 448). Eco, in his essay on *Casablanca*, is concerned with the separation of frames from the whole film; in dealing with *Wuthering Heights* we have the added separation of film from written text. The still photograph itself transforms the original text in significant ways; it gives visual shape to the image which remains implicit in the novel, of Catherine and Heathcliff out of doors as adults, and it presents them in a pose and a physical situation which invites our direct participation in their experience and implicitly denies the existence of the framing, judging voices of the novel.

In her book on feminism and cinema, Kuhn uses Lacanian psychoanalysis to argue that 'one of the central ideological operations of dominant cinema' – which would certainly include this Hollywood version of *Wuthering Heights* – 'is precisely the positioning of the viewing subject as apparently unitary' (Kuhn 1982: 210). What she means is that as we watch the film, the technique of the camera is to persuade us that we are the camera, looking directly at the figures who appear on the screen, without any such mediation as appears in Emily Brontë's novel in the form of a variety of narrators. Moreover, what she calls 'classic narrative codes' – the characteristic structure of the film plot – encourages us to identify with the characters (Kuhn 1982: 157; see also Hawkins 1990: 35). Even more crucially, she argues that this activity of looking at a human object on the screen repeats the important moment in our childhood when we begin to construct an identity for ourselves by looking at our own image in a mirror or the image of another child (Kuhn 1982: 47–9). The operation of dominant cinema is, according

Figure 12.2 Merle Oberon as Catherine and Laurence Olivier as Heathcliff on Penistone Crag, *Wuthering Heights*, directed by William Wyler, 1939.

to Kuhn, ideologically powerful because it repeats the process by which we 'recognize' who we are. This image of Catherine and Heathcliff, the lines of their bodies and the direction of their gaze repeating each other against the sky, offers us a picture of our own ideal identity, as one half of an inseparable pair who together take on sublimity. It is a picture of romantic love as a kind of heaven.

We have seen that certain 'mythic' texts become reduced, in the process of retelling, to their 'simplest memorable pattern' (Baldick 1987: 3). For the wide audience who recognize the Goldwyn cartoon or the 'Monty Python' semaphore version, the 'simplest memorable pattern' of *Wuthering Heights* derives more from this Hollywood film than from the original text. This might be explained by the fact that more people go to the cinema than read books; but the image clearly responds to a need in the viewing public to which there are clues in contemporary texts. Although Sam Goldwyn may not have known it, William Wyler's visual image matches a metaphor in an academic essay written five years earlier by Lord David Cecil, Professor of English Literature at Oxford. In his book *Early Victorian Novelists*, Cecil wrote that Catherine and Heathcliff 'loom before us in the simple epic outline which is all that we see of man when revealed against the huge landscape of the cosmic scheme' (Cecil 1934: 150–1). It was Charlotte Brontë who began the association of the novel with the landscape; in her preface to the 1850 edition of *Wuthering Heights* she writes of how her sister 'found a granite block on a solitary moor' and 'wrought' it 'with a crude chisel'. 'With time and labour, the crag took human shape; and there it stands colossal, dark, and frowning, half statue, half rock' (Brontë 1965: 41). (Figure 12.3 shows the rock, called Ponden Kirk in real life, and Penistone Crag in *Wuthering Heights*, which Charlotte might have had in mind.) Critics of the 1920s and 1930s, however, seem particularly devoted to the notion that the novel represented something at once human and superhuman. Virginia Woolf, writing in 1925, speaks of the novelist's 'struggle . . . to say something through the mouths of her characters which is not merely "I love" or "I hate", but "we, the whole human race" and "you, the eternal powers"' (quoted in Allott 1970: 1). Ernest Baker, in his standard *History of the English Novel*, makes a value judgement more clearly in line with Wyler's film: 'Emily has not merely grasped the modern idea of the supreme value of the individual soul, which realises itself in its personal life and in mutual understanding, complete harmony, virtual identity with its destined mate; she sees the personality and the consummated union as eternal

Figure 12.3 Photograph by Simon McBride of Ponden Kirk ('Penistone Crag') in *The Landscape of the Brontës*, ed. Arthur Pollard, Exeter and London: Webb & Bower with Michael Joseph, 1988. Reproduced by courtesy of Simon McBride.

facts, which mortality itself cannot annul' (Baker 1937, quoted in Lettis and Morris 1961: 50).

Behind William Wyler's film, therefore, is an ideology which puts great value on epic grandeur and cosmic scale which is nevertheless related to 'the supreme value of the individual soul, which realises itself in its personal life'. Eagleton, in his book *Literary Theory*, quotes another early Professor of English Literature at Oxford, George Gordon, who suggests a reason why this ideology is so important. In his inaugural lecture Gordon refers ironically to a growing body of feeling which can be summarized as follows: 'England is sick, and . . . English literature must save it. The Churches . . . having failed, and social remedies being slow, English literature [must] . . . save our souls and heal the State' (Eagleton 1983: 23; see also Baldick 1983). Eagleton comments: 'as religion progressively ceases to provide the . . . basic mythologies by which a socially turbulent class-society can be welded together, "English" is constructed as a subject to carry this ideological burden'. In the troubled inter-war years British educators believed that the study of English literature could encourage 'humane values' which would transcend 'narrow' class sympathies (see also Drotner 1983: 40). In this climate, literature was valued not for its realistic depiction of specific societies, but for its 'universality'. The word 'epic' figures prominently in these accounts of *Wuthering Heights*, and although 'epic' and 'universal' seem to suggest infinite openness of meaning, Mikhail Bakhtin claims that epic discourse is peculiarly dogmatic, the vehicle of ideology (see Moi 1986: 41). Although Emily Brontë's novel does not in itself conform to Bakhtin's definition of an 'epic',[3] both Cecil and Wyler are attempting to transform it into just that, and the much-reproduced picture of Catherine and Heathcliff on Penistone Crag serves as a visual image of 'consummated union as eternal fact'.

Clayton, in his book, *Romantic Vision and the Novel*, argues that *Wuthering Heights*, by contrast, fascinates because it refuses to provide this image:

> We continue to believe in the visionary existence of their bond, even when they have been divided from one another, precisely because the bond itself has never been represented. . . . If we [look] . . . for a place in the text that records an authentic moment of union, we can locate nothing but a gap, a hole in the narrative beyond which the topic of union becomes prominent. . . . The representational void is so great that William

Wyler, making his movie of *Wuthering Heights*, felt required to fill it both with a place – Penistone Crag, where the lovers meet even after their death – and with an action, a sexual embrace.

(Clayton 1987: 93, 83, 84)

Wyler, who must, in a visual medium, present a visual image of his lovers, confronts a problem which Cecil, in an essay, can evade. The recognizable figures of Laurence Olivier and Merle Oberon are clearly not simply, as Cecil suggests, 'manifestations of natural forces', who function in relation to a 'cosmic scheme' rather than to 'human civilizations and societies and codes of conduct' (Cecil 1934: 165, 150). The image of real human beings must prompt us to question their relationship with 'codes of conduct', and in what sense their union is 'consummated'.

Baker, in the passage I quoted earlier, slides from the 'mutual understanding' to the 'virtual identity' of 'destined mate[s]' as if there were no problem in this conflation, but Mitchell, in a very persuasive analysis, makes a clear distinction between these two kinds of love. One is 'legitimate or married love', which she sees as 'the triumph of sexuality over death, the species over the individual'. The other is 'romantic love', which represents 'the triumph of death over life'. She is using the word 'romantic' in its academic sense, as relating to the Romantic poets, for instance. Romantic love is a model of love which 'does not have a sexual object that is ultimately different from itself' (Mitchell 1984: 111). The object of the Romantic poets' search is the sister-muse, the alter ego, the epipsyche, not the wife, the helpmate, the little woman. It is clearly Romantic love which animates Emily Brontë's novel; Catherine in a famous speech declares that she *is* Heathcliff, while Heathcliff 'cannot live without [his] soul' (Brontë 1965: 122, 204). It is a concept of love which is both sublime and retrogressive in that it looks back to childhood and tries to deny adult separation and responsibility; but for these reasons it is hardly a concept which contributes to social cohesion. Its promise of ontological security is attractive to the needy child in all of us, and in this sense it gives form to 'universal' desires. It is not, however, an ideal to be adopted *en masse* by readers and viewers who need to live in society, where desire is normally channelled into marriage and sexuality does, on the whole, triumph over death.

We have seen that in the passages I have quoted from *Wuthering Heights* itself, what Cecil calls 'societies and codes of conduct' (Cecil 1934: 22) are very much present. Catherine and Heathcliff are

Figure 12.4 Catherine and Heathcliff on Penistone Crag: wood engraving by Clare Leighton, *Wuthering Heights*, New York: Random House, 1931, frontispiece.

'framed' by other people's behaviour (going to church and sitting in the drawing-room) and other people's judgements (they are 'savage' or 'naughty'). In relation to the 'frame' Catherine and Heathcliff stand together; mutually excluded from 'society', they assert their own centrality to a different code of values. In the novel, the meaning of their escape to Penistone Crag is that 'society' does not matter. According to the psychoanalytic model which I described earlier, they derive their sense of identity and worth not from the judgements of society but precisely from looking at each other. As Nelly says, 'they forgot everything the minute they were together again' (Brontë 1965: 87). But in order for *Wuthering Heights* to be presented as a 'great love story' of a type which will confirm rather than reject social 'codes of conduct', Catherine and Heathcliff must be brought within society and must, above all, relate to one another as *heterosexual* lovers who could, potentially, marry.

Emily Brontë's early Victorian novel draws on a rhetoric in which consummation is a matter of souls, not bodies. This discourse of Romantic love was perhaps the only challenge to 'legitimate or married love' available to a woman writer at that time. Wyler's film, however, was a product of a different age, the inter-war period, which in Britain and America was one of rapid social advance for women in society. Women were for the first time able to participate in previous male enclaves such as the law, higher education, big business. In America this development is reflected in the series of films with strong public heroines played by Katherine Hepburn. Catherine Earnshaw, in one of her inter-war manifestations, also appears as a feminist heroine. Figure 12.4 shows a wood engraving by Clare Leighton, which appears as the frontispiece to the Random House edition of *Wuthering Heights* published in 1931. Unlike the Wyler image of Catherine and Heathcliff exposed in Romantic exile against the skyline, this woodcut gives us the single figure of Catherine against the sky, while Heathcliff inhabits a lower, earthy habitat. Catherine's hair floats free, linking her with the 'elemental freedom' of the birds and the clouds. Her physique is strong; strong jaw, strong shoulders and, above all, strong legs, clad in wrinkling socks that inescapably suggest the hiker or the hoyden. Her stance is that of the conqueror – she might have her foot on a defeated lion rather than a mere rock – and her wide-spread legs disregard decorum. It is a particularly masculine position, adopted for instance by the boy scouts in Figure 12.5.[4] On the other hand, her dress, though short, is also low-cut

GLORIOUS PANORAMAS OF NATURE ARE REVEALED TO BOY SCOUT EYES

Pausing at a vantage point along the Skyline Trail, Mount Rainier National Park, Washington, a group of young naturalists contemplate the glacier-masked face of the magnificent peak which the Indians called the "Mountain That Was God." More than 500 kinds of flowers and grasses make the park a happy hunting ground for seekers of a botany merit badge.

Figure 12.5 Boy scouts, *Geographic Magazine*, vol. LXV (1934), facing p. 644.

and the shape of her hair in the picture seems like a quotation from Botticelli's *Birth of Venus* (Figure 12.6); she therefore represents both strong, independent womanhood *and* the beauty and sexuality of traditional woman. In this picture, Heathcliff is insignificant and 'consummation' must be read as an androgynous process within the figure of the woman. The androgynous heroine is just as great a threat to 'legitimate or married love' as the Romantic heroine, and Kuhn confirms that one of the major projects of 1930s cinema was to 'recuperate' the image of woman into the dominant ideology (Kuhn 1982: 34). Whether we focus on Emily Brontë's Romantic challenge, or Clare Leighton's feminist challenge, the problem posed by *Wuthering Heights* to William Wyler is, therefore, the problem of Catherine, who must be presented to the viewing public not as Heathcliff's alter ego but as the object of his desire.

Wyler's solution to this problem is to keep the 'epic sublimity' of the image of Catherine and Heathcliff on Penistone Crag, but to offer as an explanation for their exile not their own mutual scorn of 'societies and codes of conduct', but a different myth – the myth of star-crossed lovers, who would willingly conform, by marrying, if only society would let them. Wyler's version of the myth is based on class – 'the story of the stable-boy and the lady' (Bluestone, quoted in Wagner 1975: 234), and in order to give substance to this reading he presents Catherine in ringlets and silks, with chandeliers and grand pianos (which would have been quite beyond the rural gentry of Yorkshire) and exaggerates the class difference between Edgar and Heathcliff in order to emphasize the power of love to transcend class. In the meantime, however, as she vacillates between the two men, Catherine appears as 'a vulgar tease and common snob, the bitch-heroine luring her helpless male to destruction'. Wagner argues that Wyler structured his film to fit 'the quick social climbing and class mobility of America in the Thirties' (Wagner 1975: 240). But this change of focus was not restricted to America. The year 1937 saw the first performance of John Davison's English stage version of *Wuthering Heights*, in which Catherine and Heathcliff's 'scamper on the moors' becomes a weapon in the sex war.

Davison's stage directions present Catherine as 'attractive, passionate, ruthless and vital, stormy yet tender and feminine'; she is 'wearing an expensive silk dress of the period'. Edgar is 'well-dressed, and handsome in the finery of a gentleman of the period' (Davison 1937: 1). The stage format removes all the 'framing' devices of the novel; the words we hear are spoken directly by the

Figure 12.6 *Birth of Venus* by Sandro Botticelli.

characters. Moreover, in this version Catherine speaks not to her diary but to Edgar Linton, and her description of herself and Heathcliff out of doors is turned to a social purpose – to make Edgar jealous. When Edgar hears that Catherine and Heathcliff 'strolled' to the park gates on the previous night, he is 'amazed':

> *Edgar*: Why, the lodge gates . . . are quite three miles from here. Heavens, weren't you tired out?
>
> *Cathy* (*easily*): Oh, Heathcliff carried me part of the way back. It was a glorious night.
>
> *Edgar* (*a shade annoyed*): Heathcliff! carried you?
>
> *Cathy*: Oh yes, he often does . . .
>
> *Edgar*: Catherine, you shouldn't allow the fellow to be so familiar. To carry you, indeed; I hope no one saw you.
>
> *Cathy*: I don't know whether they did or they didn't. I had my eyes closed most of the time.
>
> *Edgar*: Why?
>
> *Cathy*: Don't you ever close your eyes in moments of ecstasy, Edgar?
>
> *Edgar*: Is it such ecstasy, then, to be carried over the moors by that Heathcliff fellow? Really, Catherine!
>
> *Cathy*: Oh, don't be absurd, Edgar. I was weary and . . . and footsore.
>
> (Davison 1937: 8)

Edgar here is acutely conscious of the class difference between Catherine and 'that fellow', while Catherine seems to intend to make him jealous, because later she says she might let Edgar carry her if he didn't let her fall. In order to set up this triangle situation, however, Davison has had to weaken Catherine. She agrees with Edgar that 'three miles' is enough to tire her so much that she needed to be carried, although, in the novel, there is no sign that she feels fatigue any more than Heathcliff. We have seen how Clare Leighton works on this suggestion of strength to create her feminist Catherine; in her version of the relationship it is Heathcliff who appears to be struggling with the climb! In the novel, she is beaten in the race because she is 'barefoot' (in rough country). In the play this becomes 'footsore', suggesting the delicate lady not fit for much exertion. The rhetoric of Davison's passage therefore works on our recognition of signs of both class distinction, in words like 'fellow', and conventional gender distinctions, based on words like 'tired' and 'footsore'. In order to stress the 'stable-boy and lady' theme, both the film and the play have to create gender differences which are not there in the novel.

William Wyler's film, in fact, inserts a whole scene which is not in the novel at all, showing Catherine and Heathcliff out of doors as children; significantly, however, it emphasizes not their identity with one another, but their gendered differences. At first the scene seems to follow the feeling of the novel well, showing the children, aged about twelve, dressed simply and mounted on rough farm ponies galloping across moor and rough pasture, exhilarated by speed. There seems to be neither class nor gender distinction between them until they speak. Catherine's first words, however, are, 'Heathcliff, I'll race you to the barn. The one that loses has to be the other's slave'. The introduction of a power-relationship here is quite foreign to the novel's sense of the *identity* of the two children. (As Heathcliff says in the novel, 'When would you catch me wishing to have what Catherine wanted?' (Brontë 1965: 89).) The 'stable-boy and the lady' myth, however, does require a complex adjustment of power in terms of class and gender. Heathcliff must be low enough in class terms for Catherine's love to represent a triumph over social convention, but strong enough in gender terms to be a protective husband.

In the novel, while Mr Earnshaw is alive, Heathcliff is able to dominate Catherine's brother Hindley, the legitimate son of the house. In Wyler's film, however, Heathcliff is beaten by Hindley, confirming his class inferiority, so that Catherine needs to be suddenly feminine to restore his masculine pride. Her reason for wanting to go to Penistone Crag is no longer to beat him in a race but to 'pick bluebells' (a flower, incidentally, that grows only in sheltered woodlands!), and she is prepared to be servile to get him to agree, curtseying and saying, '*Please*, m'lord?' She then persuades him to adopt the role of a knight in armour jousting with a rival to win a castle for his lady. In his book *Love in the Western World* Rougemont calls the tournament 'a physical representation of the myth' of Tristan, the 'great European myth of adultery' (Rougemont 1983: 248, 18). The tournament is therefore very appropriate to the 'stable-boy and the lady' myth as it develops later in the film, with the triangle situation between Edgar, Catherine and Heathcliff, and the children in this early scene are perceived as already joined in a sexual relation; their gender-identity has been 'naturalized'.[5] In the novel, however, Catherine's heterosexual orientation is part of her socialization, at the age of twelve, in the Linton household, and it is this which *separates* her from Heathcliff.

The tournament scene in the film ends with Heathcliff, in his role as triumphant knight, raising Catherine from her role as his 'slave' to be 'the Princess Catherine of Yorkshire'. The class issue is thus neatly solved, in fantasy; she is allowed to be a princess, but only because he has raised her to that status; her gender status, on the other hand, is established as inferior to his. The visual image with which this scene ends, with Heathcliff looking out from Penistone Crag over the distant landscape and claiming his sovereignty over it, thus includes the gender-construction of his sovereignty over Catherine. The later image of the adult Catherine and Heathcliff on Penistone Crag (Figure 12.2) might seem congruent with Cecil's 'Romantic' reading of the lovers as 'elemental forces', unrelated to 'societies and codes of conduct', if we view it as an isolated still. Implicit in the film image, however, for the viewer who has already seen the knight-and-lady scene, is Catherine's subjugation by virtue of her sex to Heathcliff's dominance by virtue of his. What has happened is that the Catherine-and-Heathcliff pair are allowed to appear to transcend class differences at the cost of accepting gender-difference as an essential part of the film's 'epic truth'. Viewers who believed themselves to be part of the 'classless society' of the 1930s could identify sympathetically with the victims of the less enlightened days of costume drama, when stable-boys could not marry ladies, but the mythic status of the pair of lovers includes gender-differences which have been naturalized as 'eternal truths', with a status which Kristeva calls, precisely, 'metaphysical' (Moi 1986: 209).

It is the 'metaphysical' status of masculinity and femininity in our culture which allows Wyler and Davison implicitly to promote 'legitimate or married love' without confronting marriage as either a sexual union or a social institution. Post-war transformations of *Wuthering Heights*, under the influence of Freud and Marx, focus more on the material conditions of 'consummation'. The change of focus is welcome in that it resists the insidious incorporation of *Wuthering Heights* into the dominant ideology. It can, however, be depressingly deterministic. Where William Wyler shows Catherine-and-Heathcliff silhouetted against the sky, Luis Buñuel's *Abismos de Pasiòn* confines all its characters to earth. His reversal of the title, from *Wuthering Heights* to *Depths of Passion*, seems abruptly to deny the mythical transcendence which the novel claims, at least at some level, for its protagonists. Made in 1952, it is, like other films of the 1950s, a film about adult sexuality, but its vaguely nineteenth-century setting, with the extrovert patriarchy of Latin countries,[6] provides the 'codes of conduct' that lead passion into the abyss. Significantly, there are no childhood scenes in this film – it begins with Alejandro/Heathcliff's return to find Catalina/ Catherine married – and the outdoor scenes show the characters plunging into the earth rather than reaching for the sky. Alejandro's brutal and sardonic 'courtship' of Isabel (Figure 12.7), takes place in an arid ravine which is only less fruitful, not less earthy, than the sunken wood where Alejandro and Catalina have a hiding-place in the roots of a tree (Figure 12.8). The film ends with the lovers dead in an underground tomb on which the heavy metal lid has just clanged shut. Visual echoes of *Romeo and Juliet* combine with the 'Liebestod' from *Tristan and Isolde* to emphasize that this story is, in Mitchell's terms, one of death-orientated love; but its imagery confines death to the tomb.

Like *Romeo and Juliet*, *Abismos de Pasiòn* has an explicitly sexual rhetoric of social compulsion and judgement. Early in the film Catalina tells Isabel that she is carrying Eduardo/Edgar's child – 'What more does he want?' In later scenes her increasingly visible pregnancy serves as a sign of her sexual appropriation, and the birth is explicitly feared as the likely cause of her death. Eduardo complains that Catalina is unfaithful to him, not in her bedroom but in her thoughts, and Ricardo/Hindley later mocks Isabel, saying that her husband Alejandro 'cheats on [her] with a dead woman'. Like *Tristan and Isolde*, the film shows lovers whose tragedy derives from the transgressive (social) nature of their (adulterous) love. Lacking the childhood scenes and the second generation, it is focused on what Rougemont calls the 'great European myth of adultery' (Rougemont 1983: 18). Its very final deaths (Catalina stiff in her coffin, Alejandro shot through the head) disallow the perennially fascinating suggestion of Emily Brontë's novel – that our heart's desire, socially unattainable, might somehow, some-where, be within our reach. Nor does it allow the consolation of Wyler's sweeter tragedy of 'star-crossed lovers', in which Catherine and Heathcliff are only unfortunate exceptions to the rule that finds our heart's desire in marriage. By contrast, Buñuel's film acts as a harsh *critique* of the norms which provide its tragic structure. Mar-riage can hardly be the lovers' goal in a world where Catalina and Isabel are the property of their husbands, and significant changes to the plot point to the robustness of this patriarchy. In the novel, Edgar and Hindley, as well as Heathcliff, die, leaving an ambiguous promise of change for Catherine's daughter. In Buñuel's film, Edu-ardo and Ricardo live to close ranks over the lovers' expunged

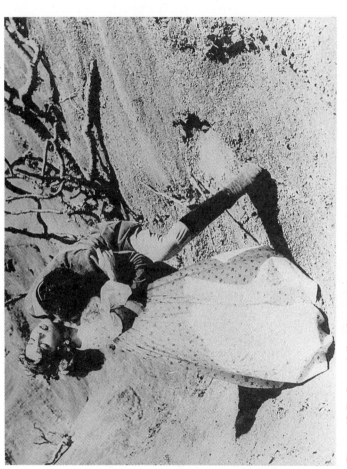

Figure 12.7 Jorge Mistral as Alejandro (Heathcliff) and Lilia Prado as Isabel in desert landscape: *Abismos de Pasiòn*, directed by Luis Buñuel, 1953.

Figure 12.8 Jorge Mistral as Alejandro and Irasema Dilian as Catalina: *Abismos de Pasiòn*, directed by Luis Buñuel, 1953.

history, and as Jose/Joseph reads from the Bible that death is God's punishment for envy and that there is no return from the grave his voice has the dignity and resonance of accepted truth.

In a complex article entitled 'Framing in *Wuthering Heights*', Matthews argues that the focus of the novel shifts from the judging voices of the 'frame' to the central pair and back, one incessantly dissolving into the other, because 'Catherine and Heathcliff's love is the ghost of the prohibitions that structure society' (Matthews 1985: 54). It is, therefore, sharply appropriate than when, in Buñuel's film, Alejandro in the tomb has a momentary vision of Catalina's ghost, the figure dissolves as we watch, reforming into that of Ricardo with a shot-gun. It is Ricardo who lets the lid clang shut to repossess the world in which Catalina's baby is 'a beautiful boy'.

Matthews argues that 'it is [the] incessant dissolving of figure into ground and back that . . . organizes our spellbinding admiration for *Wuthering Heights*' (Matthews 1985: 57). Buñuel's film, however, with its hard focus on the finality of power, resolves this restless movement and thus clangs shut the lid not only on the stiffening corpses of our lovers, but also on the transformative possibilities of Emily Brontë's text. At the beginning of this chapter I quoted Annette Kuhn, who argues that 'a society's representations of itself . . . may be seen as a vital, pervasive and active element in the constitution of social structures and formations' and that 'interventions within culture have some independent potential to transform' them (Kuhn 1982: 5, 6). Buñuel's film is valuable in that it forces us to contront the power-structures which are silently naturalized in a film like William Wyler's. If Wyler's film tries to deny the social 'frame' by endorsing love as transcendence in images of sky, air, heaven, Buñuel's reinstates the frame as earth, prison, tomb. Both films, however, have the effect of halting what Matthews calls the 'incessant dissolving of figure into ground and back' (Matthews 1985: 57) which makes *Wuthering Heights* an open rather than a closed text, and thus they present us with meanings that are more limited than those of the original. Iser suggests that it is inevitable that in the visual specificity of film, 'the vital richness of potential' in written texts 'is brutally cancelled out' (Iser 1972: 219). It is perhaps also inevitable, therefore, that my final example, which accepts the challenge to evade closure, should also be a novel: *Changing Heaven*, published in 1990 by the Canadian novelist Jane Urquhart.

Changing Heaven takes its title from one of Emily Brontë's poems:

I loved the plashing of the surge,
The changing Heaven, the breezy weather.

(Hatfield 1941: 96)

In one way it is a novel about the weather, and it certainly deals
with characters out of doors. Much of the novel is devoted to a
conversation on Haworth Moor between the ghost of Emily Brontë
and the ghost of a lady balloonist called Arianna Ether who was
killed near Penistone Crag at the turn of the century. There is also
a modern woman academic who is obsessed with *Wuthering Heights*
and goes to live nearby. The point about the title is that each of
these speakers (and Branwell Brontë, and the male lovers of the
balloonist and the academic) has her own idea of heaven, and most
of them are heavens of love. In a *reductio ad absurdum* of the
echoing lines, the skyward gaze of Wyler's lovers, the novel vividly
and wittily demonstrates that romantic love, 'the triumph of death
over life . . . does not have a sexual object that is ultimately different from itself' (Mitchell 1984: 111). Emily tells Arianna how her
brother Branwell constructed the image of his lost mistress so that
she became 'his perfect prison. An exact reproduction of himself
one week before he died' (Urquhart 1990: 139). Arianna tells Emily
how her lover required that she lose her name, her job, her family,
to become the white, ethereal image of his ideal, ascending into
the sky in 'the apotheosis of Arianna' (Urquhart 1990: 26). Not
content, however, with constructing her aerial persona and her
'skyey' habitat, he cannot rest until he has caused her death, when
she becomes perfect, the unattainable object of his obsessive desire.
In Wyler's film, Heathcliff follows the ghost of Catherine to a
snowy death on Penistone Crag; in *Changing Heaven* the balloonist
pursues his creation, like Frankenstein his monster, into the frozen
wastes of the Arctic, dropping messages of love from his balloon.

Changing Heaven deconstructs notions of 'eternal truth'. Even
the 'elemental' landscape of the Yorkshire moors becomes part of
Wuthering Heights' construction. Emily tells Arianna, 'It is hard
work, too, building landscape. The rocks were particularly difficult,
and that is what Mr Capital H was made out of – different shapes
of black stone. And he was obdurate, unyielding . . . Practically
unkillable!' (Urquhart 1990: 179–80). If this version of Emily Brontë
claims responsibility for having 'made' a 'practically unkillable'
myth, she is also shown as having changed her mind. By the end
of the novel even her ghostly presence is wearing thin, and the

present-day heroine, Ann, learns that 'Mr Capital H' will no longer serve as her ideal of love.

Matthews implies that our dreams of heaven cannot genuinely change because 'the oppressions of society not only compromise our present, they condition the dreams of its reversal' so that 'all that beckons to us as the beyond is the blank inverse of what is within' (Matthews 1985: 54). If ghosts and prohibitions, however, 'incessantly dissolve' into one another, there is no way of assigning primacy to either. Our dreams may be shaped by 'the oppressions of society', but this is a reciprocal interaction, in which the discourse of dreams can 'shape forms of consciousness and unconsciousness, which are closely related to the . . . transformation of our existing systems of power' (Eagleton 1983: 210). The rhetoric of our desires, the intensity with which we tell ourselves stories of tragic love, is a social force which erodes the prohibitions that structure tragedy, just as weather, as it 'wuthers' round obstructive crags, makes new shapes of 'obdurate' landscape. Society, like landscape, changes slowly, but our weathered crags no longer have quite the contours seen by Emily Brontë. As we read old stories, we half-recognize the landscape of past prohibitions, but our pleasure comes from moving with the narrative as it wuthers through to its appropriate heaven. The danger of *Wuthering Heights*, for modern readers, is that we locate our pleasure not in its restless movement, but in its culturally specific heaven. Ann, in *Changing Heaven*, craves identity with her lover – 'she wanted him to become her' (Urquhart 1990: 237) – but the social landscape has changed since *Wuthering Heights*, eroded in part by the force of desire which breathes in Clare Leighton's woodcut and batters against Buñuel's prison. Instead she finds love in a new shape, neither 'Romantic' nor 'legitimate', between adults with separate identities, who do not belong to each other, who do not mirror each other, whose love does not require the death of either. And their intercourse begins in discourse – telling stories about the weather.

Changing Heaven is a wonderful, polyvocal book, in which 'eternal truths' become stories and the 'timeless' Emily Brontë is a whimsical ghost who vanishes into landscape. As we listen to its new storytellers giving new shapes to old desires, we are content to let her go. 'When ghosts become landscape, weather alters, the wind shifts, and heaven changes' (Urquhart 1990: 258).

NOTES

1 I hope to do this for both *Wuthering Heights* and *Jane Eyre* in a book which I am preparing for the Harvester Press.
2 A third, reminiscent source is a few sentences from the adult Catherine's delirious speech in chapter 12, where the feathers from her pillow remind her of how Heathcliff as a boy once set a trap for birds on the moor (Brontë 1965: 160).
3 'The organizational principle of epic structure . . . remains monological. . . . Within monologism, we detect the presence of the "transcendental signifier" and "self presence" as highlighted by Jacques Derrida. . . . Epic logic pursues the general through the specific; it thus assumes a hierarchy within the structure of substance. Epic logic is therefore causal, that is, theological; it is a *belief* in the literal sense of the word' (Kristeva, paraphrasing Bakhtin, in Moi 1986: 48).
4 Drotner, in her study of girls' magazines from the inter-war period, provides plenty of evidence for the ideological changes which lie behind Clare Leighton's picture. Girls were for the first time joining the Girl Guides, going camping, and, at least in fantasy stories, living gypsy-like, adventurous lives free from parental control and chaperonage (Drotner 1983: 33–52).
5 Freud, too, argues that 'normal' femininity and masculinity are formed during the Oedipus complex, the 'family romance' which is the basis of all such triangle-plots, and Rougemont says that 'the essential triangle (Father/Mother/Son) . . . is the poem of Western culture' (Rougemont 1983: 371).
6 Made in Mexico, it was never released in Great Britain.

13　Weathertexts on Spanish, French and English language television

Jerry Booth

Weather forecasts are public-service broadcasting *par excellence*. The weather affects everybody, and from the sample of Spanish, French and British stations viewed, broadcasters take very few liberties with it. Furthermore, it is an area of public-service output where, unlike news, which in other senses it resembles, sponsorship is not seen as a threat. It may be seen either as the thin end of the wedge of sponsored programming on public-service networks, or as an example of the fact that there need be no contradiction between private interests and public service.

This chapter started from a notion that, given that basic meteorological information was the same for everybody, weather forecasts might provide an acid test of different presentation styles, not only across channels, but also across nations. There certainly are different styles which will be explored, but there is also evidence of a mission to inform which determines the scripting and presentation of the meteorological information at the heart of all the broadcasts viewed.

The differences in perspective offered by the national broadcasts seem to have more to do with geography than politics. British forecasts tend to pay more attention to mainland weather at holiday times and the weekends, and the overall picture does include Newfoundland. One might argue that this showed Britain's insularity or was a parallel for its government's stance on Europe, but it is more likely to be a reflection of the Atlantic climate. Similarly, the presence of North Africa in French and Spanish broadcasts might be seen as a post-colonial mirage, but again it is more likely to be proximity.

FORECASTING, METEOROLOGY AND FORMS OF EXPLANATION

Weather has always been an outward and visible sign of largely invisible changes which affect us all. In the west popular explanations for shifts in climate and the weather have, along with many other phenomena, largely moved from religious, through 'folk' to human causes. Examples of the association of weather and religion abound: sometimes weather is a divine instrument, at others aspects of it define the gods themselves.

The shift from divine, through traditional folk to more 'rational' forms of explanation is common to all forms of knowledge, and has of course been part of a general widening of geographical and conceptual horizons. More recently, since the Second World War, we have seen popular explanations for perceived climatic shifts moving from anxieties about nuclear testing to more focused ecological concerns about carbon monoxide, other oil derivatives and CFCs in the context of the ozone layer. In some ways, then, ecology has started to supply a new source of explanation and meaning and part of its appeal lies in the link it provides between long-term, invisible change and the short-term, visible changes provided by weather.

So, whilst ecological theories do not make quite the same claims to explanatory reach as religion, they are nevertheless invoked to deal with unusually hot summers, high winds and concerns about water. They are also, in principle if not in practice, less crude in the sense that they do not require the large ontological jumps between the cosmic and the everyday characteristic of divine explanations or the essentially vague connections between fallout and climate. Familiarity with weather forecasting and thereby meteorology has doubtless helped this shift from 'folk' to 'scientific' forms of explanations for a series of phenomena by providing part of the explanatory bridge between planetary and everyday events. The desire for an overall explanation still exists, but meteorology provides what Merton (1949) called 'theories of the middle range', which are not insignificant in convincing both scientists and lay-people of a discipline's claims to legitimacy. Meteorology provides part of a scientifically legitimated explanatory link between the global and the individual levels.

PREDICTION AND LEGITIMACY

The presence of forecasts in the mass media means that as a science meteorology gets an unusual amount of public exposure, and in this context science does not seem to have swept all before it. Stories of the countryman-forecaster who has consistently 'out-predicted' the weathermen or the depth to which snails in the Po valley have burrowed are constantly challenging the legitimacy of the forecasters. Competing 'folk' predictions and explanations of weather have traditionally tended to be based on localized experience and it has been suggested that scientific reasoning has become the approved way of providing convincing arguments which downgrade such contextualized argument and knowledge.[1]

The persistence of these populist challenges to science is arguably only encouraged by the contrast between the probabilistic nature of meteorological predictions and the impression of infallibility which the degree of exposure, coupled with the new technology of presentation, creates. Whatever philosophers of science may think, in the popular mind scientific legitimacy is still attached to predictive accuracy, and here meteorology has a problem. Given popular interest in the weather and its role in the media generally, meteorology is even more exposed than social sciences: the inaccuracy of weather forecasts will get a laugh in almost any language.

It may be true that no other science parades its predictions so publicly or so often, but then few others have been helped to develop the battery of techniques that weather presenters deploy. Access to a vast public may be a mixed blessing, but their mere presence on screen lends the forecasters and by extension their discipline a degree of legitimacy. Few scientists enjoy a daily relationship with a very large audience unmediated by other television professionals, and meteorology has undoubtedly benefited from this exposure. It has been able to develop visual and verbal languages specifically designed to communicate with the layman so that, as sciences go, meteorology, or at any rate its predictions, are relatively 'user-friendly'. In a world where science relies on political support, a high public profile can be very useful: there is a link between the forms of communication meteorology employs and the support that it can claim. This is not, of course, separate from its use-value, but other forms of science which might contribute more to the sum of human happiness do not have quite the same place in the public eye or mind.

NEW TECHNOLOGY

Looking at forecasts from Spain, France and the UK it is obvious that satellite technology has made a difference both to the area covered and the ways in which it is depicted. All the forecasts now start with a satellite perspective, whether it be global, hemispherical or continental. They constantly provide images of the world which link the national with the international, and indeed the global.

Satellite pictures and information now provide the dominant perspective for television forecasts both in scientific and graphic terms. They add a sense of immediacy in their rendition of the developing weather, and are uniquely able to convey the dynamics of the weather systems. Although the images used in forecasts only occasionally consist of photographs taken by satellites, the derived and enhanced presentations that appear on our television screens only serve to underline the role that technology now plays in forecasting. It associates meteorology with the developments in space travel and technology which have been an important part of the culture of the last half of the twentieth century.

Satellite images are now used to show cloud cover in most of the more extended forecasts, and time-lapse photography is often employed to show the developing situation. This gives a strong sense of the movement of weather systems, difficult to convey in the presentations which relied on magnetic symbols being moved around a map by the presenter. The clockwise and anticlockwise movements of air around high- and low-pressure areas can be seen clearly and the movement of weather systems is graphically demonstrated rather than merely indicated by the presenter's hand.

The sense of 'realism' in bulletins given by the graphics is defined by this satellite-eye view, and these images in turn provide a familiar form through which audiences gain an understanding of satellite technology. Whether it harks back to religious imagery or not, the extra-terrestrial perspective gives a powerful endorsement to the information in the bulletins.

PRODUCTION CONTEXT AND PURITY OF FORM

On television the weather forecast is usually scheduled with – often after – the news, because in a sense it *is* news. However, from the point of view of its collection the weather is a less complicated, and therefore analytically a less 'distorted' form. News has to be gathered and processed, and although much of it is predictable, newsgathering can never be entirely routine. The preparation of weather forecasts, on the other hand, is a familiar routine where the source (the meteorological office) sends the necessary information when it is required so that the process of production for the screen, page or microphone can be done at a fixed time every day.

The fact that the source of information has a vested interest in its accuracy, together with the predictability of the production process, mean that the interpretation and presentation of the weather forecast is more 'pure' than that of the news. News gathering and news processing unavoidably distort the facts and events that are presented. News sources often have their own reasons for providing information in a particular way, journalists have an interest in pushing their stories, editors have to work under another set of constraints: wholly objective news reporting is a myth, if only because of the number of gatekeepers through whose hands it passes. The people who produce the weather in the media all draw their information from the same source; their job is to present it in the manner they feel is most appropriate for their particular medium or channel. It is in this sense that the presentation of the weather forecast may be seen as a pure form; it provides a sort of controlled experiment of the art of presentation in a highly specific context. It is interesting to reflect on the fact that the 'purest' forms of public-service broadcasting (public-service announcements, for example) are those where the information comes largely unadulterated from outside agencies.

TITLES

There is usually some separating device between the previous programme, generally the news, and detailed consideration of the weather maps. It may consist of an animated or still sequence with music or a 'sting', and might feature the presenter in some form or another.

In Britain the BBC favours watercolour scenes of the countryside as background for the presenter introducing the forecast. This has a rather traditional, even old-fashioned feel as well as introducing the presenter on his or her own. It evokes a sort of intimacy, especially when it is contrasted with the ITV bulletin, now sponsored by Powergen. This latter has music over the titles which feature the globe, clouds and spinning titles before it cuts to the presenter.

TV5 (France) uses the station logo on a starlit background which is then joined by the word 'METEO' on a background of clouds and blue sky in a moving panel. A changing chord accompanies this sequence, which combines the 'technological' and the 'natural'. TF1 (France) has a pan across water with the reflection of trees and drops falling into it. This combines the natural and the technological in one image since the form of the image is too perfect to seem 'natural'.

Consistent with the breadth of its coverage, Galavision's title-sequence has a Mercator projection of the world superimposed over symbols of clouds and the sun which orbit rapidly behind it. 'EL ESTADO DEL TIEMPO' is then superimposed in gold reflective sanserif capitals over the whole. Its bulletin is also unique in having a music track under the voice speaking the forecast.

TVE's bulletin (Spain) starts with a flower, followed by a stylized sun, and then in the bottom half of the screen a stop-frame photographic animation of growing mushrooms and other plants while the words 'EL TIEMPO' in sanserif capitals come in from the right and the presenter standing in front of a relief backdrop with isobars, and a large A and B denoting *alta* (high) and *baja* (low) in blue and red.

So most of the sequences include some kind of computer-generated animation and combine the 'natural' (whether it be a plant or a map) with the more obviously symbolic (whether it be isobars, stylized suns, clouds or rain). Sanserif 'metallic' capitals seem to be favoured for the type. Although the representations of the 'natural' vary, the static watercolour backdrop stands out because it has quite a different feel from the animated sequences. The watercolour is hardly a televisual form and its two-dimensionality and use as a background for the presenter in medium shot harks back to the theatre at a time when most studio set-ups strive for three-dimensionality. The TVE sequence, with its jerky stop-frame animation, manages to show natural forms whilst overriding their naturalness, and then its two-dimensional relief backdrop for the presenter emphasizes the measurements forecasters use. The overall effect of these isobar reliefs is organic though, especially when contrasted with some of the more high-tech graphics elsewhere.

Most of the title-sequences, then, express the natural in a deliberately representational form. The images may be of what we think of as natural objects, but they are produced in such a way as to denaturalize them. The overall message is of technology being used to explain and predict natural phenomena. The differences are in the means by which this is achieved: TF1's pan is hyper-real, TV5's uses the more familiar grammar of the vision mixer's desk, the moving panel, and TVE's is a rostrum stop animation which is better established than any of them. The British stations offer both ends of the spectrum, ITV's global and computer-generated high-tech, and the BBC's watercolour.

TYPE

Title type for Galavision (Spanish language) and TF1 uses capitals and a metallic surface. TF1's letters are tilted from flat, Galavision's fill the bottom half of the screen but do not themselves move. TV5 has 'METEO' in a metallic rectangle which moves across the screen and finally tilts to upright. The use of animated type gives an impression of higher production values than still or scrolled titles. At the beginning and end of bulletins, the presenter's name may appear, and in the case of TF1 a more personalized touch is sometimes given by the presenter's signature being animated over the end titles.

Once the bulletin has come down to the particular nation-state it is common to see a title indicating the day and time to which the map and narration are referring. Other forms of typographic information may include the station logo superimposed in a corner. Galavision's hemispherical forecast has a strip along the bottom of the screen where the temperatures in world capitals are scrolled from right to left, and in the bottom left-hand corner of the screen the bulletin's title 'El Estado del Tiempo' and the name of the country to which it refers, hence 'Estados Unidos' when North America is being dealt with.

Figures are obviously important, conveying as they do wind speed and temperature. They vary in colour and density, but they have not sacrificed clarity for style, and, when they appear, in all cases they dominate the maps.

MAPS

The maps which supply much of the backdrop and context for all the other information in the bulletins vary in colour and detail. British channels seem to favour the green and pleasant land image with blue for the sea. The western hemispheric projection on TV5 uses brown for the land masses and has basic relief information as well as cross-hairs for the intersection of latitude and longitude lines. Nighttime bulletins on TF1 use a map which stresses human rather than physical features and combines this with a sense of immediacy by having a dark European land mass with what seem to be pinpoints of light clustering around the centres of population. Galavision favours dark brown and physical relief, but this 'naturalism' is rather offset by the use of a variety of graphic devices to fill the area of the sea. For the North American continent the top half of the screen has scrolling clouds whilst the bottom half is occupied by a blue venetian-blind effect. There is also a cut from a partial view of the whole continent to a map which is seen to stop at the 49th parallel. When the bulletin moves on to Central America, the Caribbean and the Pacific seem to share a sort of diaphanous fog, and South America is seen from a satellite perspective which clearly stresses the curvature of the earth and sets the land mass in the context of space rather than the sea. When the bulletin moves on to the 'old continent' (that is, Europe), it reverts to an overhead shot and the sea is just plain blue without any animation.

The maps provide the dominant colours; they are the backdrop against which the presenters and the graphics have to operate. As we have seen they may privilege the human or the physical, the technical or the 'natural', and they may be used to shift the perspective. For example, there is a tendency for hemispherical perspectives to stress 'naturalism', with the use of brown for the land and the use of shading for high ground, but when the bulletin goes on to the national forecast this is usually abandoned in favour of a non-naturalistic palette containing purples and greens. It is generally at this point that specific predictions are made, and the visual and verbal tone of the core of the forecast. From the flowing contours of pressure systems and perhaps cloud systems moving across the map many bulletins change to figures, arrows and more angular symbols. At the same time the language becomes more constrained and specific and less discursive. Here at the heart of the bulletin the language and the symbols together may objectively create a high degree of redundancy, but the intention is clearly to reinforce the predictions.

PRESENTERS

Television is supposed to be a personality medium, so weather presenters could become a very significant feature of the bulletins; in fact they are constrained by the production context, and

increasingly overshadowed by the graphics they employ. Short bulletins on all channels can and do deliver the forecast with only a
voice-over, and usually dispense with any background explanation
of the overall situation. This seems to be a perfectly adequate
method of getting the information across, and there is no intrinsic
reason why the more elaborate forecasts could not use a voice-
over. Although it is an empirical question, it seems likely that the
sophisticated graphics now employed convey most of the information to the viewer, but the flavour of the bulletin can be and is
affected by the presenter.

Presenters can provide a note of spontaneity, although it is tightly
circumscribed by the medium shot and the time in which they have
to deliver their core script. The open-handed circling gesture seems
universal and, aside from that, dress and coiffure offer the most
visual scope for individuality. Presenters may be allowed their introductions and their codas, but the central part of the bulletin has
little verbal redundancy (this may be why people find it so hard to
remember specific predictions). The forecast itself is the core of all
bulletins, and none of those viewed allowed performance or production to detract from the basic job of getting this across. The
verbal 'frills' are confined to the beginning and end of the bulletin,
the core remains tightly scripted and generally rather dense.

These introductions and codas, however, are not simply there to
allow the presenters room to express themselves; they often serve
a purpose. Weather forecasts provide a useful buffer, saving or
spending time to correct schedules which have gone awry. So presenters may be asked to extend or curtail their introductions or
summaries according to the needs of the control room; the ability
to ad lib is as useful for weather presenters as it is for continuity
announcers.

In the days before computer graphics, when the presenter used
a pointer and moved magnetic symbols around a map of the British
Isles, the dominant style might best be described as schoolmasterly
(all the presenters were men). Since then the bulletin has not
entirely lost its pedagogic flavour, but the technology and general
changes in television presentation have certainly set it apart from
most schoolrooms. Often the presenter has time for a general introduction before the graphics become the focus of attention, and this
helps to establish the link with the audience. This time is often
employed to outline what has been happening in the last twelve or
twenty-four hours.

The styles of presentation and the degree of 'personalization' do, of course, differ. The least presenter-oriented is Galavision, where the forecast is introduced by a presenter who does the voice-over, but who is not seen during the bulletin. TVE's weather presenters have their names together with the station logo along the bottom of the screen at the beginning of their bulletin, and they are able to be fairly expansive although not anecdotal in their coverage. The most potential for stardom amongst the bulletins watched is provided by the French language stations. TV5's bulletin tends to be introduced with a medium close-up of the presenter leaning on a sort of lectern, sometimes with a neutral backdrop, sometimes in front of a hemisphere with Europe at its centre. The introduction may be done with a smile and even an exhortation to get out the swimming costumes and sunshades before continuing with the detail of weather movements followed by the predictions. At the end of the bulletin the presenter's signature adds to the personal touch. It is, however, TF1 which allows most scope for presenters to stamp their personality on the bulletins. One presenter's trademark is wearing a buttonhole often featured in big close-up at the start of the bulletin as a link into the forecast. A flavour of these introductions may be provided by the example of a pun on the word *buissonnant*, meaning 'bushy', applied to the plant in the top pocket of the presenter's suit-jacket and the same word used as an adjective to describe cumulus clouds. The presenters of TF1's bulletin do perform more than the other presenters in terms of interpolations and the amount of movement they allow themselves in front of the charts, as well as in their links at the beginning and end. Another TF1 presenter, at the end of the bulletin, where sun and moon setting and rising times are given under the date and the saint's day, felt moved to say that the saint in question had absolutely no possible link with any aspect of the weather.

On British television some weather presenters have become personalities in their own right, and they are now used as people with whom the audience is expected to identify.[2] They write books, are featured in articles in the listings magazines and even appear on chat shows: they form part of a channel's brand image. In Britain at least, many of these presenters are personnel from the Meteorological Office who have volunteered for the job and part of their appeal is their perceived 'ordinariness' compared with most of the other presenters used on national channels. For example, presenters with strong regional accents were accepted by the public in weather forecasts while letters were still being written about news presenters' accents being 'incomprehensible'. Much of this added up to a sort of 'lovable boffin' image which accepted, and indeed to some extent encouraged, minor eccentricities. Different cultures have different sensibilities when it comes to the line between permitted eccentricity and a lack of seriousness.

Presenters do not have an easy task. They must deliver a tightly scripted text in synchronization with increasingly sophisticated and often animated graphics.[3] Aside from this they may have to keep an eye on the studio floor manager, who may ask them to speed up or fill in to put the schedule back on course. They add a human dimension to balance the highly technical impression given by the rest of the bulletin; they may be there to symbolize the fact that even the most comprehensive data-gathering coupled with the most sophisticated computer models requires human knowledge of the peculiarities of national climates to produce an accurate forecast.

STUDIO PRODUCTION: CAMERA MOVEMENT

Visual language reflects different assumptions about the appropriate balance between populism and propriety. British forecasts do not normally employ any camera movement; changes are provided by the generated image and the viewer's perspective does not vary. Contrast this with the bulletin already alluded to on TF1 which, after the titles, cut to a big close-up of the presenter's buttonhole and then zoomed back to frame the presenter, thereafter continuing rather more conventionally. Such informality as there may be in British bulletins is normally confined to the spoken word. This, to British audiences at least, gives a less contrived feel because, whilst the spoken word is perceived as spontaneous, using camera movements requires planning.

In theory it would be perfectly possible to use the camera to highlight the areas or features the forecaster was dealing with. This would give the forecast a different feel, and add marginally to the time and trouble needed to put it together. One only has to consider the possibilities of multiple camera positions, zooms and dolly shots to realize that the economy of the weather bulletins gives them an air of seriousness appropriate to 'factual' programming. Simply offering close-ups of regions would not unduly upset this impression, but it might detract from the notion of national weather which the channels seem keen to put over. TF1, whose forecasts allow their presenters more 'performance room', also varies the effects. One bulletin which has the presenter leaning casually in front of a map of the hemisphere fades her out to reveal the half globe. In general, however, it is the graphics which are faded in and out, and the main transition used is the cut. The main sense of movement is provided by the graphics in the maps.

Most of the bulletins analysed came from national channels and the forecasts are one way of reinforcing that national character. Galavision's coverage of the weather in both North and South America and Europe carries an equally strong message about its intended reach. In this context it is worth noting in passing that Spain and France (the square and the hexagon) fit and fill the television screen much more easily than the UK. The UK television weather map illustrates perfectly the country's maritime climate, as well as its insularity. A summary of the features analysed can be seen below in Table 13.1.

FACTUAL PROGRAMMING: A SERIOUS BUSINESS?

Style of presentation needs to take account of the bulletin's context, and since the weather is usually preceded by and linked with the news, it tends to take its cue literally and metaphorically from the news. News bulletins often end with a phrase such as 'And now the weather' before the cut from one to the other. Newsreaders are nearly always sitting at desks, usually with technological hints of the newsgathering process around them (monitors and key-boards), and the fact that weather presenters are normally standing sets them apart, and puts them in a different frame. News presen-ters sit behind a desk where the most expressive use of their hands is to tidy their notes at the end of the bulletin; weather presenters can use their upper bodies, arms and hands to refer to the graphics which come up behind them. In principle, then, there is more room for performance, but in practice factual programming norms limit this.

Depending on how it is done, the link between the news and the weather may provide a note of informality. The link may introduce the weather presenter, and the informality may be increased by comments about the weather from the newscaster to which the weather presenter may respond. As we have seen, it is at the beginning and end of the forecasts that 'performance room' is allowed: the predictions remain sacrosanct.

Handovers of this nature may be prompted as much by rivalry as by the friendship that this sort of introduction normally connotes: preparing to deliver a set piece can be disrupted by having to respond in a more informal register. The most common form of

Table 13.1 Summary of analysis

	BBC	ITV	TV5	TF1	TVE	Galavision
Overall perspective	continental	continental	hemispherical	hemispherical	continental	global
Animation	static	computer	panel movement	hyper-real track	stop-frame	–
Map colour						
Land	green	green	brown	dark with lights	–	brown
Sea	blue	blue	–	–	–	scrolling clouds and venetian blind
Presenter performance, presence and prominence	discursive freedom	discursive freedom	discursive freedom	discursive freedom	name in titles	voice-over
Camera movement	none	none	none	zoom	none	–

professional disruption is aimed at sports presenters, whose tone and language are frequently ridiculed.

CONCLUSION

Forecasts demonstrate the application of science and its instruments to natural phenomena and are therefore at some level always dealing with the borders between the natural, which is not controllable, and the 'rational', which attempts to impose order upon it. The forecast literally superimposes measures of barometric pressure, temperature, wind speed, etc., which signify weather systems on territorial maps to make the weather visible and comprehensible. Developments in television graphics, not to mention satellites, have allowed the bulletins to show the dynamics of the weather in a way which other media are unable to match.

There are a number of ways of achieving the aims of television forecasts, but what was striking was the structural similarity between the material from Spain, Britain and France. The central message of the bulletins is prediction rather than explanation. This 'core' message is usually contained in a tightly scripted bulletin backed up with highly visible symbols and measures which relate to the felt effects of weather rather than the underlying causes. Hence barometric pressure is not dealt with in as much detail as wind speed, for example; high- and low-pressure areas are usually shown separately from the forecast of what is likely to happen, and measures of pressure only occasionally appear on the screen.

There is a discernible difference between the graphic style of the overall situation which provides the explanatory background and that of the national predictions which follow. The overall movement of weather systems tends to be shown by animated sequences which, in contrast to the national picture at least, are more 'realistic' than symbolic. So, for example, clouds tend to be seen as such – with darker areas within them designating rain – and moving, whereas once the bulletin moves on to the national picture, clouds are likely to appear as much more regular and symbolic forms, which often remain static. The national maps change for different times of the day, and so do not attempt to show the continuous movement more characteristic of the presentation of the overall situation.

Television forecasts embody a message about the relationship between technology and nature, and they provide several different kinds of image. After the titles, the extra-terrestrial fluid 'realism' of the satellite imagery gives way to the more symbolic and static presentations used for the national predictions. Isobar lines may provide a symbolic link between the two, sharing the fluidity of the moving systems in outline, but imposing numerical order on them. In some bulletins the cloud movements fade to reveal the isobar lines 'underneath' them, providing a graphic illustration of the connections between the two. Once on to the national charts, the measurements relating to temperature and wind speed imply understanding through quantification, and their prominence (through size and colour) literally and metaphorically overlays the 'natural', because irregular, forms of the maps.

Developments in satellite technology have enhanced the possibilities of the 'mission to explain' which arguably forms part of contemporary notions of public-service broadcasting. Forecasts no longer give a purely national view, all provide a continental context, and some give a hemispherical and even global picture. They have become showcases for the latest developments in television graphics, which have contributed to a dynamic and broader view of the weather. The extent to which their audiences are better informed about the weather and its causes is an empirical question, but what seems clear is that so far this particular piece of public-service broadcasting has been able to thrive in what is often seen as a hostile environment.

NOTES

1 L. Hunter, paper given at Leeds University, December 1990.
2 The presenter who 'failed' to predict the 1987 hurricane in the south of England was blamed personally in the popular press.
3 As a rule, the viewer sees the presenter standing in front of a map, but in most cases this is simply a blue background which picks up images from another source. The presenter can only tell where she or he is pointing by referring to a monitor which gives him or her the viewer's perspective. This has the advantage that the presenter does not really need to look away from camera, although if the body is not at all inclined towards the map it can look rather robotic. Like many performances, what looks natural is carefully contrived and takes on its own reality.

14 The power of a dress: the rhetoric of a moment in fashion

Prudence Black and Stephen Muecke

EXPOSITIO

This chapter will present the rhetorical analysis of a photograph, a famous press photograph of Jean Shrimpton wearing a mini-skirt in Melbourne in 1965 (Figure 14.1). The paradigm we are working within is the post-structuralist analysis of the rhetoric of images (Barthes 1977), so the emphasis will be on the image as a *text*, but not the structuralist version of text as a self-contained system of meanings organized around binary oppositions. The analysis will extend formal relations within the text along vectorial lines outside the text to those relations of context offered by history and society and which we think are crucial to understandings of how the text functions.

WAYS OF TALKING FASHION: THREE MODELS

Within the field of the critical analysis of fashion we have three models to follow (for a fuller discussion see Black 1990). In addition there is the non-critical field of fashion discourse (of which some examples below) which is merely narrative and/or descriptive and is congruent with the commercial aims of the fashion industry. A critical analysis will subsume the objects of fashion, as discursive artifacts, under a broader theoretical framework. Barthes's (1985) *The Fashion System*, for instance, is a structural and textual model which deals with the singularities of the *grammar* of fashion discourse, a universalizing theory separate from any particular fashion institution or historical moment in fashion even though he was dealing with certain French fashion journals. Since we will be trying to deal with the 'phenomenology of the moment' here we will clearly not follow this approach. Then there is the early cultural

Figure 14.1 Jean Shrimpton at the 1965 Melbourne Cup. Reproduced courtesy of The Herald and Weekly Times Ltd, Melbourne, Australia.

studies approach of Hebdige (1979), where icons of dress became signifiers for a resistant or liberatory practice: punks' pins and rasta locks were the way for a younger, displaced generation to reject an older, conservative generation. Where Barthes had critical distance from his object, Hebdige has political involvement: his objects are positively valorized as modernist and transgressive. The third model is similarly involved; it is the critique of high fashion as a conspiracy of an elite, and here we cite Silverman's (1987) *Selling Culture* as a good example, as she makes intimate connections between Diana Vreeland, the Reagans, Yves Saint Laurent and the Big Stores in the United States. This elite is taken to task, from a liberal point of view, for irresponsibly fantasizing and appropriating others' styles and images.

We will talk about our little mini-skirt from a fourth position, in such a way as to provide a context for the critical discussion of fashion history: the chapter is within the field of the cultural history of the 1960s in this sense, and it is hard to forge this position because it is within the broad mainstream of fashion rather than at the punk or elite fringes. We will not make grand critical claims for an everyday object like the mini-skirt but we will bear in mind the importance of ornament and dress as social signifiers; always different across cultures and history, essential to self-image, of major financial import, and so on. And our mini is also a pretext for a meditation on the importance of rhetoric as a recent theoretical movement which can renovate post-structuralist practice in the reading of images.

THE ANALYSIS

The function of the text for rhetorical analysis involves, according to the classical formula, 'seeking the available means of persuasion'. We take this to mean that the pivotal element in rhetorical analysis is the audience. How this audience is constituted is clearly important, and terms like 'persuasion' will need to be theorized not as psychological but as textual and historical at the same time. We do not want to say that the whole text has a general effect on a subject. We want to say that parts of the text encounter the partially formed subject in the process of social communication.

We will therefore argue against the utility of setting up a *general* rhetorical model for language or communication functions: we would argue that each text needs to be taken in its own historical and social context, and that while a linguistic model of language suggests that there are general features of language that are paradigmatically shared by (all) texts, analysis along those lines produces results *for linguistics*, but not for cultural studies, which might use rhetoric to study the particular instances of *texts in use*. In and around these texts we would discern effects of truth or power which might be engendered by, for instance, appeals to authority, or common sense, or logic, or poetic truth. Our analysis therefore involves an understanding of the desiring subject as engaged via psychic mechanisms of identity (mimesis) or resistance (aggression) in a process of becoming.

It is for this reason that rhetoric is the study of figures of 'speech' (and by speech we mean articulation as *connection between different bodies, corporeal and otherwise*), or parts of speech, the available moves in a Wittgensteinian language game. The analysis is directed not so much to the author as to the reader, we speak of ends rather than origins, mechanisms of reception rather than expression, speech *occasions* rather than general theories of language. In this sense we could locate our project as being sympathetic to both the ethnography of speaking – Hymes and his 1964 model for the analysis of the speech event (see Hymes 1972 for a survey of the field) – and to Foucault, with his account of discourse, which had as its aim to restore to language its status as *event*. So the analysis will draw on the elements of the *occasion* and the text it demands, the *figures* of the text itself, and the unique character of the statement the occasion produces.

The statement (*énoncé*) articulates speaking positions (*énonciation*), creating a particular historically construed audience. The statement is essentially rare in its distribution in time and space, so the analysis of communication involves explaining the uneven distribution of texts and meanings: why did a particular discourse of popular culture flourish during the 1960s? How did its mobilization by certain speakers for certain audiences become a plausible rhetorical move?

The statement, in its Foucauldian appearance, is thus an ideal unit for the analysis of fashion, grasping the rarity of the object within the knowledge-producing institutions of society (discursive formations) and carrying with it the articulation of audiences' desires-to-become or desires-to-know. The photograph we are looking at comes, after all, at a turning point in the history of the evolution of styles; it is a pivot around which an audience divided itself and a new generation began to find an identity. In this connection it is worth bearing in mind from the outset the simple demographic fact that the hump of the post-war baby-boomers were in their late teens when the photograph was taken.

THE NARRATIVE: 'WHO'S THAT GIRL?'

Jean (The Shrimp) Shrimpton appeared at the Melbourne Cup in 1965, wearing a mini-skirt four inches above the knee. Or so goes the story. Somewhere down the track popular memory scrambled this story. *That* mini-skirt which we all remember, the plain white shift with the small motif of embroidered beads was not what she wore to the Melbourne Cup. On Tuesday, Melbourne Cup day 1965, she wore a neat, little, three-piece suit of grey and beige tweed with an ice-blue Breton, beige gloves and stockings. She carried a light-chocolate-coloured handbag. This outfit was by no means extraordinary although some people commented that the skirt was 'too short'. What was extraordinary was her prior appearance on the Saturday at the Derby, Flemington, wearing the now-famous mini. The events of the day resulted in a fashion image which has become fixed as a crucial moment in Australian fashion history.

The fact that the occasions were confused is not so unusual given the mythology at work. Derby day, Saturday, is merely the tease towards Cup day; it has none of the grandeur or status as *event* of the Melbourne Cup, which is televised nationally, publicized world-wide and is a recognized fashion venue. While The Shrimp appeared throughout the three days of the Melbourne Cup Carnival – that is, all the races over the week – the popular image of her remains as wearing *that* dress on Melbourne Cup day – almost all Australian fashion books, social histories and even next-door neighbours will confirm this. This is perhaps a small point to make, but the way images are anchored on to a broader framework, their mode of signification, is attached not to the object, Jean Shrimpton or the dress, but to a concept, and in this case it is the rapid insertion of the mercurial Shrimpton into the national event as a historical moment or (static) monument. With the Shrimpton image it is not the actual race day but the National Occasion which fuels the myth, and the portable narrative becomes one of transgression of this national/conservative image.

The photograph (Figure 14.1) has been reproduced in most books on Australian fashion history, and been used to discuss the photographic image in many Fine Arts and Design courses. It is a news-pictorial from the Melbourne *Sun*, a photograph in many ways similar to others taken on the same occasion by the popular press, with The Shrimp as central character, a full-length shot and in this instance with a backdrop of the members' stand (other photographs are very similar, although the backdrop looks like the famous rose garden which borders the enclosure). She is at a slight angle, her body frozen in mid-movement, one knee slightly bent, her hands free. Her eyes look to the side, her hair is swinging across her shoulders so that she looks disengaged, carefree, even 'liberated'. She is wearing a sleeveless dress, two-tone sling-back shoes, a man's watch, and is carrying a dark handbag. The background is a mass of faces in the members stand, most of them women wearing either prescription glasses or sun-glasses. All eyes are on Jean Shrimpton, but her gaze dances gaily off in another direction.

The attention to a fashion event had not had such a run since Queen Elizabeth alighted from the royal barge eleven years before. There were certainly many publicized fashion occasions after this; the appearance of the bikini on the Gold Coast in the early 1950s, and then in 1964, just the year before The Shrimp's appearance, a King's Cross stripper wore the latest fashion; a topless dress on the Manly ferry. None of these received the national exposure that the Queen and The Shrimp did. Even the Queen's later visit in 1963 had none of the hysteria and expectation she had received on that first royal visit in 1954. Rumour has it that they were saving it all up for the Beatles' tour the following year. The editress (*sic*) of the women's section of the *Herald* reported the arrival of the Queen, and we quote some of the article as a way of allowing the discourses of fashion to dialogue with each other.

Then she came ashore, matching the golden day – every woman's dream of beauty.

As she took up her position under the gleaming white canopy decorated with golden crowns, she put her hand up her back to make sure the collar of her dress was flat.

Her dress was simplicity itself, a flutter of champagne chiffon printed in gold which had a tinge of green. The pattern was of golden wheat ears, which took movement as the fabric rippled in the slight breeze. Her little hat was a pretty conceit which showed her soft, wavy hair. Off white petals, laid one upon another, it had an organdie rose finished with a gold leaf at one side.

Poised, youthful, feminine, perhaps slightly withdrawn into her own pools of silence from which she gains such strength, the Queen might have been any young woman on a great occasion.

(*Herald*, 4 February 1954)

While the Queen managed to set the standard that was expected of her, the same cannot be said in relation to The Shrimp. An article from the *Sun* of 3 November 1965 read more like Cicero's account of Antony vomiting 'before an assembly of the Roman people, while performing a public duty, while master of the horse' (Quintilian 1922: VIII.IV.6–9) The article quotes Lady Nathan, the then Lady Mayoress of Melbourne:

> If Miss Shrimpton wants to wear skirts four inches above the knees in London, that's her business. But it's not done here. We all took exception to her not wearing hat or gloves on Saturday. But she wore them yesterday. Surely, you have respect for the country you visit and wear the right thing. I feel we know so much better than Miss Shrimpton.

Lady Nathan, wearing an imported French mushroom ostrich-feather hat, also denied that Australian women dressed over-elaborately although there were 'a few novelties'. 'We dress for our climate,' she said. In an earlier comment Lady Nathan said, 'We all dress correctly here. This Shrimpton is a child and she showed very bad manners.'

THE RHETORIC OF THE IMAGE

How does one begin to ask questions about the rhetoric of an image? Rhetoric has been defined as the art of fine speaking or, as Aristotle put it, 'the art of finding in any case the available means of persuasion'. Classical rhetoricians argued through the ages about the honourability of applied rhetoric. Was it something used just to ornament vocal exchange, was it a form of trickery and what moral type of character could deliver it? There was the theoretical or analytical side of discovering what were the available and appropriate means best suited to construct a rhetoric; on the other hand, for theorists like the Roman rhetorician Quintilian, it was a more technical or pragmatic approach dependent on an extensive training of subjects to prepare them to deliver rhetoric for specific domains like the law, literature and education, and in this way the whole person was formed by rhetoric.

Eagleton has made a precise connection between ancient rhetoric and contemporary critical practice:

> The most widespread early criticism on historical record was not, in our sense, 'aesthetic': it was a mode of what we would now call discourse theory, devoted to analysing the material effects of particular uses of language in particular social conjunctures. It was a highly elaborate theory of specific signifying practices – above all of the discursive practices of the judicial, political and religious apparatuses of the state. Its intention, quite consciously, was to theorize systematically the articulations of discourse and power, and to do so in the name of political practice: to enrich the political effectiveness of signification.
>
> The name of this form of criticism is rhetoric. . . . Text-books on rhetoric are the densely codified manuals of such politico-discursive education; they are hand-books of ruling-class power.
>
> (Eagleton 1982)

Rhetoric is rarely used to address problems of text/image relations, but the contemporary preponderance of audio-visual media urges us to apply rhetoric to visual images.[1] Rhetoric provides a form of identification; it informs as well as persuades. In relation to the Shrimpton photograph, rhetorical analysis would ask this question: how does this particular fashion image address a particular audience? What *structure* of address is implied? This is the motif we are looking for, not strictly the *internal* relations of a text, but text/image/subject relations.

Here we need to make a passing mention to Barthes's 'Rhetoric of the image'. In that article Barthes performs a now exemplary semiotic analysis of an image. The advertisement for Panzani pasta products is read in terms of its linguistic and iconic messages. For Barthes, at the level of mass communications, 'the linguistic message is indeed present in every image' (Barthes 1977: 38). He sees the linguistic message as one way of 'fixing' a chain of floating signifieds around a text. This 'fixing' of the visual image by the verbal rhetoric is a form of analysis which is easily applied to newspaper captions, advertisements and films. But images do not always need to rely on written texts to secure a meaning, to be secondary. The Shrimpton image can stand on its own, in the sense that an image's meanings are no more indeterminate than those of a linguistic text; it still has an audience which construes a meaning, even though that audience never approaches the image innocently, uncontaminated by other verbal and visual texts.

Barthes's 'internal' reading tells us more about the conventions of constructing the advertisement with its structural signification than it does about the much broader ways in which it can be received and understood. For instance, a semiotic reading *à la* Barthes does not address subjectivity. It does not tell us how a certain image addresses a particular audience and how an image can be received by different audiences.

THE GODDESS OF RHETORIC: PERSUASION

Rhetoric was often represented during the Middle Ages as a tall and beautiful lady. Her robes are sumptuously adorned with the figures of speech, and in her hand she carries weapons with which to wound her adversaries. These weapons are wielded in judicial rhetoric and in demonstrative orations which are devoted to censure and condemnation.

(Dixon 1971: 53)

And so stands Jean Shrimpton, a good five feet nine inches tall, those Medusa locks swinging across the shoulders of her stark, white dress. Far from sumptuous adornment, there is only the discretion of the beaded motif. And the weapons to wound her adversaries? Leaving aside the lone handbag against the gaze of many, there is only that strangely quantifiable danger, the hemline measured in inches, above or below the knee, a quantification which would seem to derive from a military disciplining of the body. (At this time, as boys' hair threatened to become longer, it was policed in terms of inches above the collar.) The measurement is not for the interest of the couturier. The measurement *is* the danger, the progressive transgression of limits to such an extent that the hiking of the mini-skirt beyond all limits will eventually destroy the notion of fashion as transgression by inches.

Is she taking charge of the critics of classical rhetoric by making use of devices to serve her own end, to speak things as they are not and thereby excite the passions (Quintilian 1922: I, II.XVII.24–9)? These 'devices' at her disposal might also be termed 'ornaments of style'. Her modernist minimalism is also part of her fashion armoury. As Quintilian stated: 'For all ornament derives its effect not from its own qualities so much as from the circumstances in which it is applied, and the occasion chosen for saying anything is at least as important a consideration as what is actually said' (Quintilian 1922: XI.I.6–10). One of the ornaments of style in the Shrimpton image is her dress. Maggie Tabberer, Australian fashion writer, had a front-page story (much to her surprise) in the afternoon edition of the *Daily Mirror*. She had this to say about the dress:

> Well, frankly I'm disappointed. Here I was waiting with bated breath for that fabulous Jean Shrimpton to hit the local fashion scene. When she did – bang, fizzle. That's what this dress is, a big fizzle! I can't think what I expected her to wear for her big appearance at the Melbourne racing carnival but her very nothing little white dress certainly fell short of my expectations. Now speaking of things being short what did you think of that hemline? Four inches above the beautiful knees.
>
> (*Daily Mirror*, 1 November 1965)

(Tabberer then went on to make the *faux pas* of her fashion career when she suggested that the mini-skirt would never catch on.)

It is the very nothingness of that little white dress which speaks so much to that particular occasion. It is not a 'flutter of champagne chiffon' but a plain cotton, the cut of the dress even more simple than the plainest empire-line. There are no sleeves and the beaded motif becomes the jewellery absent from the rest of her body.

This fashion image as a representation of fashion is 'making a statement'. And here it is not so great a hop to cross from Quintilian's 'ornament of style' to Foucault to describe what we mean by a fashion 'statement'. For Foucault any statement belongs to a discursive formation, by which it is also defined (Sheridan 1980: 100). As a 'fashion statement', The Shrimp's dress can only appear within an associated field:

> a complex made up of all the other formulations among which the statement appears and forms one element . . . and this network embraces not only an immediate, apparent context, but also those other past formulations to which it refers, if even implicitly, and those future formulations that it makes possible.
>
> (Sheridan 1980: 100)

The appearance of The Shrimp wearing that simple shift on Derby day cannot be read alone, it has to be understood in terms of a particular woman on a particular occasion, including the conditions making possible that particular dress and that particular hairstyle. And why was the audience so receptive to a young fashionable woman?

Her dress, on that occasion, was to be read for all the things it was not. The dress worn on another occasion, and therefore under new circumstances, would constitute a different statement. This was the case on Oaks day, but this time not only the occasion changed but the fashion statement changed; the same little, white, shift dress was worn with a jacket and stockings; it became acceptable.

The Shrimp's dress forms a part of a discursive formation. To put it more simply, this means an intertextuality which has the characteristics of constantly rearticulating subjectivity and objectivity. An example of this using a fashion description would be: The dress is unrestrained, and so is she, the dress is pure white, she is natural to the core, the dress is cool and bare, there is a nakedness to her image, the dress has simple lines, she has no contrived elegance, the dress flows from the figure, her shape can take it.

But this is sounding like a structuralist semiotic reading with the signifiers 'natural', 'unrestrained', 'simplicity' producing themselves against an array of implied opposites such as 'constraint', 'convention', etc. What we had intended with that description was to detail how subjectivity can meet objectivity through those discourses such as sexuality, health, youth, nature and transgression of morals. The Shrimp's sexuality and morality are articulated through a breaking of social codes and rules by wearing that type of fashion; the nakedness of her body, the lack of stockings, etc. And her beauty does not just indicate her health but sets up new definitions of what is possible in terms of beauty and even in terms of how a body should look in relation to a particular fashion.

Rhetorical analysis of images would try to combine a reading of those socially and historically determined discourses such as sexuality, health, beauty, morality with a more social semiotic or textual account. So, while the rhetoric of an image might be addressing something in a new form, it must still, if it is to be received at all, be recognizable as a mobilization of discourses around a particular image. These rhetorical characteristics can then be identified using not the structural semiotic account of the early Barthes but a more *social* semiotic, which would take into consideration not a fixed account attributed to the text itself but an analysis of the text and its effects in the production of meaning (Hodge and Kress 1988: 12). It is the specific discourses which construct the meaning around an image, which enable a particular audience to be addressed, and in the case of Jean Shrimpton, that audience was divided.

SCANDALIZED AND SEDUCED: THAT MOMENT CALLED THE 1960s

How does this 'fashion statement' articulate itself in such a way that it can divide an audience by seducing one section of it, while scandalizing the other?

Jean Shrimpton did not just wear a dress; she created an event. And if we were to elaborate Melbourne Cup popular history, the Governor General of Australia, Sir John Kerr, was not just drunk; he also created an event. Many people have disgraced themselves at the Melbourne Cup and there have been times before when fashions have shocked the racing crowd. But these two events in particular became moments in history. Not just the powerful subjectivities of the individuals concerned produced the events; they were also powerful in the sense that they left a remainder to be gathered up. They became *overcoded* not just as texts, but as text/images, subjects/objects. They became 'rare' statements, now constantly repeatable in the very contexts where the makers of rhetoric argue for what needs to be known, historically, about the 1960s, and how that story needs to be told. So for a Stanley Fish, The Shrimp might be like 'the force that pulls us away from the centre and into its own world of ever-shifting shapes and shimmering surfaces' (Fish 1990: 206).

Juxtaposition is important in the reading of this image as transgressive and unique. Juxtaposition is an old merchandizing technique – the placing of dissimilar objects alongside each other such that any inerest an item might intrinsically lack can often be solved by an unexpected juxtaposition (see Sennett 1977 for more about retail practices in the mid-1900s). Different *contexts* are juxtaposed in this image as intertext, or, to put it another way, the image mobilizes adjacent discourses. The Shrimp has no hat and gloves; she is wearing no jewellery except for a man's watch; her legs and shoulders are so bare; her limbs look so long; her hair is uncoiffured; her stance is so relaxed compared with the women behind her who appear armed with their gloves and glares, hats and hairdos, earrings and pearls, collars and sleeves. She is on her own, central to the image, while the other women are clustered together. She looks different but she deviates. Here we use the notion of deviancy to mean a departure from a recognized norm. It is a deviancy which appealed to some and appalled others. A closer look at the photograph and one can see the amused looks of the younger women compared to the glares and frowns of the older contingent. It is a moment which we can, as history has, fetishize as the stylistic take-over of one generation from another.

Maggie Tabberer remembers the shock of the event because it was so totally unexpected (from an interview with Maggie Tabberer, August 1990). This may seem surprising given the publicity and excitement which preceded the arrival of the young English model who had that year been named 'The Face'. She had been asked to Australia to publicize the Melbourne Cup Carnival and to present the awards at the Fashions in the Field contest. Prior to her arrival Jean Shrimpton had said that she knew very little about the Melbourne Cup. She was expected to present the final prizes in categories which included the most elegant hat section, ensembles under 50 guineas and ensembles over 50 guineas. Her appearance in a 3 guinea dress and not the slightest gesture of a hat put her eligibility low in the stakes of those categories.

The *Australian Woman's Day*, 8 November 1965, had Jean Shrimpton on the front cover with the lead article 'The report: the Bishop v. the Archbishop on the pill'. Not only did the 1960s introduce us to Jean Shrimpton, who was that subtle combination of the gamine looks of Audrey Hepburn ('The Face' of the 1950s) combined with the sexuality of Brigitte Bardot, but it was an era of liberation regarding contraception and the ways and places one could discuss sex. Responding to a comment that her appeal lay in a combination of sex and the little-girl look, she said that it was not really sex: 'It's just a breeze coming in the window that is vaguely sexual, that's all' (*Mirror*, 17 August 1965).

But sexuality was used by The Shrimp as part of her version of beauty to determine a relationship with the camera, the fashion press and the public. There was, at the time, the beginnings of flamboyant sexualized behaviour of model and photographer in the studio (or at least it came to be *represented* that way, and this behaviour was partly technologically determined by the appearance of fast, portable cameras): she had an important relationship with David Bailey, the Cockney photographer who became the subject of Antonioni's film *Blow Up*. He saw in her a new look which combined youth, elegance, sophistication and sexuality. And Bailey was the first to admit it was not the clothes that he wanted to photograph. Indeed he was the one who said, 'Well, a frock's a frock isn't it?' (Mulvagh 1988: 240).

Not only was it a matter of sexuality; both Bailey and The Shrimp represented a different class to the fashion world. Coming from a lower-middle-class background, Jean Shrimpton described her look as 'not beatnik and not classical exactly – but more beatnik than classical' (Harrison and Bailey 1983: 30). She did not have that unattainable look of Audrey Hepburn; she was the 'real thing' for a younger audience.

It was the period of time that Diana Vreeland, the editor of American *Vogue*, called a 'youth-quake'. What was fashionable was youth. In America the young Jackie Kennedy set a new standard by being unashamedly fashionable, not just 'well dressed'. Hers was top-to-toe fashion – with her pill-box hats, bouffant hairdo, Chanel-style suits – right down to the simple slip-on shoes.

Young people who were 'in' had to have the 'switched-on look'. It became an expected part of youth that they should be fashionable, and that fashion was not for just a special occasion; it was to be worn on the street, on the bus, and it did not have to be expensive. This fashion democracy was certainly the pioneering philosophy behind Bazaar, the clothes boutique which Mary Quant set up in Kings Road, Chelsea, in 1965.

The Shrimp created not a gentle breeze, but a gale force in the Australian fashion climate. By breaking convention at a sacred event, she scandalized those who believed in those conventions. One Toorak matron echoed what was obviously the thought of others: 'I'm afraid this girl and what she stands for will never take on in Melbourne' (*Sun*, 2 November 1965).

Paris responded to the conservatism of Melbourne society (and there were other similar reactions from overseas) through the voice of Yves St Laurent: 'It is women like those who are an obstacle to any progress in fashion. I am all against the convention that certain types of function demand certain types of dresses' (*Sun*, 10 November 1965). Yves St Laurent may have had a vague idea about the provincial conservatism of the Victorian Racing Club. After all, it was going to take them another twenty years before gender segregation was stopped in the members' area of the club.

While those scandalized feared the breaking of rigid society codes, they were also in awe of the actual dress. How could one sit down properly? (And there is a photograph of The Shrimp demonstrating how it can be done; sitting on the tailboard of a station wagon, sipping champagne.) What sort of underwear could be worn? It was an entirely different matter for those who were seduced by this event. The possibility of not having to wear stockings (and anyway weren't there these new things called tights?), the comfort of a more natural style of underwear (hadn't someone invented the 'no-bra bra'?) and the relief of not having to worry about keeping gloves to a pair and snowy white, were desperately appealing for many young women.

The rhetoric of the image seduced one audience to be something different and it scandalized the other section to try to hold on to what they were before. The rhetoric in this instance can be seen as an attempt to disturb the field by upsetting or traversing the range of choices. There is nothing so unusual about this; that is what rhetoric otherwise coined the 'modern art of everyday expression' is all about (Certeau 1988: 101).

One can read fashion as rhetoric in its attempts to produce a repertoire of the different ways in which one can be original. Even when it is not being particularly original, rhetoric is a way of inscribing desire. Setting the past against the future, it overturns time; the fashion image is always an image of becoming. It does not seem to matter in these 'postmodern times' that things can be worn and presented simultaneously – a 1960s' mini-skirt with a 1970s' black leather jacket. With postmodernism (one could argue) fashion has become more circular and spatial than with modernism, which pursued the new along a linear time-line, with each new object overturning the last.[2]

But these questions are strictly academic – they turn around the ways of thinking about fashion. These ways of thinking are not given by the object, but by how it is read – then and now. The Shrimpton 'moment' had a particular rhetorical structure of address. It split an audience and marked the moment for a rebellious youth generation to flow into a field of becoming which was marked by transgression and liberation, arguably central notions in the rhetoric of 1960s' modernism.

In its appearance here and now other considerations apply. Over twenty years later, history or cultural studies can start to see the moment as significant – in women's history and in fashion history. Fashion is a field which notoriously lacks everyday *critical* discourses. We have been trying to talk fashion without resorting to the liberatory 'semiotic delinquency' of Hebdige and the punks, or to the establishment conspiracies of Diana Vreeland's critics. We are dealing with a more diffuse middle ground of fashion, and a particular historical moment which seems to relate only to its own singularities. Here, it seems, there is no 'maxi theory' to cover a range of such events – the theory we have been working with to cover this story is minimal and rhetorical, and for this reason we have had to keep it relatively short.

NOTES

1 But see Hodge and Kress (1988) and Kress and van Leeuwen (1991).
2 'It seems that modernity simultaneously sets into motion a linear time, which is that of technical progress of production and history, and a cyclical time, which is that of fashion' (Baudrillard, quoted in Pefanis 1991: 72).

Bibliography

Adams, H. (ed.) (1971) *Critical Theory Since Plato*, New York: Harcourt Brace Jovanovich.

Alexander, R.J. (1984) *Primary Teaching*, London: Holt, Rinehart & Winston.

Allott, M. (1970) *Wuthering Heights: A Casebook*, Basingstoke: Macmillan.

Andrews, R. (ed.) (1989) *Narrative and Argument*, Milton Keynes: Open University Press.

―――― (1991a) *The Problem with Poetry*, Buckingham: Open University Press.

―――― (1991b) 'Rhetoric and composition', *Typereader* 6, Geelong: Centre for Studies in Literary Education, Deakin University.

Apple, M. (1979) *Ideology and Curriculum*, London: Routledge & Kegan Paul.

Applebee, A.N., Langer, J.A. and Mullis, I.V.S. (1986) *The Writing Report Card Writing Achievement in American Schools*, Princeton, NJ: The National Assessment of Educational Progress.

Aristotle (1924) *Rhetoric*, trans. W.R. Roberts; *De Poetica*, trans. I. Bywater, in *Works*, vol. 11, Oxford: Oxford University Press.

―――― (1926) *The 'Art' of Rhetoric*, trans. J.H. Freese, London: Heinemann.

Aronowitz, S. and Giroux, H. (1991) *Postmodern Education: Politics, Culture and Social Criticism*, Minneapolis: University of Minnesota Press.

Baker, E. (1937) *The History of the English Novel*, 10 vols, London: H.F. & G. Witherby, vol. VIII.

Bakhtin, M.M. (1981) *The Dialogic Imagination*, ed. M. Holquist, trans. C. Emerson and M. Holquist, Austin, Tex.: University of Texas Press.

Baldick, C. (1983) *The Social Mission of English Criticism*, Oxford: Clarendon Press.

―――― (1987) *In Frankenstein's Shadow: Myth, Monstrosity and Nineteenth-Century Writing*, Oxford: Clarendon Press.

Baldwin, C.S. (1989) *Ancient Rhetoric and Poetic*, Gloucester, Mass.: Peter Smith.

Ball, S. (1990) 'Management as moral technology: a Luddite analysis', in S. Ball (ed.) *Foucault and Education*, London: Routledge.

Bambrough, R. (1974) 'Conflict and the scope of reason', University of Hull, St John's College Lecture.

_____ (1975) 'Comment: ideology and the modes of explanation', in S. Korner (ed.) *Explanation*, Oxford: Basil Blackwell.

Barnes, D., Britton, J. and Rosen, H. (1969) *Language, the Learner and the School*, Harmondsworth: Penguin.

Barthes, R. (1966) 'Introduction to the structural analysis of narratives', Birmingham: University of Birmingham, Centre for Contemporary Cultural Studies.

_____ (1975) *The Pleasure of the Text*, trans. R. Miller, New York: Hill & Wang.

_____ (1977) 'Rhetoric of the image', in S. Heath (ed.) *Image, Music, Text*, London: Fontana.

_____ (1985) *The Fashion System*, trans. M. Ward and R. Howard, London: Jonathan Cape.

Basseches, M. (1984) *Dialectical Thinking and Adult Development*, Norwood, New Jersey: Ablex Publishing.

Bereiter, C. (1980) 'Development in writing', in L.W. Gregg and E.R. Steinberg (eds) *Cognitive Processes in Writing*, Hillsdale, NJ: Lawrence Erlbaum.

Bergonzi, B. (1990) *Exploding English: Criticism, Theory, Culture*, Oxford: Clarendon Press.

Berkenkotter, C. (1981) 'Understanding a writer's awareness of audience', *College Composition and Communication* 32: 388–99.

Berlin, J.A. (1985) 'Rhetoric and poetics in the English department: our nineteenth-century inheritance', *College English* 44: 521–33.

_____ (1987) *Rhetoric and Reality: Writing Instruction in American Colleges, 1900–1985*, Carbondale, Ill.: Southern Illinois University Press.

_____ (1991) 'Rhetoric, poetic, and culture: contested boundaries in English studies', in R. Bullock and J. Trimbur (eds) *The Politics of Writing Instruction: Postsecondary*, Upper Montclair, NJ: Boynton/Cook.

Berrill, D.P. (1990a) 'What exposition has to do with argument: argumentative writing of sixteen-year-olds', *English in Education*, 24(1): 77–92.

_____ (1990b) 'The development of written argument at eleven, sixteen and twenty-two years of age', unpublished doctoral dissertation, University of East Anglia.

_____ (1991) 'Metaphors of literacy: argument is war – but should it be?' Paper presented at the International Language and Literacy Convention, Norwich.

Biggs, J.B. and Collis, K.F. (1982) *Evaluating the Quality of Learning: The SOLO Taxonomy*, New York: Academic Press.

Bineham, J.L. (1990) 'The Cartesian anxiety in epistemic rhetoric: an assessment of the literature', *Philosophy and Rhetoric* 23(1): 43–62.

Black, P.S. (1990) 'Decor for the body: ways of talking mainstream fashion', unpublished paper.

Blegvad, E. (1978) *Burnie's Hill*, London: Fontana.

Bloom, H. (1975) *A Map of Misreading*, Oxford: Oxford University Press.

Booth, W. (1961) *The Rhetoric of Fiction*, Chicago: University of Chicago Press.

Bottery, M. (1988) 'Educational management: an ethical critique', *Oxford Review of Education* 14(3).

Brantlinger, P. (1990) *Crusoe's Footprints: Cultural Studies in Britain and America*, New York: Routledge.

Brémond, C. (1973) *Logique du récit*, Paris: Editions du Seuil.

Britton, J., Burgess, T., Martin, N., McLeod, A. and Rosen, H. (1975) *The Development of Writing Abilities (11–18)*, London: Macmillan Educational.

Brontë, E. (1965) *Wuthering Heights*, Harmondsworth: Penguin.

Burke, K. (1978) 'Rhetoric, poetics, and philosophy', in D.M. Burks (ed.) *Rhetoric, Philosophy and Literature: An Exploration*, West Lafayette, Ind.: Purdue University Press.

Butler, D. (1991) *My Brown Bear Barney*, London: Hodder & Stoughton.

Calkins, L.McC. (1986) *The Art of Teaching Writing*, Portsmouth, NH: Heinemann.

Campbell, R. (1989) *Oh Dear*, London: Campbell Blackie.

Caro, R. (1974) *The Power Broker: Robert Moses and the Fall of New York*, New York: Alfred A. Knopf.

Cecil, Lord D. (1934) 'Emily Brontë and *Wuthering Heights*', in *Early Victorian Novelists*, London: Constable.

Certeau, M. de (1988) *The Practice of Everyday Life*, trans. S. Rendall, Berkeley: University of California Press.

Chapman, G. *et al.* (1989) *Monty Python's Flying Circus: Just the Words*, vol. 1, London: Methuen.

Cicero (1954) *Ad Herennium* (trans. H. Caplan), London: Heinemann.

Clarke, S. (1984) 'An area of neglect', *English in Education* 18(2): 67–73.

Clayton, J. (1987) *Romantic Vision and the Novel*, Cambridge: Cambridge University Press.

Connor, U. (1990) 'Linguistic/rhetorical measures for international persuasive student writing', *Research in the Teaching of English* 24(1): 67–87.

Consigny, S. (1989) 'Dialectical, rhetorical, and Aristotelian rhetoric', *Philosophy and Rhetoric* 22(4): 281–7.

Cook, J. *et al.* (1980) *Writing: An Educational Perspective*, Norwood, SA: Australian Association for the Teaching of English.

Culler, J. (1975) *Structuralist Poetics: Structuralism, Linguistics and the Study of Literature*, London: Routledge & Kegan Paul.

―――― (1982) *On Deconstruction*, Ithaca, NY: Cornell University Press.

Davison, J. (1937) *Wuthering Heights: A Play from the Novel by Emily Brontë*, London: Frederick Muller.

Derrida, J. (1976) *Of Grammatology*, trans. G. Spivak, Baltimore, Md: Johns Hopkins University Press.

―――― (1978) *Writing and Difference*, trans. A. Bass, London: Routledge & Kegan Paul.

Dixon, John (1991) *A Schooling in English*, Buckingham: Open University Press.

Dixon, J. and Stratta, L. (1986a) *Writing Narrative – and Beyond*, Ottawa: CCTE Publications.

―――― (1986b) 'Argument and the teaching of English', in A. Wilkinson (ed.) *The Writing of Writing*, Milton Keynes: Open University Press.

Dixon, P. (1971) *Rhetoric*, London: Methuen.

Donaldson, M. (1978) *Children's Minds*, London: Fontana.

Drotner, K. (1983) 'Schoolgirls, madcaps, and air aces: English girls and their magazine reading between the wars', *Feminist Studies* 9(1).

Eagleton, T. (1982) 'The end of criticism', *English in Education* 16(1).

—— (1983) *Literary Theory*, Oxford: Blackwell.

—— (1991) 'The enemy within', *NATE News*: 5–7.

Eco, U. (1979) *The Role of the Reader*, Bloomington: Indiana University Press.

—— (1984) '*Casablanca*: cult movies and intertextual collage', in D. Lodge (ed.) (1988) *Modern Criticism and Theory*, London: Longman.

Edel, A. (1967) 'Reflections on the concept of ideology', *Praxis* 4.

Elbow, P. (1973) *Writing Without Teachers*, London: Oxford University Press.

Fairclough, N. (1989) *Language and Power*, London: Longman.

Fish, S. (1980) *Is There a Text in This Class?* Cambridge, Mass.: Harvard University Press.

—— (1990) 'Rhetoric', in F. Lentricchia and T. McLaughlin (eds) *Critical Terms for Literary Study*, Chicago: University of Chicago Press.

Flavell, J.H. (1963) *The Developmental Psychology of Jean Piaget*, Princeton, NJ: Van Nostrand.

Foucault, M. (1970) *The Order of Things*, London: Tavistock.

Fox, C. (1989a) 'Children thinking through story', *English in Education* 23(2).

—— (1989b) 'Divine dialogues', in R. Andrews (ed.) *Narrative and Argument*, Milton Keynes: Open University Press.

—— (1990) 'The genesis of argument in narrative discourse', *English in Education* 24(1).

Freedman, A. and Pringle, I. (1984) 'Why students can't write arguments', *English in Education* 18(2).

—— (1985) *A Comparative Study of Writing Abilities in Two Modes at the Grade 5, 8 and 12 Levels*, Toronto: Ministry of Education.

Gates, R.L. (1988) 'Causality, community, and the canons of reasoning: classical rhetoric and writing across the curriculum', *Journal of Advanced Composition* 8(1–2): 137–45.

Geuss, R. (1982) *The Idea of a Critical Theory*, Cambridge: Cambridge University Press.

Gibson, R. (1986–92) *Shakespeare and Schools*, Cambridge: Cambridge Institute of Education.

—— (1992) *Romeo and Juliet*, Cambridge: Cambridge University Press.

Gibson, W. (1950) 'Authors, speakers, readers and mock readers', *College English* 11: 265–9.

Gilbert, P. (1987) 'Post reader-response: the deconstructive critique', in B. Corcoran and E. Evans (eds) *Readers, Texts, Teachers*, Upper Montclair, NJ: Boynton/Cook.

—— (1989) *Writing, Schooling and Deconstruction: From Voice to Text in the Classroom*, London: Routledge.

—— (1991) 'Writing pedagogy: personal voices, truth telling and "real" texts', in A. Luke and C.D. Baker (eds) *Towards a Critical Sociology of Reading: Papers of the 12th World Congress of Reading*, Amsterdam: John Benjamins.

Gilbert, P. and Taylor, S. (1991) *Fashioning the Feminine: Girls, Popular Culture and Schooling*, Sydney: Allen & Unwin.

Gorman, T.P., White, J., Brooks, C., MacLure, M. and Kispal, A. (1988) *A Review of Language Monitoring 1979–1983*, London: Assessment of Performance Unit, HMSO.

Gormley, M. (1990) 'Cartoon strip', *Hardwords* 1.

Graves, D. (1982) *Writing: Children and Teachers at Work*, London: Heinemann.

—— (1983) *Writing: Teachers and Children at Work*, Exeter, NH: Heinemann Educational.

Gretz, S. (1986) *Teddy Bears 1 to 10*, London: Blackie.

Grice, H.P. (1975) 'Logic and conversation', in P. Cole and J.L. Morgan (eds) *Syntax and Semantics*, vol. III: *Speech Acts*, New York: Academic Press.

Grimaldi, W.M.A. (1972) *Studies in the Philosophy of Aristotle's Rhetoric*, Wiesbaden: Franz Steiner Verlag.

Gross, J. (ed.) (1991) *The Oxford Book of Essays*, Oxford: Oxford University Press.

Habermas, J. (1971) *Toward a Rational Society*, London: Heinemann.

Hall, S. (1977) 'The hinterland of science: ideology and the "sociology of knowledge" ', in *On Ideology*, Birmingham: University of Birmingham Centre for Contemporary Cultural Studies.

Harrison, B. (1983) *Learning Through Writing*, London: NFER-Nelson.

Harrison, M. and Bailey, D. (1983) *Black and White Memories: Photographs 1948–1969*, London: Dent.

Hartnett, A. and Naish, M. (1977) 'Educational theory: bromide and barmecide', *Journal of Further and Higher Education* 1(3).

Hatfield, C.W. (ed.) (1941) *The Complete Poems of Emily Jane Brontë*, New York: Columbia University Press.

Hawkes, T. (1983) 'Skull caps' (review of Eagleton's *Literary Theory*), *New Statesman*, 3 June 1983.

Hawkins, H. (1990) *Classics and Trash*, Hemel Hempstead: Harvester.

Hayes, S. and Craig, H. (1989) *This is the Bear*, London: Walker Books.

Hays, J.N. (1988) 'Socio-cognitive development and argumentative writing: issues and implications from one research project', *Journal of Basic Writing* 7(2): 42–67.

—— (forthcoming) 'Intellectual parenting and a development feminist pedagogy of writing', in J. Emig and L. Phelps (eds) Modern Language Association.

Hays, J.N., Brandt, L.M. and Chantry, K.H. (1988) 'The impact of friendly and hostile audience on the argumentative writing of high school and college students', *Research in the Teaching of English* 22(4): 391–416.

Hebdige, D. (1979) *Subculture: The Meaning of Style*, London: Methuen.

Henriques, J. *et al.* (1984) *Changing the Subject*, London: Methuen.

Hernadi, P. (1990) *The Interpretation of Rhetoric and the Rhetoric of Interpretation*, Durham, SC: Duke University Press.

Hesse, D. (forthcoming) 'The recent rise of "literary nonfiction": a cautionary assay', *Journal of Advanced Composition*.

Hodge, R. and Kress, G. (1988) *Social Semiotics*, Cambridge: Polity Press.

Homer (1963) *The Odyssey*, trans. R. Fitzgerald, New York: Doubleday.

House, E.R. (1980) *Evaluating with Validity*, London: Sage.

Hutchins, P. (1973) *Goodnight Owl!* London: Bodley Head.

—— (1976) *Don't Forget the Bacon*, London: Bodley Head.

Hymes, D. (1972) 'Toward ethnographies of communication: the analysis of communicative events', in P.P. Giglioli (ed.) *Language and Social Context*, Harmondsworth: Penguin.

Inglis, F. (1985) *The Management of Ignorance*, Oxford: Basil Blackwell.

Iser, W. (1972) 'The reading process: a phenomenological approach', in D. Lodge (ed.) (1988) *Modern Criticism and Theory*, London: Longman.

—— (1978) *The Act of Reading: A Theory of Aesthetic Response*, Baltimore, Md: Johns Hopkins University Press.

Johnson, N. and Mandler, J. (1980) 'A tale of two structures', *Poetics* 9: 51–86.

Jones, N. (1991) 'A map of reading', in P. Dougill (ed.) *Developing English*, Buckingham: Open University Press.

Joseph, Sister M. (1947) *Shakespeare's Use of the Arts of Language*, New York: Columbia University Press.

Kauffman, C. (1981) 'Poetic as argument', *Quarterly Journal of Speech* 67(4): 407–15.

Keith, G. (1991) 'Language study at key stage 3', in R. Carter (ed.) *Knowledge About Language and the Curriculum*, London: Hodder & Stoughton.

Kinneavy, J.L. (1985) 'Deconstructing the rhetoric/poetic distinction: the Platonizing of rhetoric and literature', *Dieciocho* 8(1): 70–7.

Kintgen, E. (1983) *The Perception of Poetry*, Bloomington: Indiana University Press.

Knoblauch, C.H. and Brannon, L. (1984) *Rhetorical Traditions and the Teaching of Writing*, Upper Montclair, NJ: Boynton/Cook.

Kolakowski, L. (1980) 'Why an ideology is always right', in M. Cranston and P. Mair (eds) *Ideology and Politics*, European University Institute, Sijthoff Alphen Aandenrijn.

Kress, G. (1985) *Linguistic Processes in Sociocultural Practice*, Geelong: Deakin University Press.

—— (1989) 'Texture and meaning', in R. Andrews (ed.) *Narrative and Argument*, Milton Keynes: Open University Press.

Kress, G. and van Leeuwen, T. (1991) *Reading Images*, Geelong: Deakin University Press.

Kroll, B.M. (1984) 'Writing for readers: three perspectives on audience', *College Composition and Communication* 355(2): 172–85.

Kuhn, A. (1990) [1982] *Women's Pictures: Feminism and Cinema*, London: Pandora Press.

Labov, W. and Waletsky, J. (1967) 'Narrative analysis: oral versions of personal experience', in J. Helm (ed.) *Essays of the Verbal and Visual Arts*, Seattle: University of Washington Press.

Lakoff, G. and Johnson, M. (1980) *Metaphors We Live By*, Chicago: University of Chicago Press.

Lamb, C.E. (1991) 'Beyond argument in feminist composition', *College Composition and Communication* 4(1): 11–24.

Lettis, R. and Morris, W.E. (eds) (1961) *A Wuthering Heights Handbook*, New York: The Odyssey Press.

Lloyd-Jones, R. and Lunsford, A.A. (1989) *The English Coalition Confer-ence: Democracy through Language*, Urbana, Ill.: National Council of Teachers of English.

Macrorie, K. (1980) *Searching Writing*, Rochelle Park, NJ: Hayden.

Mandler, J. and Johnson, N. (1977) 'Remembrance of things parsed: story structure and recall', *Cognitive Psychology* 9: 111–51.

Martin, B. (1971) 'Progressive education *versus* the working class', *Critical Quarterly* 13(4).

Martin, B. Jr (1986) *Brown Bear, Brown Bear, What Do You See?* London: Picture Lions.

Martin, W. (1986) *Recent Theories of Narrative*, Ithaca, NY: Cornell University Press.

Matthews, J.T. (1985) 'Framing in *Wuthering Heights*', *Texas Studies in Literature and Language* XXVII.

Maybin, J. (1991) 'Children's informal talk and the construction of meaning', *English in Education* 25(2).

Meek, M. (1988) 'How texts teach what readers learn', in M. Lightfoot and N. Martin (eds) *The Word for Teaching is Learning*, London: Heinemann.

Mellor, B. (1987) *Reading Stories*, Scarborough, WA: Chalkface Press.

—— (1989) *Reading Hamlet*, Scarborough, WA: Chalkface Press.

Merton, R.K. (1949) *Social Theory and Social Structure*, New York: Free Press.

Michael, B. and Jackson, B. (1990) *The Foundations of Writing, parts 1 and 2, Teachers' Handbook*, Glasgow: Jordanhill College Publications.

Michael, B. and Michael, M. (1990) *Young Writers Look At . . . Wind, Water, Places to Go*, Glasgow: Jordanhill College Publications.

Miller, D. (1972) 'Ideology and the problem of false consciousness', *Political Studies* 20.

Mitchell, J. (1984) *Women: The Longest Revolution*, London: Virago.

Moffett, J. (1968) *Teaching the Universe of Discourse*, Boston: Houghton Mifflin.

—— (1981) *Active Voice*, Upper Montclair, NJ: Boynton/Cook.

Moi, T. (ed.) (1986) *The Kristeva Reader*, Oxford: Blackwell.

Morgan, G. (1989) 'Sharing the vision', in C. Riches and C. Morgan (eds) *Human Resource Management*, Milton Keynes: Open University Press.

Mulvagh, J. (1988) *Vogue History of 20th Century Fashion*, London: Viking.

Murray, D. (1982) *Learning by Teaching*, Upper Montclair, NJ: Boynton/Cook.

—— (1991) 'Layering: writing the fully developed text', workshop presented at the First National Writing Conference, Winnipeg, Canada.

Nadeau, R. (1952) 'The Progymnasmata of Aphthonius', in *Speech Monographs*, 19, pp. 264–85.

Naish, M., Hartnett, A. and Finlayson, D. (1976) 'Ideological documents in education: some suggestions towards a definition', in A. Hartnett and M. Naish (eds) *Theory and the Practice of Education*, vol. II, London: Heinemann.

Nash, W. (1980) *Designs in Prose*, London: Longman.

North West Educational Management Centre (1990) 'The effective middle manager', course run for Wirral LEA, March 1990.

Ovens, J. (1989) *Talk About Poetry*, Dundee: SCCC Publications.

Pattison, S. (1991) 'Strange theology of management', *Guardian*, 27 May 1991.

Pavel, T. (1986) *Fictional Worlds*, Cambridge, Mass.: Harvard University Press.

Peel, E.A. (1971) *The Nature of Adolescent Judgement*, London: Staples.

Pefanis, J. (1991) *Heterology and the Postmodern*, Durham, SC: Duke University Press.

Perry, W.G. (1970) *Forms of Intellectual and Ethical Development in the College Years: A Scheme*, New York: Holt, Reinhart & Winston.

Pratt, M.L. (1977) *Toward a Speech Act Theory of Literary Discourse*, Bloomington: Indiana University Press.

Pringle, I. and Freedman, A. (1985) *A Comparative Study of Writing Abilities in Two Modes at the Grade 5, 8 and 12 Levels*, Toronto: Ontario Ministry of Education.

Propp, V. (1968) *Morphology of the Folktale* (American Folklore Society Bibliographical and Special Services No. 9) 2nd edn., Austin: University of Texas Press.

Quintilian (1922) *The Institutio Oratoria of Quintilian*, vol. IV, trans. H.E. Butler, London: Heinemann.

Reid, I. (ed.) (1986) *The Place of Genre in Learning: Current Debates*, Geelong: Deakin University Press.

Riches, C. and Morgan, C. (eds) (1989) *Human Resource Management in Education*, Milton Keynes: Open University Press.

Ricoeur, P. (1984) *Time and Narrative*, vol. 1, Chicago: University of Chicago Press.

Ritchie, J.S. (1989) 'Beginning writers: diverse voices and individual identity', *College Composition and Communication* 40(2): 152–74.

Ross, A. (1989) *The Root of the Matter*, Edinburgh: Mainstream.

Rougemont, D. de (1983) *Love in the Western World*, Princeton, NJ: Princeton University Press.

Rubin, D.L., Piche, G.L., Michlin, M.L. and Johnson, F.L. (1984) 'Social cognitive ability as a predictor of the quality of fourth-graders' written narratives', in R. Beach and L. Bridwell (eds) *New Directions in Composition Research*, New York: Guilford Press.

Rumelhart, D. (1975) 'Notes on a schema for stories', in D.G. Bobrow and A. Collins (eds) *Representation and Understanding*, New York: Academic Press.

Sampson, G. (1921) *English for the English*, Cambridge: Cambridge University Press.

Scruton, R. (1987) 'Expressionist education', *Oxford Review of Education* 13(1).

Sennett, R. (1977) *The Fall of Public Man*, Cambridge: Cambridge University Press.

Sheeran, Y. and Barnes, D. (1991) *School Writing*, Buckingham: Open University Press.

Sheridan, A. (1980) *The Will to Truth*, London: Tavistock.

Silverman, D. (1987) *Selling Culture: Bloomingdale's, Diana Vreeland and the New Aristocracy of Taste in Reagan's America*, New York: Pantheon Books.

Simon, R. (1984) 'Signposts for a critical pedagogy: a review of Henry Giroux's *Theory and Resistance in Education*', *Education Theory* 34(2).

Skinner, Q. (1980) 'Language and social change', in L. Michaels and C. Ricks (eds) *The State of the Language*, Berkeley: University of California Press.

Slevin, J. (1988) 'Genre theory, academic discourse, and writing within disciplines', in L.Z. Smith (ed.) *Audits of Meaning*, Portsmouth, NH: Boynton/Cook.

Smith, B.H. (1978) *On the Margins of Discourse*, Chicago: University of Chicago Press.

Squibb, P.G. (1977) 'Some notes towards the analysis of the social constructions of the "less able" or "backward" child', *Journal of Further and Higher Education* 1(3).

Stein, M.L. and Glenn, C.G. (1979) 'The role of structural varieties in children's recall of simple stories', paper presented to the Society for Research in Child Development, New Orleans.

Stoppard, T. (1975) *Travesties*, London: Faber.

Stratta, L. and Dixon, J. (1987) 'Writing about literature: monitoring and assessment', in B. Corcoran and E. Evans (eds) *Readers, Texts, Teachers*, Upper Montclair, NJ: Boynton/Cook.

—— (1992) 'Genre theory: what does it have to offer?' *English in Education* 26(2).

Summers, A. (1991) 'Unofficial stories in the classroom', *English in Education* 25(2): 24–31.

Taylor, M. (1991) 'Books in the classroom and "knowledge about language" ', in R. Carter (ed.) *Knowledge about Language and the Curriculum*, London: Hodder & Stoughton.

Terman, L. and Merrill, M. (1937) *Measuring Intelligence*, London: Harrap.

Thompson, J.B. (1984) *Studies in the Theory of Ideology*, Cambridge: Polity Press.

Urquhart, J. (1990) *Changing Heaven*, London: Hodder & Stoughton.

Vickers, B. (1988) *In Defence of Rhetoric*, Oxford: Clarendon Press.

Vygotsky, L.S. (1962) (1986) *Thought and Language*, Cambridge, Mass.: MIT Press.

Wagner, G. (1975) *The Novel and Cinema*, London: Associated University Presses.

Welch, K.E. (1990) *The Contemporary Reception of Classical Rhetoric: Appropriations of Ancient Discourse*, Hillsdale, NJ: Lawrence Erlbaum Associates.

Wells, G. (1989) *The Meaning Makers*, London: Hodder & Stoughton.

Wilkinson, A. (1989) 'Our first great conversationalists', *English in Education* 23(2).

—— (1990) 'Argument as a primary act of mind', *English in Education* 24(1).

Wilkinson, A., Davies, A. and Berrill, D. (1990) *Spoken English Illuminated*, Milton Keynes: Open University Press.

Wilkinson, A., Barnsley, G., Hanna, P. and Swan, M. (1980) *Assessing Language Development*, Oxford: Oxford University Press.

Williams, R. (1976) *Keywords*, London: Croom Helm.

Wilson, E. (1985) *Adorned in Dreams: Fashion and Modernity*, London: Virago.

Wilson, P.S. (1969) 'Child-centred education', in *Philosophy of Education Society of Great Britain, Proceedings of the Annual Conference*.

Winterowd, W.R. (1968) *Rhetoric: A Synthesis*, New York: Holt, Reinhart & Winston.

Wittgenstein, L. (1958) *Philosophical Investigations*, Oxford: Basil Blackwell.

Young, P. and Tyre, C. (1989) *Dyslexia or Illiteracy? Realising the Right to Read*, Milton Keynes: Open University Press.

Index

Ad Herennium 126
advertisements 129
Alexander, R. J. 46
Allais, A. 144–5, 148
antithesis 160, 162–3
argumentation 8–9, 81–101, 116–28
Aristotle 4, 9, 19ff., 82, 124, 126
assertion 93–4
audience 67ff., 82, 85, 98

Bakhtin, M. M. 6–9, 180
Bambrough, R. 44
Barnes, D. 8
Barthes, R. 150, 212, 219–20
Berkenkotter, C. 98–9
Berlin, J. 20–1
binarism 61–2, 68–9, 72–3
Bloom, H. 150
Booth, W. 141
Bottery, M. 52
Bourdieu, P. 44–5
Brannon, L. 22ff.

camera movement 207–8
'capable reader' 146–7
ceremonial rhetoric 29
Cicero 9
cinema 172ff.
classical rhetoric 4, 220–1
cognition 83–4, 85
collaboration 105
competence 146
composition 20
computers 65
critical discourse theory 79
Culler, J. 63–4, 152

definition of rhetoric 4–5
Derrida, J. 62–3, 68, 70
Dhondy, F. 3
dichotomies 68–9, 73
difference 62
digital codes 61–2
dispositio 7, 13, 123ff.
Dixon, J. 8, 9
dominant reading 149
domination 44–5

Eagleton, T. 5–6, 9, 19, 20, 174, 180, 219
Eco, U. 143–6, 174, 176
egocentrism 81ff., 95–7
Elizabethan rhetoric 170
elocutio 7
emotional appeal 166
enactment 156–71
'English', nature of 9–11
enthymeme 34
episode 118
equivocation 161
essay 36, 103, 123–4
exposition 102–15

fashion 212–27
feminism 176ff., 183
Foucault, M. 215, 221

gender 183–9
genre 9, 78–9, 139

hendiadys 158–9
Hernadi, P. 6
history of rhetoric 59–60

ideology 43–8, 178–80
imagery 160–1
images 172–96, 197–211, 212–27
implicature 145
Inglis, F. 51
inner speech 97
intelligence testing 48–51
intertext 129ff., 172–96, 222
inventio 7, 12, 20
Isocrates 3

juxtaposition 223

Knoblauch, C. 22ff.
knowledge about language 138
Kroll, B. 81–2
Kuhn, A. 174, 176–8, 185, 193

language study 1
listing 160
literary discourse 174, 176–8, 185, 193

Macbeth 159–70
managerialism 61–8
manuals 12, 170
maps 203–4
Martin, B. 53
Maybin, J. 8
Meek, M. 130, 132–3
metaphors of argument 100–1
mimesis 27
Morris, C. 2
myth 174

narrative 1, 8, 25, 116–28, 135, 137
Nash, W. 5
news 200–1, 208
non-fiction 102–15

Odyssey, The 153–5
oxymorons 158

paired reading 136
Pavel, T. 11–12
pedagogy 12, 70, 67–80, 104–5, 138–40, 151–5, 205
personal writing 72
persuasion 4, 28, 29–30, 32, 45, 130, 139–40, 147, 149, 156, 159–60
Piaget, J. 96–7, 101

planning 124
Plato 2, 25, 51
poetics 19, 20, 24
poetry 74–6, 138
presenters 204–7

reading 139–55
reading autobiographies 151–2
'real world' 21
reciprocity 6, 136, 141
repetition 160
rhythm 135, 168–9
Ricoeur, P. 25–6
Ross, A. 134

school texts 74, 75ff.
scientific discourse 63–4
self-persuasion 166–70
sexuality 224
Shakespeare, W. 156–71
Shrimpton, J. 212–27
site 79
Skinner, Q. 40–2
spectacle 159
'stage' 118
Stoppard, T. 42
structure 1, 91, 116–28
stylistics 6–7
syntax 135–6

tableaux 162
teacher–student relationships 65–6, 73, 76, 77–8, 114–15
text 79, 67–80
title sequences 201–3
topoi 26
tropes 65
Turtles, Teenage Mutant Ninja 134
type 203

university 59, 61ff., 64, 89–101
Urquhart, J. 193–5

'voice' 67–80
Vygotsky, L. 96–7, 101, 147–8

weather forecasts 197–211
Wells, G. 131
Williams, R. 40–1
Winterowd, R. 4
Wuthering Heights 172–96